Second Edition

Greek
for the
REST of US

Also by William Mounce

Basics of Biblical Greek: Grammar
Basics of Biblical Greek: Workbook
A Graded Reader of Biblical Greek
The Analytical Lexicon to the Greek New Testament
Biblical Greek: A Compact Guide
The Morphology of Biblical Greek
The Interlinear for the Rest of Us
The Zondervan Greek and English Interlinear New Testament (NASB/NIV)
Mounce's Complete Expository Dictionary of Old and New Testament Words
Pastoral Epistles (Word Biblical Commentary)
The Crossway Comprehensive Concordance of the Holy Bible

Second Edition

Greek
for the
REST of US

The Essentials of Biblical Greek

William D. Mounce

ZONDERVAN

Greek for the Rest of Us
Copyright © 2013 by William D. Mounce

This title is also available as a Zondervan ebook. Visit www.zondervan.com/ebooks.

Requests for information should be addressed to:

Zondervan, *Grand Rapids, Michigan 49530*

Library of Congress Cataloging-in-Publication Data

Mounce, William D.
    Greek for the rest of us: the essentials of biblical Greek / William D. Mounce—Second edition.
      p. cm.
    Includes index.
    ISBN 978-0-310-27710-1 (softcover)
    Biblical—Grammar. 2. Bible. New Testament—Language, style. I. Title.
  PA817.M655 2013
  487'.4—dc23   2013023352

---

14 15 16 17 18 19 20 /DCI/ 22 21 20 19 18 17 16 15 14 13 12 11 10 9 8 7 6 5 4 3 2

for Big Terry

who deeply desires to know God's Word better
but who does not have the time to learn traditional Greek

Codex Sinaiticus is an important majuscule manuscript from the 4th century. The images posted here are from the full-sized black and white facsimile of the manuscript produced in 1911 by Kirsopp Lake and Clarendon Press. The Codex Sinaiticus Project website (http://codexsinaiticus. org) has new images and information about this manuscript.

Table of Contents

Preface

When people learn that I am a Greek teacher, one of the more common responses is, "I have always wanted to learn Greek." (It may not be the most common, but it has happened repeatedly.) I always ask them why they want to learn Greek. To date, only one person has said he really wants to learn the language. What they want is to understand the Bible better, and especially to know what the Greek words behind the English translation mean.

In a perfect world, we would all know Greek and be able to understand the Bible better because we would not rely on translations. But the world is not perfect, and many people are not able to spend the years required to learn Greek properly, even those who have a seminary education.

As I thought about how I might help the situation, I came to the conclusion that if people knew a little about Greek and a lot about how to use the good biblical study tools, they could in fact glean much from the Bible and from other resources that are otherwise beyond their grasp. This includes:

- making sense of the information that Bible software shows
- finding what the Greek words mean
- seeing the author's flow of thought and his central message
- understanding why translations are different
- reading good commentaries and using other biblical tools that make use of Greek

Several years ago I wrote *The Interlinear for the Rest of Us: The Reverse Interlinear*, which helps people get to the Greek behind the English (and this data is used by some of the Bible software programs), and now I am writing this text to help you learn how to use *IRU* and other such tools.

There are, of course, many dangers in relying on tools rather than fully learning Greek, and I expressed those concerns in the preface to *IRU*. My fear is that people will think they know Greek well enough to come up with their own interpretations without commentary support. However, this is the same concern I have for all my first-year Greek students learning Greek in a traditional manner. Alexander Pope once said, "A little knowledge is a dangerous thing." But as I indicated in *IRU*, I saw that it is a little bit of arrogance that is dangerous. So I offer this text, trusting that you will recognize the limits of the approach.

GRU is divided into three sections.

- **Foundational Greek** teaches you enough Greek so you can use the Bible study software, understand a Strong's Bible, and do Greek word studies.

- **Church Greek** teaches you more Greek so you can understand a reverse interlinear and use better reference works, especially commentaries.

- **Functional Greek** teaches you even more Greek so you can be comfortable working with a traditional interlinear and go even deeper into the best commentaries.

The greatest challenge of the book was to find good examples of what I am teaching, especially for the homework assignments. All homework assignments are posted on the online class, *www.teknia.com/greekfortherestofus*. This allows me to continually update my work. Please keep an eye on the website as I am continually tweaking and upgrading it.

The online course is comprised of three smaller courses that correspond to these three sections of this text. These will help you walk through this textbook. I also am doing a three-part video series that works its way through the textbook. They can be purchased at the online class.

There are, in fact, many helps on the website. Go to the chapter you are currently studying and see what is there. You will find resources such as study notes, summaries, all the vocabulary words (and you can hear me say the words), all the homework exercises, fun things to do, and perhaps most important, a summary of all the grammar (available at the last lecture of Functional Greek).

Of the many people I would like to thank, most goes to my Greek assistant Matt Smith for his many hours of help, to my colleagues Lynn Losie, Doug Stuart, and Daniel Wallace for their help, to my editor Verlyn Verbrugge, and to many students who patiently endured while I changed my mind on how to teach this material. The two Western Seminary classes that helped the most were the D.Min class with Lew Dawson, and the M.Div class of 2012–13 with Paul Alexander, Steve Davis, Mike Dedera, Lucas Howard, Aaron Larson, Nick Marks, Phil Rankin, Joshua Smith, and Katy Shaw. Thanks also to the many laypeople who read the text, and to Robin, my wife, who patiently encouraged me to finish the task well.

I have relied quite heavily on the work of my friend Daniel Wallace and his grammar, *The Basics of New Testament Syntax.* Many of the grammatical categories and examples I use are from his work, and this should prove an easy transition for you to move from *Greek for the Rest of Us* to his work. I would encourage you to do so. If you are especially adventureous, you should use his full grammar, *Greek Grammar Beyond the Basics.*

I will primarily be using Accordance to illustrate Bible software, but you can also use Logos, The Bible Study App (from OliveTree), WORDsearch, BibleGateway.com, and possibly others.

It has been rewarding to teach this book many times in many venues (churches, weekend retreats, seminaries, etc.). As a result, I radically altered the order of the material in the second edition. This allows you to set three different goals; and no matter how far you work into the book, what you learn will help you go deeper in your Bible study.

I am also thankful that Lee Fields has written the Hebrew counterpart, *Hebrew for the Rest of Us.* My old Appendix on Hebrew can still be downloaded from the online class, but I encourage you to study his book.

I trust that you will find this a valuable resource as you work to understand the Word of God better.

Bill Mounce
Washougal, WA

Abbreviations

Bible Versions

ESV	English Standard Version
KJV	King James Version
NASB	New American Standard Bible (1995)
NEB	New English Bible
NET	New English Translation
NIV	New International Version (2011 edition)
NIV (1984)	New International Version (1984 edition)
NIrV	New International Reader's Version
NKJV	New King James Version
NLT	New Living Translation
NRSV	New Revised Standard Version
RSV	Revised Standard Version
TEV	Today's English Version
TNIV	Today's New International Version

Book Abbreviations

BBG	*The Basics of Biblical Greek* (William Mounce, Zondervan)
BNTS	*The Basics of New Testament Syntax* (Daniel Wallace, Zondervan)
BDAG	*A Greek-English Lexicon of the New Testament and Other Early Christian Literature* (3rd ed.; revised and edited by Frederick Danker, University of Chicago)
GGBB	*Greek Grammar Beyond the Basics* (Daniel Wallace, Zondervan)
IRU	*Interlinear for the Rest of Us: A Reverse Interlinear for New Testament Word Studies* (William Mounce, Zondervan)
MRINT	*Mounce Reverse-Interlinear New Testament* (a module for Accordance)

Other Abbreviations

e.g.	for example	i.e.	that is (used for a restatement)
f	one following page	v	verse
ff	more than one following page	vv	verses

What Would It Look Like
If You Knew a Little Greek?

What will you be able to do when you are done working through this text that, perhaps, you cannot do now?

1. How do I use my software? Software has progressed so far that now it can be a significant tool in your Bible study. This is a pleasant improvement since I wrote the first edition of *GRU*. You can call up a verse and mouse-over an English word, and the software will show you all sorts of dazzling information. But what does it all mean?

If you check out John 3:16 in the MOUNCE-NT translation, you might see something unusual, not "For God so loved the world" but "For this is how God loved the world" followed with a colon.

> MOUNCE-NT ▾
>
> John 3:16 ¶ "For this is how God loved the world: he gave his one and only Son that everyone who believes in him should not perish but have eternal life.

You can look over at your Greek text and see what Greek word is being translated, but if you don't know the Greek alphabet that doesn't help.

> GNT-T ▾ A A
>
> John 3:16 οὕτως γὰρ ἠγάπησεν ὁ θεὸς τὸν κόσμον, ὥστε τὸν υἱὸν τὸν μονογενῆ ἔδωκεν, ἵνα πᾶς ὁ πιστεύων εἰς αὐτὸν μὴ ἀπόληται ἀλλ᾽ ἔχῃ ζωὴν αἰώνιον.

If you look in the Instant Details window (I am using Accordance software), it gives you some

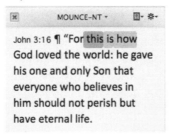

> this is how GK G4048 οὕτως houtōs
>
> [GNT-T] οὕτως houtōs Adverb (intensity) thus, so, in this way

more information about this Greek word. But what does "Adverb (intensity)" mean, and why can the MOUNCE-NT translation treat it so differently than other translations (except the NET)?

If you have a real Greek dictionary, you could double click οὕτως and see a fuller definition of the word, but can you understand it?

By the time you are done with *GRU*, all

> **οὕτω/οὕτως** adv. of οὗτος (Hom.+ gener. 'so'); the form οὕτως is most used, before consonants as well as before vowels; the form οὕτω (En 98:3 before a vowel; EpArist only before consonants) in the NT only Ac 23:11; Phil 3:17; Hb 12:21; Rv 16:18 w. really outstanding attestation and taken into the text by most edd.; by others, with t.r., also Mt 3:15; 7:17; Mk 2:7; Ac 13:47; Ro 1:15; 6:19 (B-D-F §21; W-S. §5, 28b; Mlt-H. 112f; W-H. appendix 146f. Also in ins [s. Nachmanson 112], pap [Mayser 242f; Crönert 142] and LXX [Thackeray p. 136] οὕτως predominates)
>   **1. referring to what precedes,** *in this manner, thus, so*

these mysteries and many more will be made clear!

2. You will discover the meaning of the Greek words that lie behind the English. This is called doing "word studies." Without knowing Greek or without learning how to use the study tools, the best you can do is learn what the English word means. But as you will see, words have a range of meanings. Think through all the ways we use the word "can" and "run." Words don't have exact counterparts in different languages. The range of meaning of an English word will almost never be the same as the range of meaning for the Greek word behind the English. We call this the word's "semantic range." So just because an English word can have a certain meaning, it is by no means certain that the Greek behind it has that specific meaning.

A good example of this is the Greek word σάρξ, *sarx*. This word can be translated many different ways because English has no exact counterpart to it. In as short a book as Galatians we find *sarx* translated by the NIV (1984, changed in the 2011 edition) as "flesh," "human effort," "illness," "man," "no one," "ordinary way," "outwardly," "sinful nature," and "that nature." All these English words partially overlap in meaning with *sarx*, but none is an exact equivalent.

Another example is in 1 Corinthians 7:1.

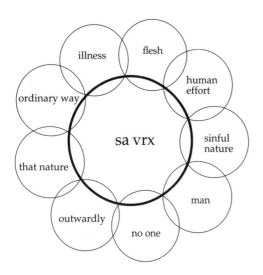

The RSV translates, "It is well for a man not to *touch* a woman." Lots of good youth group talks on dating come out of the word "touch." But guess what? The NIV (1984) translates 1 Corinthians 7:1 as, "It is good for a man not to marry." Wait a minute! Are we talking about dating or are we talking about marriage? The fact of the matter is that *haptesthai* can mean "to touch," or it can be speaking of marriage or even sexual relations (see the NIV 2011). Translators have to pick one meaning or the other.

There is another example later on in the same chapter. The RSV translates 1 Corinthians 7:36 as,

> If any one thinks that he is not behaving properly toward his betrothed, if his passions are strong, and it has to be, let him do as he wishes: let them marry—it is no sin.

Paul has been encouraging people not to marry in order to be more involved in the gospel ministry, but then he says that if that's not your gift, if your passions are strong, then there is nothing wrong with getting married. Go ahead and marry your "betrothed." "Any one" refers to the fiancé. However, when you read the same verse in the NASB it reads,

> But if any man thinks that he is acting unbecomingly toward his virgin *daughter*, if she is past her youth, and if it must be so, let him do what he wishes, he does not sin; let her marry.

The italics in the NASB's translation indicate that it has added a word, but the difference is more than that. The question is, who is the "man"? In the NASB, Paul is thinking of a father/guardian who believes his daughter's fiancé is acting improperly. Either way you look at this verse, it can be confusing.

Another example is John 3:16.

> For God so loved the world that he gave his one and only Son, that whoever believes in him shall not perish but have eternal life (NIV).

What does "so" mean? Most readers think it means "a lot." That's about the only way someone would read the English. But did you know that the Greek word behind "so" most likely means, "in this way"? "For God loved the world *in this way:* he gave...." The giving of his Son shows *how* God loved the world, *not how much.* (This is why the footnote in the ESV reads, "Or *For this is how God loved the world.*")

My favorite example when it comes to translating words is Matthew 26:27, which talks about the Lord's Supper. The KJV says,

> Drink ye all of it.

My dad tells the story of how, when he was younger, he made sure he drank every last little bit of grape juice in the communion cup. He would shake it until every drop was gone; he was going to obey Scripture and drink "all of it." Only one problem: that's not what the verse means. The "all" means "all of you," not "all the liquid." The RSV translates, "Drink of it, all of you."

So as we learn about Greek and translations, we'll see why these types of differences occur, and give you the tools to help you determine what the Greek really means.

3. *You will also learn the basics of exegesis.* "Exegesis" is a fancy word for Bible study. Using a methodology I call "phrasing," you will learn to divide a biblical story into smaller, more manageable, units, locate the main thought, and see how the other statements in the passage relate to the main point. You will then lay the passage out visually in a way that helps you see the author's flow of thought. This is the best way to help you learn what good commentary writers are trying to do.

For example, below is the salutation from Jude. How many main thoughts are there, and how many descriptions of the recipients does the author include?

The salutation breaks down into three sec-

1:1	Jude,	
	a servant of Jesus Christ and	
	a brother of James,	
	To those	
	who have been	called,
	who are	loved by God the Father and
		kept by Jesus Christ:
1:2	Mercy, peace and love be yours in abundance.	

tions: author; recipients; greeting. Jude tells us three things about the recipients: they have been called; they are loved by God; they are kept by Jesus.

4. *You will often be able to understand why translations are different.* How many times have you been in a Bible study where the leader is discussing a verse, but your Bible appears to say something considerably different? How can the translations be so different? What does the verse really say? Let me give you a few examples.

Luke 2:14 is one of the better-known verses in the Bible. In the KJV it reads,

> Glory to God in the highest, and on earth peace, good will toward men.

Is there anything in this verse that bothers you? It is a statement of blessing, and God's angels say, "peace, good will toward men." Does God's peace extend to all people? "Peace" is a marvelous biblical concept that designates a cessation of hostility between God and us; it's the result of justification (Rom 5:1).

The RSV says,

> Glory to God in the highest, and on earth peace among men with whom he is pleased!

Here, peace isn't extended to all people, but only to those who are the recipients of God's pleasure. Why are the KJV and the RSV different? The answer is that the Greek manuscripts are different at this verse. Some have *eudokias* with the "*s*" (the Greek sigma), which is followed by the RSV; others have *eudokia*, which is followed by the KJV. The "*s*" completely changes the meaning. (I will discuss the issue of different Greek manuscripts in chapter 31.)

Another example is Mark 16. If you are reading Mark 16 in the RSV, after the women see that the tomb is empty, the Bible says,

> And they went out and fled from the tomb; for trembling and astonishment had come upon them; and they said nothing to any one, for they were afraid.

The gospel ends at verse 8 on a note of fear. But let me tell you a story that is related, although it won't sound like it at first. Have you ever seen those movies they often show in high school sociology class about the snake people of the Appalachians? They handle rattlesnakes as part of their church worship, and they don't die. They also drink poison, and they don't die. Why are these people doing this? Why are my cousins doing this? (They actually are my cousins, by the way. My family is from Gravelswitch, Kentucky.) "Because the Bible says so," they would respond. If you are reading the KJV, it doesn't stop at verse 8 but goes on to verse 20. Verses 17–18 say,

> And these signs shall follow them that believe; In my name shall they cast out devils; they shall speak with new tongues; They shall take up serpents; and if they drink any deadly thing, it shall not hurt them; they shall lay hands on the sick, and they shall recover.

Wouldn't you like to know whether these verses truly belong in the Bible or not?

Here is a more subtle example. In 2 Corinthians 1:15 the ESV reads,

> Because I was sure of this, I wanted to come to you first, so that you may have a second experience of grace.

Sounds as if Paul is talking about a second work of grace subsequent to conversion. But see how other translations handle the passage.

> In this confidence I intended at first to come to you, so that you might twice receive a blessing (NASB).
>
> Because I was sure of this, I wanted to come to you first, so that you might have a double pleasure (RSV).
>
> Because I was confident of this, I wanted to visit you first so that you might benefit twice (NIV).

Since none of the other translations give any suggestion of a second work of grace, it is doubtful that the ESV means to suggest this. (I can say this with full certainty, since I was one of the twelve translators of the ESV.)

So what are we going to do with these differences? First of all, we will work to understand why they are different. Second, we will learn to pull the translations together. So often in Bible study when the translations are different, we seem content to let them say different things. Rather, what we need to do is use the different translations to come together and arrive at a common meaning, a meaning that perhaps has several nuances that the different translations are trying to convey.

5. *The final thing that I am going to help you learn is how to read good commentaries.* Let's say you're going to have a Sunday School lesson on Romans 1:17 and you need the help of a commentary. (A commentary is a book that explains what each verse means.) One of the best commentaries on Romans is by C. E. B. Cranfield, so let's say you pick it up and try to read his discussion of the verse. Here is a small part of his discussion (pp. 95-96).

> The other main disagreement concerns the question whether in the phrase δικαιοσύνη θεοῦ in 1.17; 3.21, 22 (cf. 10.3) θεοῦ is to be understood as a subjective genitive or as a genitive of origin, or—to put it differently—whether δικαιοσύνη refers to an activity of God or to a status of man resulting from God's action, righteousness as a gift from God. In support of the view that θεοῦ is a subjective genitive and δικαιοσύνη refers to God's activity, a number of arguments have been advanced: (i) That in 3.5 (θεοῦ δικαιοσύνη) θεοῦ must be a subjective genitive (cf. also 3.25, 26) ....

Does this make sense? Probably not right now. But by the end of this text you will know what a subjective genitive and a genitive of origin are. You'll know what a genitive is. I want you to know enough about English and Greek grammar so that you can pick up an excellent commentary and be able to follow the discussion.

Stated in reverse, I don't want you to make silly mistakes that come from misreading commentaries or misapplying Greek grammar. For example, you probably know the passage, "Are all apostles? Are all prophets? Are all teachers? Do all work miracles? Do all speak in tongues?" (1 Cor 12:29). Have you ever heard anyone claim the answer is "Yes," and insist that a "real" Christian must have spoken in tongues once? I have. But when you get your commentary on 1 Corinthians out, you will read something like this: "Questions preceded by μή expect a negative answer." What does that mean? It means that Greek can indicate whether the person asking the question expects the answer "Yes" or "No." (We do this in English by adding a phrase, like: "All don't speak in tongues, do they?") In 1 Corinthians 12:29, the Greek indicates that Paul's expected answer is, "No."

Limitations

There are limitations to our approach, but they are the same limitations placed on any first-year Greek student. You are at the beginning stages of learning Greek, and my concern is that you will forget that you know only a little. I'm going to give you the ability to sound authoritative by citing Greek words and grammar, and perhaps be completely wrong. I actually put off writing this book for several years because of this concern, but I finally came to the conclusion, as I've said, that it's not a little Greek that proves dangerous. It's a little bit of pride that proves dangerous.

If you don't respect the fact that you are only starting to learn Greek, then these tools can become just another way in which you can be wrong. I know a well-known speaker who was talking about how a Christian should not incur debt. I believe in debt-free living, so don't misunderstand me at this point, but the problem was in how he used Romans 13:8: "Owe no one anything, except to love each other, for the one who loves another has fulfilled the law" (ESV). He claimed something like the following.

> Now what's really important in Romans 13:8 is that there are three negations. Unlike in English, where if you have two negations they cancel each other out, in Greek when you have double negations they pile up on each other making the statement stronger. Paul has three negations in Romans 13:8 and he's making the point that it's really a sin ever to go into debt.

But the fact of the matter is that there are no negatives in this verse in the sense this author speaks of negatives. (You will find μή used once in the idiom εἰ μή, *except*, and twice as parts of words meaning *to no one* and *nothing*). In none of these situations do the rules the speaker was citing apply. He is teaching thousands of people, and he's wrong. So I say as a gentle warning: please remember what we're doing and what we're not doing. We're learning to use the tools; we're trying to follow good commentaries; we're trying to understand what words mean. We're not learning enough Greek to make complicated grammatical pronouncements that aren't supported by the commentaries.

I remember when I was in seminary sitting in the balcony of a large and well-known church listening to the preacher say, "Well, the Greek says this and the Greek says this." And I'm looking at the Greek and I say (I hope to myself), "You're wrong, you're wrong, you're wrong." He didn't really know Greek, but he was using it—it seemed to me—to elevate himself in a position of authority over his people. He should have been more careful, and more humble.

Jehovah's Witnesses are another good example of misusing Greek. They will cite John 1:1—"In the beginning was the Word and the Word was with God and the Word was *a god*"—and argue that there is no word "the" before "God." Jesus is not "the" God but "a" god, a created god. But if they really knew Greek, they wouldn't make such a horrible and obvious mistake, for two reasons. (1) There's technically no such thing as the word "the" in Greek. There is a word, ὁ, that can be translated as "the," but it can also be translated as "my," as "your," or as many other words. There is no exact equivalent for the word "the" in Greek. (2) Grammatically the Greek explicitly states that Jesus is, in our language, "the God" (cf. *GGBB*, pp. 266-269).

One last illustration. Last year I was sitting at my desk grading papers, minding my own business, and I received a phone call from an elderly gentleman. He started talking and was evidently lonely so I listened, and within ten minutes he had accused every translator of being intentionally deceitful, of not knowing what they were doing, of mistranslating God's Word, and God was going to curse them. I said,

> Well, Sir, do you know any translators?
>
> No, I've never met any of them.
>
> Well, I know a lot of them, and they are godly men and women who would

never mistranslate anything on purpose, and they know a lot more Greek than you.

Well, they don't translate 2 Peter 3:5 properly. The Greek says God created "die-uh" [his mispronunciation of the Greek] water. The earth is formed *through* water. "Die-uh" means "through" and so in this verse Peter is saying that God created the world "through" water, and everyone is translating it "out of" water.

He was absolutely insistent that *dia* meant "through," and he went through a fifteen-minute discussion in physics. (I didn't have any idea what he was talking about.) When he finally paused for a breath, I said, "First of all, it's pronounced 'dia.' There's a good chance that if you can't pronounce it, then you probably don't know what it means."

(I was a little frustrated.) Then I tried to explain that all words have a range of meaning. *Dia* can mean "through," but it can also mean "out of" or "by," and the translators must make an interpretive decision as to which word they use. (By the way, the ESV did agree on "through," so he should be happy.) I tried to impress on him the fact of how dangerous it was to slander Christian brothers and sisters and to accuse them of intentionally doing things wrong when he didn't know what he was talking about.

So why should you learn a little Greek, if it is possible to make these types of errors? Because the personal rewards of deepening your biblical study are so great that it is worth the effort. Just remember the importance of humility (Phil 2:1-13) and meekness (Matt 5:5), and that while knowledge puffs up, love builds up (1 Cor 8:1).

Online and Video Resources for Learning

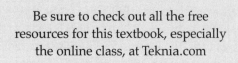

Be sure to check out all the free resources for this textbook, especially the online class, at Teknia.com

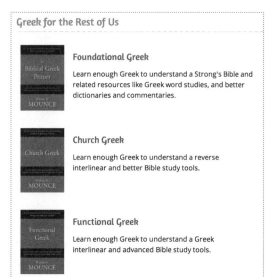

Greek for the Rest of Us

Foundational Greek

Learn enough Greek to understand a Strong's Bible and related resources like Greek word studies, and better dictionaries and commentaries.

Church Greek

Learn enough Greek to understand a reverse interlinear and better Bible study tools.

Functional Greek

Learn enough Greek to understand a Greek interlinear and advanced Bible study tools.

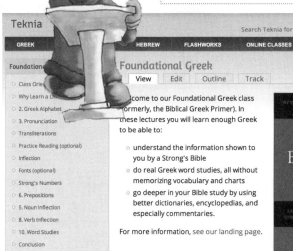

Teknia

Search Teknia for [   ] -Any- [Search]

GREEK   HEBREW   FLASHWORKS   ONLINE CLASSES   STORE

Foundational...

- Class Orie...
- Why Learn a L...
- 2. Greek Alphabet
- 3. Pronunciation
- Transliterations
- Practice Reading (optional)
- Inflection
- Fonts (optional)
- Strong's Numbers
- 6. Prepositions
- 5. Noun Inflection
- 8. Verb Inflection
- 10. Word Studies
- Conclusion

Foundational Greek

[View] Edit   Outline   Track

...come to our Foundational Greek class (formerly, the Biblical Greek Primer). In these lectures you will learn enough Greek to be able to:

- understand the information shown to you by a Strong's Bible
- do real Greek word studies, all without memorizing vocabulary and charts
- go deeper in your Bible study by using better dictionaries, encyclopedias, and especially commentaries.

For more information, see our landing page.

How to Navigate

You can start by clicking the Table of

Foundational Greek

In these 9 hours of video lectures and screen casts (formerly, the Biblical Greek Primer), Dr. Mounce will teach you enough Greek so you can go deepen in your Bible Study, but without all the time and memory work required by traditional Greek learning approaches.

You will be able to:

- Understand your Strong's Bibles
- Do Greek word studies
- Use better commentaries and dictionaries

You can view the first three lessons for free in our online class. To purchase the class, you have two options.

You can also purchase Bill's video lectures over the book for individual or group use. Tell your discipleship pastor that this is the tool for learning Greek and deeper Bible study in the church!

Part I

Foundational Greek

This is your first of three passes through the Greek language. This is the easiest of the three sections of the book, although it may be more challenging if you have never learned a foreign language. In Foundational Greek we will be meeting the basic concepts that make up the Greek language, so be ready potentially for some new ideas but not a lot of memorization. We will be learning the following:

- Greek alphabet and transliteration
- How to pronounce Greek
- What inflection is (and Strong's numbers)
- Basics of the Greek noun and verbal system
- How to do Greek word studies

Chapter 1

The Greek Language

The Greek language has a long and rich history stretching all the way from the thirteenth century BC to the present. The earliest form of the language is called "Linear B" (13th century BC).

The form of Greek used by writers from Homer (8th century BC) through Plato (4th century BC) is called "Classical Greek." It was a marvelous form of the language, capable of exact expression and subtle nuances. Its alphabet was derived from the Phoenicians. Classical Greek existed in many dialects of which three were primary: Doric, Aeolic, and Ionic (of which Attic was a branch).

Athens was conquered in the fourth century BC by King Philip of Macedonia. Alexander the Great was Philip's son and was tutored by the Greek philosopher Aristotle. He set out to conquer the world and spread Greek culture and language. Because Alexander spoke Attic Greek, it was this dialect that was spread. It was also the dialect spoken by the famous Athenian writers. This was the beginning of the Hellenistic Age.

As the Greek language spread across the world and met other languages, it was altered (which would happen to any language). The dialects also interacted with each other. Eventually this adaptation resulted in what we call Koine Greek. "Koine" (κοινή) means "common" and was the common, everyday form of the language, used by everyday people. It was not considered a polished literary form of the language, and in fact some writers of this era purposefully imitated the older style of Greek (which is like someone today writing in King James English). Koine unfortunately lost many of the subtleties of classical Greek. For example, in classical Greek ἄλλος meant "other" of the same kind while ἕτερος meant "other" of a different kind. If you had an apple and you asked for ἄλλος, you would receive another apple. But if you asked for ἕτερος, you would be given perhaps an orange. Some of these subtleties come through in the New Testament but not often. It is this common, Koine Greek that is used in the Septuagint (the Greek translation of the Old Testament), the New Testament, and the writings of the Apostolic Fathers.

For a long time Koine Greek confused many scholars because it was significantly different from Classical Greek. Some hypothesized that it was a combination of Greek, Hebrew, and Aramaic. Others attempted to explain it as a "Holy Ghost language," meaning that God created a special language just for the Bible. But studies of Greek papyri found in Egypt over the last one hundred years have shown that Koine Greek was the language of the everyday people used in the writings of wills, letters, receipts, shopping lists, etc.

There are two lessons we can learn from this. As Paul says, "In the fullness of time God sent his Son" (Gal 4:4), and part of that fullness was a universal language. No matter where Paul traveled he could be understood.

But there is another lesson here that is perhaps a little closer to the pastor's heart.

God used the common language to communicate the gospel. The gospel does not belong to the erudite; it belongs to all people. It now becomes our task to learn this marvelous language so we can make the grace of God known to all people.

By the way. I often hear that we should learn Latin because it is the basis of English. Not true. English is a Germanic language and Latin is a Romance language.

Languages can be grouped into families. There is a hypothetical base language we call "Proto-Indo-European." It developed into four language groups.

- Romance languages (Latin, French, Italian, Portuguese, Romanian, Spanish, and others)

- Germanic languages (English, Danish, Dutch, English, German, Gothic, Norwegian, Swedish, and others). Technically the base language for this group is called "Proto-Germanic."

- Old Greek (Linear B, Classical, Koine, Byzantine, Modern Greek)

- Aryan (Iranian, Sanskrit)

There was a lot of borrowing between Romance and Germanic languages (think where the countries are located), and both of these language groups borrowed from Greek. English especially was heavily influenced by other languages. This can be illustrated by words they have in common.

- From Greek (didactic, apostle, theology)

- From Latin (aquarium, name, volcano)

- From French (closet, resume, prestige)

On the other hand, Hebrew and Aramaic come from another family called the Semitic languages, and there was little borrowing between them and the Proto-Indo-European languages. Almost every Aramaic word would sound strange to you (and English to them).

So why learn Greek rather than Latin? I learned Latin and read Caesar's *Gallic Wars*; it was interesting. I learned Greek and read the Bible; it was life changing.

Chapter 2

The Greek Alphabet

In this chapter we will learn the twenty-four letters of the Greek alphabet and the transliteration of each.

Introduction

2.1 A transliteration is the equivalent of a letter in another language. For example, the Greek "beta" (β) is transliterated with the English "b." Because they have the same sound, it is said that the English "b" is the transliteration of the Greek "beta." It is common in modern texts to set off a transliterated word in italics.

> Jesus' last word from the cross was *tetelestai*.

This does not mean that a similar combination of letters in one language has the same meaning as the same combination in another.

> kappa + alpha + tau (κατ) does not mean "cat."

Some word study books and commentaries avoid the Greek form and give only the transliteration.

Alphabet Chart

2.2 Below I have listed the letter's name, its transliteration, the small and capital Greek form, and its pronunciation. The website will help you with the pronunciation of the alphabet and the reading exercises in the following chapters.

Name	Translit.	Small	Capital	Pron.	As in
Alpha	*a*	α	A	a	as in father
Beta	*b*	β	B	b	as in Bible
Gamma	*g*	γ	Γ	g	as in gone
Delta	*d*	δ	Δ	d	as in dog
Epsilon	*e*	ε	E	e	as in met
Zeta	*z*	ζ	Z	z	as in daze
Eta	*ē*	η	H	e	as in obey

Theta	*th*	θ	Θ	th	as in thing
Iota	*i*	ι	I	i	as in intrigue
Kappa	*k*	κ	K	k	as in kitchen
Lambda	*l*	λ	Λ	l	as in law
Mu	*m*	μ	M	m	as in mother
Nu	*n*	ν	N	n	as in new
Xi	*x*	ξ	Ξ	x	as in axiom
Omicron	*o*	ο	O	o	as in not
Pi	*p*	π	Π	p	as in peach
Rho	*r*	ρ	P	r	as in rod
Sigma	*s*	σ/ς	Σ	s	as in sit
Tau	*t*	τ	T	t	as in talk
Upsilon	*u/y*	υ	Y	u	as the German ü
Phi	*ph*	φ	Φ	ph	as in phone
Chi	*ch*	χ	X	ch	as in loch
Psi	*ps*	ψ	Ψ	ps	as in lips
Omega	*ō*	ω	Ω	o	as in tone

Learning the capital letters is not as critical right now, but they are easy and you might as well learn it all now.

> **D**ifferent books may follow slightly different transliteration schemes. Be sure to check the book's scheme before looking up a word. If you would rather learn modern Greek pronunciation, see this chapter in the online class.

Helps

2.3   The vowels are α, ε, η, ι, ο, υ, ω. The rest are consonants.

2.4   Sigma is written as ς when it occurs at the end of the word, and as σ when it occurs elsewhere: ἀπόστολος.

2.5   υ is transliterated as "*u*" if it is preceded by a vowel (εὐαγγέλιον → *euangelion*), and "*y*" if it occurs as a single vowel (μυστήριον → *mystērion*).

2.6   Do not confuse the η (eta) with the English "n," ν (nu) with "v," ρ (rho) with "p," χ (chi) with "x," or ω (omega) with "w."

2.7   Notice the many similarities among the Greek and English letters, not only in shape and sound but also in their respective order in the alphabet. The Greek alphabet can be broken down into sections. It will parallel the English for a while,[1] differ, and then begin to parallel again. Try to find these natural divisions.

Pronouncing the alphabet

2.8   In pronouncing the Greek letters, use the first sound of the name of the letter. Alpha is an "a" sound (there is no "pha" sound); lambda is an "l" sound (there is no "ambda" sound).

2.9   There is some disagreement among scholars on the pronunciation of a few letters, but I have chosen the most common. This is a different pronunciation scheme than is used by modern Greek, which is a much more beautiful pronunciation than the traditional suggests.

> **Y**ou can download a chart from the online class in both traditional pronunciation as well as modern. You can also listen to me and a modern Greek speaker work through the alphabet, and all the vocabulary on the website has both pronunciations.

2.10   γ usually has a hard "g" sound, as in "get." However, when it is immediately followed by γ, κ, χ, or ξ, it is pronounced as "n." ἄγγελος is pronounced "angelos" (from which we get our word "angel"). The γ pronounced like "n" is called a **gamma nasal** and is transliterated as "n" (*angelos*).

2.11   The ι can be either short or long, like the two i's in the English "intrigue." When you are memorizing vocabulary and not sure how to pronounce an ι, just listen to how your teacher pronounces the words (or to me on the website).

Miscellaneous

2.12   **Iota subscript**. Sometimes an iota is written under the vowels α, η, or ω (ᾳ, ῃ, ῳ). This iota is not pronounced, but it does affect the word's meaning. It normally is not transliterated. The vowel combination is called an "improper diphthong."

---

[1]   Of course, Greek isn't actually following English since Greek was created before English; it just looks that way to us.

2.13   **Capitals**. Originally the Greek Testament was written in all capital letters without punctuation or spaces between the words. For example, John 1:1 began,

ΕΝΑΡΧΗΗΝΟΛΟΓΟΣ

The cursive script was created before the time of Christ but became popular in the ninth century. In cursive the letters are connected, like our present-day handwriting. Spaces were also added between words. In Greek texts today, John 1:1 begins,

εν αρχη ην ο λογος

In our Greek texts today, capitals are used only for proper names, the first word in a quotation, and the first word in the paragraph.

> **T**he first capital letters were written with straight lines, which were easier to carve into writing material like rock. In the first century AD, a modified style of capital letters was created called "uncial". These letters had more curves so they could be more easily written on the newer writing materials such as papyrus and parchment. The earliest New Testament documents are called uncials. In the 8th to the 9th century, cursive script was written smaller and in a style that could be written faster, saving both time and parchment. This script is known as "minuscule"; there are currently 2,867 New Testament minuscule manuscripts.

Exercises

2.14   All the exercises are available on the class' website, at:

www.teknia.com/greekprimer
(or click on Greek for the Rest of Us)

This is true for all chapters.

Chapter 3

Pronunciation

Just as it is important to learn how to pronounce the letters, it is also important to pronounce the words correctly. But in order to pronounce a Greek word you must be able to break it down into its syllables. This is called "syllabification." We will also learn about accents and punctuation.

Diphthongs

3.1 A **diphthong** is a combination of two vowels that produce one sound. The second vowel is always ι or υ. Be sure to listen to me pronounce the Greek words in the online class.

αι	as in aisle	αιρω
ει	as in eight	ει
οι	as in oil	οικια
αυ	as in sauerkraut	αυτος
ου	as in soup	ουδε
υι	as in suite	υιος
ευ, ηυ	as in feud	ευθυς / ηυξανεν

Breathing marks

3.2 Greek has two **breathing marks**, "rough" and "smooth." Every word beginning with a vowel or ρ has a breathing mark. (I omitted them in the previous examples.)

The **rough breathing mark** is a ʽ placed over the first vowel or initial rho, and adds an "h" sound to the word.

ὑπερ	→	*hyper*
ῥαββι	→	*rhabbi*

As you can see, the rough breathing mark is transliterated as an *h* and is placed before the transliterated vowel (but after the initial ρ).

The **smooth breathing mark** is a ’ placed over the first vowel and is not pronounced or transliterated.

ἀποστολος	→	*apostolos*
αὐτος	→	*autos*

Either breathing mark is placed before an initial capital letter.

Ἰσραηλ	→	*Israēl*
Ἰεροσόλυμα	→	*Hierosolyma*

Either breathing mark is placed over the second vowel of an initial diphthong.

αἰτεω	→	*aiteō*
Αἰτεω	→	*Aiteō*
Αἱ	→	*Hai*

John 1:1 looks like this with breathing marks.

> Ἐν ἀρχῃ ἠν ὁ λογος

Syllabification

3.3   Greek words syllabify basically the same way as English words do. Therefore, if you "go with your feelings," you will syllabify Greek words almost automatically. If you practice reading the examples below and listen to the reading exercises in the online class, you should pick it up. I will mark the syllables below with a space. The two most basic rules are:

- There is one vowel or diphthong per syllable (just like in English).

- A single consonant goes with the following vowel (e.g., αὐ - τός, not αὐτ - ός).

I included the interlinear translation for the fun of it.

John 3:16	οὕ τως	γὰρ	ἠ γά πη σεν	ὁ	θε ὸς	τὸν κό σμον,	ὥσ τε[2]	τὸν	υἱ ὸν
	so	for	he loved	the	God	the world	so that	the	son

τὸν	μο νο γε νῆ	ἔ δω κεν,	ἵ να	πᾶς	ὁ	πι στεύ ων	εἰς	αὐ τὸν
the	only	he gave	so that	each	the	one who believes	in	him

μὴ	ἀ πό λη ται	ἀλλ’	ἔ χῃ	ζω ὴν	αἰ ώ νι ον.
not	he might perish	but	he might have	life	eternal

---

2   For the rule governing this word's syllabification, see 3.8, rule 7.

1 John 1:9	ἐ ὰν	ὁ μο λο γῶ μεν	τὰς	ἁ μαρ τί ας	ἡ μῶν,	πι στός	ἐ στιν
	if	we confess	the	sins	our	faithful	he is

	καὶ	δί και ος,	ἵ να	ἀ φῇ		ἡ μῖν	τὰς	ἁ μαρ τί ας
	and	just	so that	he might forgive		to us	the	sins

	καὶ	κα θα ρί σῃ	ἡ μᾶς	ἀ πὸ	πά σης	ἀ δι κί ας.
	and	he might cleanse	us	from	all	unrighteousness

Eph 2:8	Τῇ	γὰρ	χά ρι τί	ἐ στε	σε σω σμέ νοι	δι ὰ	πί στε ως·
	by the	for	grace	you are	saved	through	faith

	καὶ	τοῦ το	οὐκ	ἐξ	ὑ μῶν,	θε οῦ	τὸ	δῶ ρον.
	and	this	not	of	you	of God	the	gift

Accents

3.4   Almost every Greek word has an accent mark. It is placed over a vowel and shows which syllable receives the emphasis when you say the word.

name	*pitch*	*example*
acute	voice rose	αἰτέω
grave	voice dropped	θεὸς
circumflex	voice rose and dropped	Ἰησοῦς

Originally the accent was a pitch accent, the voice rising (αὐτός), falling (θεὸς), or rising and falling (Ἰησοῦς) on the accented syllable. A few centuries after the writing of the New Testament, most believe the pitch accent was shifted to stress, like Modern English.

Here is John 1:1 as it actually is written in modern texts.

Ἐν ἀρχῇ ἦν ὁ λόγος

The point here is to be consistent. If you do not consistently stress the correct syllable, it will be difficult to communicate with others.

3.5 Here are the verses we saw earlier but now with accents. Read them, this time paying attention to which syllable receives the stress.

John 3:16 οὕτως γὰρ ἠγάπησεν ὁ θεὸς τὸν κόσμον, ὥστε τὸν υἱὸν τὸν μονογενῆ ἔδωκεν, ἵνα πᾶς ὁ πιστεύων εἰς αὐτὸν μὴ ἀπόληται ἀλλ᾽ ἔχῃ ζωὴν αἰώνιον.

1 John 1:9 ἐὰν ὁμολογῶμεν τὰς ἁμαρτίας ἡμῶν, πιστός ἐστιν καὶ δίκαιος, ἵνα ἀφῇ ἡμῖν τὰς ἁμαρτίας καὶ καθαρίσῃ ἡμᾶς ἀπὸ πάσης ἀδικίας.

Eph 2:8 Τῇ γὰρ χάριτί ἐστε σεσωσμένοι διὰ πίστεως· καὶ τοῦτο οὐκ ἐξ ὑμῶν, θεοῦ τὸ δῶρον.

There is an interesting true story about a cannibal tribe that killed the first two missionary couples who came to them. The couples had tried to learn their language, but could not. The third brave couple started experiencing the same problems with the language as had the two previous couples until the wife, who had been a music major in college, recognized that the tribe had a very developed set of pitch accents that were essential in understanding the language. When they learned the significance these accents played in that language, they were able to translate the Bible into that musically-minded language. Luckily for us, while Greek accents were pitch, they are not that important.

Punctuation

3.6 The comma and period are the same in Greek as they are in English. However, a period above the line is the Greek semicolon, and an English semicolon is the Greek question mark.

Punctuation	Greek
θεός,	χομμα
θεός.	περιοδ
θεός·	σεμιχολον
θεός;	question mark

Vocabulary

3.7 There is vocabulary for this chapter at the online class.

Advanced Information: Syllabification Rules

3.8   Some people prefer to learn the actual rules for syllabification instead of trusting their instincts. Here are the basic rules.

1. There is one vowel (or diphthong) per syllable. (Therefore, there are as many syllables as there are vowels/diphthongs.)

    ἀ κη κό α μεν   μαρ τυ ροῦ μεν

2. Two consecutive vowels that do not form a diphthong are divided.

    ἐ θε α σά με θα   Τι μο θέ ῳ

3. A single consonant goes with the following vowel.

    ἐ ω ρά κα μεν   ἀ πό στο λος

    By "single consonant" I mean that the following letter is not a consonant. (The ρ, κ, and μ in ἑωράκαμεν are single consonants.) If you find two or more consonants in a row that form a single sound, they are called a "consonant cluster." (The στ in ἀπόστολος form a consonant cluster.)

    If the consonant is the final letter in the word, it goes with the preceding vowel.

    ἐ κεῖ θεν   ἡ μῶν

4. A consonant cluster that does not form a single sound is divided, and the first consonant goes with the preceding vowel.

    ἔμ προ σθεν   ἀρ χῆς

5. A consonant cluster that forms a single sound goes with the following vowel.

    Χρι στός   γρα φή

6. Double consonants are divided. (A "double consonant" is when the same consonant occurs twice in a row.)

    ἀ παγ γέλ λο μεν   παρ ρη σί α

7. Compound words are divided where joined.

    ἀντι χριστός   ἐκ βάλλω

Chapter 4

English Grammar: Noun Inflection

We will learn the causes of inflection in the English word system: case, number, gender.

4.1   Sometimes the form of a word changes, such as when it performs different functions in a sentence or when it changes its meaning. This is called "inflection."

For example, the personal pronoun is "he" if it refers to a male and "she" if it refers to a female. It is "she" when it is the subject of the sentence (e.g., "*She* is my wife."), but inflects to "her" when it is the direct object (e.g., "The teacher flunked *her*.") If the king and queen have one son, he is the "prince," but if they have two, they are "princes." If their child is a girl, she is a "princess." All these changes are examples of inflection.

The third-person pronoun is one of the most inflected words in English. (I will discuss the labels for this chart later in the chapter.)

	masculine	*feminine*	*neuter*
subjective singular	he	she	it
possessive singular	his	her	its
objective singular	him	her	it
subjective plural	they	they	they
possessive plural	their	their	their
objective plural	them	them	them

4.2   **Noun**. A noun is a word that stands for someone or something (i.e., a person, place, or thing).

Bill threw his big black *book* at the strange *teacher*.

Causes of Inflection

4.3   The following grammatical concepts can affect the form of an English noun.

4.4   Nouns perform different functions in a sentence. These different functions are categorized in "cases." In English there are three cases: subjective, possessive, and objective.

4.5   If a word is the *subject* of a verb, it is in the **subjective** case.

> *He* is my brother.

The subject is what does the action of an active verb and usually precedes the verb in word order.

> *Bill* ran to the store.

> The *ball* broke the window.

Word order shows that both "Bill" and "ball" are the subjects of their verbs. If it is difficult to determine the subject, ask the question "who?" or "what?" For example, Who ran to the store? Bill. What broke the window? The ball.

4.6   If a word shows *possession*, it is in the **possessive** case.

> *His* Greek Bible is always by *his* bed.

 You can put "of" in front of the word, an apostrophe s after the word, or just an apostrophe if the word ends in "s."

> The Word *of God* is true.

> *God's* Word is true.

> The *apostles'* word was ignored.

4.7   If a word is the *direct object,* it is in the **objective** case. The direct object is the person or thing that is directly affected by the action of the verb. This means that whatever the verb does, it does it to the direct object. It usually follows the verb in word order.

> Robin passed her *test.*

> The waiter insulted *Hayden.*

Test and *Hayden* are the direct objects. You can usually determine the direct object by asking the question "what?" or "whom?" Robin passed what? Her test. The waiter insulted whom? Hayden.

case	function	example
Subjective	subject	He borrowed my computer.
Possessive	possession	He borrowed my computer.
Objective	direct object	He borrowed my computer.

Other than pronouns, most English nouns do not change their form as they perform different functions. For example, the word "teacher" stays the same whether it is the subject ("The *teacher* likes you.") or the direct object ("You like the *teacher*."). However, to form the possessive, "teacher" adds an "apostrophe s" ("She is the *teacher's* pet.").

4.8   The **indirect object** is the person or thing that is indirectly affected by the action of the verb. This means that the indirect object is somehow involved in the action described by the verb, but not directly.

For example, "Karin threw Brad a ball." The direct object is "ball," since it is directly related to the action of the verb; it is what was thrown. But "Brad" is also related to the action of the verb, since the ball was thrown to him. "Brad" is the indirect object. If Karin threw Brad, then "Brad" would be the direct object.

One way to find the indirect object is to put the word "to" in front of the word and see if it makes sense.

"Karin threw Brad a ball."

"Karin threw to Brad a ball."

To whom did Karin throw the ball? To Brad. "Brad" is the indirect object.

English does not have a separate case for the indirect object. It uses the same form as the direct object (objective case).

4.9   **Word order**. This is an important point. English uses the order of words to determine which word is doing the action of the verb, receiving the action, etc. Adjectives are placed before the word they modify. As we will see in the next chapter, Greek uses a different linkage system to indicate which words are doing what, not word order.

4.10   **Number**. Inflection can also be caused by a word's "number," which refers to whether a word is singular (referring to one thing) or plural (referring to more than one thing). English generally inflects a word relative to number one of two ways. Most words add an "s" to make the word plural.

Students should learn to study like this *student*.

Some words change an internal vowel or some other part of the word.

The *woman* visited the *women*.

The *child* joined in playing with the *children*.

4.11 **Gender**. Some words, mostly pronouns, inflect depending upon whether they are referring to a masculine, feminine, or neuter object. This is called "natural gender."

> *He* gave *it* to *her*.

"He," "it," and "her" are forms of the same pronoun, the third person singular personal pronoun. They are masculine, neuter, and feminine, respectively.

We refer to a man as "he" and a woman as "she." If a word refers to neither a masculine nor feminine thing, then it is neuter. We refer to a rock as an "it" because we do not regard the rock as male or female.[3]

Another example is the word "prince." If the heir to the throne is male, then he is the "prince." If the child is female, she is the "princess."

Most English words do not change to indicate gender. "Teacher" refers to either a woman or a man.

---

[3] My guess is that the older style of referring to a boat or a country as a "she" is on its way out of the language.

Chapter 5

Greek Grammar: Nouns

In Greek, we don't use word order to determine the function of a word. Rather, the Greek words will "inflect" to show their function; and they use something called "case endings" to do so. The case ending is a suffix attached to the end of the word. If you see the word θεοί, the ι would tell you that the word is plural and is functioning as the subject of a verb.

There are four cases: nominative (indicating subject), accusative (direct object), dative (indirect object), and genitive ("of").

Greek Inflection

5.1 **Stem**. The basic form of a noun is called the "stem." For example, the stem of the Greek word for "God" is θεο. I'll put an asterisk before a stem to make this clear (*θεο).

5.2 **Case endings**. Unlike English, most Greek nouns and adjectives change their form depending on their function in the sentence. They do this by using case endings, which are suffixes added to the end of the stem.

If a word is the subject of a verb, the writer will put it into the nominative case by adding a nominative case ending onto the stem. ς can be used as a nominative case ending for some words. In John 3:16, which word is the subject?

John 3:16   ἠγάπησεν   ὁ θεὸς   τὸν κόσμον
                   loved   *God*   the world
            God loved the world.

This is the first time I have used this layout for a verse, so let me explain what I am doing.

The first line is the Greek. To save space, and because it is often not translated, I have usually kept ὁ (in all its forms) with the following word (e.g., ὁ is with θεός, and τόν is with κόσμον).

The second line is a word-for-word translation of the Greek. I have italicized the translation of the Greek word that I am using for the illustration. For example, because I am talking about the subject, "God" is italicized.

The third and following lines (if present) are normal translations of the verse. The first translation has been chosen to illustrate the point I am making. If there is only one translation, it is generally my own. If there are more than one, it means I am using two (or more) translations to illustrate a point, and I use the abbreviation to identify which translation I am using (see page x for a list of abbreviations). Usually the difference will be one of clarity; one translation will bring out the nuance of the construction and the other will leave it vague. Rarely do translations contradict each other.

In traditional approaches to Greek, we would see the ς case ending, recognize that this may indicate the word is in the nominative case (because we memorized it), and conclude that it is the subject of the verb. For our Foundational Greek approach, we use the tools to tells us the word is in the nominative, but you still need to understand the process.

Notice that word order does not identify the subject. In our example, θεός comes after the verb, but it is the case ending that tells us θεός is in the nominative and therefore is the subject of the verb.

5.3   The only way to determine the subject of a Greek sentence is by the case endings since the subject can occur before or after the verb.

Take the following four sentences, for example. How do we know that they are all saying that God loves the world, and not that the world loves God?

ἀγαπᾷ   ὁ Θεός   τὸν κόσμον.
loves   the God   the world
ἀγαπᾷ τὸν κόσμον ὁ Θεός.
τὸν κόσμον ὁ Θεὸς ἀγαπᾷ.
ὁ Θεὸς ἀγαπᾷ τὸν κόσμον.

We know θεός is the subject because ς is a case ending indicating the subject of the verb. Although the order of the words is different, each example has the same basic meaning.

5.4   **Gender**. A noun is either masculine, feminine, or neuter. It has only one gender and it never varies.

Most Greek nouns do not follow natural gender. In other words, the gender of a word has no necessary connection to the meaning of the word.

- For example, ἁμαρτία is a feminine noun meaning "sin," although "sin" is not a female concept.

- ἁμαρτωλός is a masculine noun meaning "sinner," although "sinner" is not a masculine concept.

- πνεῦμα is a neuter word meaning "spirit," but the Holy Spirit is not a thing; he is a "person."

However, you will see natural gender in pronouns (αὐτός, "he"; αὐτή, "she") and words like "brother" (ἀδελφός, masculine) and "sister" (ἀδελφή, feminine).

5.5 **Number**. Instead of adding an "s" to a word as we do in many English plurals, Greek indicates singular or plural by using different case endings. The difference between the singular and plural here is indicated by the case endings ς and ι.

| ἀπόστολος | → | apostle |
| ἀπόστολοι | → | apostles |

5.6 **Gloss**. When a tool like Accordance gives you a short definition of a word, it is probably the word's gloss. This is not meant to be used in translation and Bible study. A gloss is a rough approximation of what the Greek word means, and any Bible study requires you to look up the word in a Greek dictionary and get a better understanding of the word's range of meaning.

5.7 **Parsing**. Your Bible study tools will "parse" the noun for you. This means they will tell you its case, number, gender, lexical form (see 5.10), and perhaps other pieces of information such as its meaning. Different tools follow different patterns; they will not necessarily be case, number, gender.

5.8 There are basically four cases in Greek: nominative, accusative, dative, and genitive.

Nominative

5.9 The normal use of the nominative case is to designate the *subject* of a verb.

Rom 10:9   ὁ θεὸς   αὐτὸν   ἤγειρεν   ἐκ   νεκρῶν
God   him   raised   from   dead
God raised him from the dead.

Who raised him? God raised him. "God" is the subject.

> id you notice how *subject* is italicized in 5.9? In 5.12 you will see that *direct object* is italicized. The reason is that these are the technical terms used to describe a specific grammatical construction. The commentaries will use these terms, so you need to be learning them.

You will come across words listed as nominative that will not be functioning as the subject of the verb. When this happens, tell yourself to have a little humility and realize that this is one of the grammatical constructions you have not yet learned. This is also true of the other cases; I am only showing you here a selection of the use of each case. There is much more to learn in Church Greek and Functional Greek.

5.10 **Lexical form**. The lexical form of a noun is its nominative singular form. If you see the inflected form ἀπόστολοι, which is nominative plural, it would be listed in the lexicon under ἀπόστολος.

This is important to know because if you want to do a word study, you will need to know the lexical form of the word. If you tried to look up the word ἀπόστολοι in a word study book, you would not find it.

Accusative

5.11 A word is put into the accusative case to indicate it is the *direct object*.

John 3:16	ἠγάπησεν	ὁ θεὸς	τὸν κόσμον
	loved	God	*the world*

God loved *the world*.

What did God love? He loved the world. "World" is the direct object.

Dative

5.12 The dative case is used to indicate the *indirect object*.

Matt 2:13	ἄγγελος	κυρίου	φαίνεται	κατ᾽ ὄναρ	τῷ Ἰωσὴφ
	angel	of the Lord	appeared	in a dream	*to Joseph*

An angel of the Lord appeared *to Joseph* in a dream.

"Joseph" is indirectly connected with the action of the verb "appeared."

Genitive

5.13 The Greek genitive case functions much like the English word "of" and the posessive case. Greek puts a word in the genitive case by adding genitive case endings onto the end of the word.

5.14 The **head noun** is the word that the word in the genitive is modifying. In the phrase "love of God," "love" would be the head noun and "God" would be in the genitive.

In English the possessive case can be indicated by the apostrophe. "Everyone breaks God's laws." Greek, however, does not have the apostrophe, and so all Greek constructions are in the form "of ...."

5.15 The most common use of the genitive is when the word in the genitive gives some description of the head noun. You will often find "of" used to translate this use (*descriptive*).

> *Rom 13:12*   ἐνδυσώμεθα   τὰ ὅπλα   τοῦ φωτός
> Let us put on   the armor   *of light*
> **Let us put on the armor *of light*.**
>
> τοῦ φωτός is in the genitive, and ὅπλα is the head noun. "Light" is describing something about the head noun "armor."

5.16 When personal pronouns are used to mean "my," "your," "his," etc., they will be in the genitive. However, in Greek they generally come after the head noun (*possessive*).

> *Matt 2:15*   ἐξ   Αἰγύπτου   ἐκάλεσα   τὸν υἱόν   μου.
> out   of Egypt   I called   son   my
> **Out of Egypt I called *my* Son.**
>
> *1 Tim 5:23*   οἴνῳ   ὀλίγῳ   χρῶ διὰ   τὸν στόμαχον   καὶ τὰς   πυκνάς   σου   ἀσθενείας.
> wine   little   use   because of   the   stomache   and the   frequent   *your*   illness
> **Use a little wine because of your stomach and *your* frequent illnesses.**

Vocabulary

5.17 There is vocabulary for this chapter in the online class.

Chapter 6

Prepositions

Prepositions and their objects form a prepositional phrase, and the preposition controls the case of its object.

English

6.1   A preposition is a word that indicates the relationship between a noun (or pronoun) and other words in the sentence.

> The book is *under* the table.

The preposition "under" describes the relationship between "book" and "table."

6.2   The noun that follows the preposition is called the **object of the preposition**.

> The flashlight is under the *bed*.

> She went through the *woods* to Grandma's house.

6.3   English requires the object of all prepositions to be in the objective case. You would not say, "The book is under he." You would say, "The book is under him." "He" is subjective and "him" is objective.

6.4   The preposition, its object, and any modifiers are together called the **prepositional phrase**.

> The flashlight is *under the bed*.

> She went *through the woods* to Grandma's house.

Greek

6.5   Greek prepositions can have a wide range of meanings. The preposition ἐν can mean "in," "among," "into," "with," "because," "while," etc. In many instances the meaning will be obvious, but in others the decision will be necessarily interpretive.

6.6 A preposition "governs" the case of its object. In other words, the case of the preposition's object is determined by the preposition.

6.7 Prepositions like εἰς take their object in the accusative case.

Matt 2:11   ἐλθόντες   εἰς   τὴν οἰκίαν   εἶδον   τὸ παιδίον
              going   into   *the house*   they saw   the child
              On coming *to the house*, they saw the child.

6.8 Some prepositions like ἐν take their objects in the dative case.

Matt 3:6   ἐβαπτίζοντο   ἐν   τῷ Ἰορδάνῃ   ποταμῷ   ὑπ᾽ αὐτοῦ
         they were baptized in   *the Jordan*   river   by   him
         They were baptized by him in *the river Jordan*.

6.9 Some prepositions like ἀπό take their object in the genitive case.

Rom 7:6   νυνὶ   δὲ   κατηργήθημεν   ἀπὸ   τοῦ νόμου
         now   but   we were released   from   *the law*
         But now we have been released from *the Law*.

Vocabulary

6.10 There is vocabulary for this chapter in the online class.

Chapter 7

English Grammar: Verb Inflection

English verbs have person and number, as well as tense, voice, and mood. You will also be introduced to the concept of "aspect."

7.1 **Verb**. A verb is a word that describes an action or a state of being.

Tom *hit* the ball.

Greek *is* the heavenly language.

7.2 **Person**. There are three persons: first, second, and third.

■ *First person* is the person speaking ("I," "we").

I am the teacher.

We are the students.

■ *Second person* is the person being spoken to ("you").

You are the student.

You are the best students.

■ *Third person* is everything else ("he," "she," "it," "they," "book"). You can also say that third person is that which is spoken about.

This *book* is wonderful.

7.3 **Number**. If the subject of a verb is third person singular, English generally inflects the present active verb by adding "s."[4]

I kick the ball.	We kick the ball.
You kick the ball.	You kick the ball.
He kicks the ball.	They kick the ball.

---

[4] This is a characteristic of the present active. Other tenses are not affected. We say, "I loved," and, "He loved."

There is no such thing as case or gender in verbs; they belong to the noun system.

7.4   **Agreement**. Verbs must agree with their subject. You would not say "Bill *say* to the class that there *is* no tests."

- Since "Bill" is singular third person, you would say, "Bill *says* to the class."

- Because "tests" is plural, you would say, "There *are* no tests."

The presence or absence of the "s" at the end of the verb, and the difference between "is" and "are," are examples of agreement.

7.5   **Tense**. "Tense" in English refers to the *time* when the action of the verb takes place.

- If you study your Greek right now, the verb is in the present tense ("study").

- If you are planning on doing it tomorrow, the verb is in the future tense ("will study").

- If you did it last night, the verb is in the past tense ("studied").

In other words, in English the terms "tense" and "time" refer to the same thing.

7.6   English verbs divide into three forms: the present, past, and past participle. These are called the verb's "principal parts." Many verbs do not have three distinct forms.

tense	"to swim"	"to eat"	"to walk"	"to read"
present	swim	eat	walk	read
past	swam	ate	walked	read
past participle	swum	eaten	walked	read

All other tenses are formed from one of these tenses, often with the aid of a helping word (e.g., "will," "have").[5]

7.7   **Voice**. The voice of a verb refers to the relationship between a verb and its subject.

- When a verb is **active**, the subject is doing the action of the verb.

   "I *walk* the dog."

   "They *called* the preacher."

   "I" is the subject of the verb "walk," which means it is doing the action of the verb.

---

[5]   The basic rule in older English for the future tense is that "shall" is used for the first person and "will" for the second and third. "I shall work hard." "You will work hard." "He will slack off." That distinction has generally fallen into disuse today.

- When a verb is **passive**, the subject of the verb is receiving the action. English forms the present passive by adding the helping verb "am / is / are" or "am / are being" to the past participle.

> Fido *is walked* by Tyler.
>
> They *are being called* by the preacher.

"Fido" is the subject of the verb "is walked," but "Fido" is not doing the action of the verb "walked." The action of the verb is being performed by "Tyler," and it is being done to the subject, "Fido."

You can often tell if a verb is passive by placing "by" after the verb and seeing if it makes sense. "I was hit." "I was hit by what?" "I was hit by the ball." "Was hit" is a passive verb.

When you use a helping verb to form the passive voice, the time of the verbal construction is determined by the helping verb, not the main verb. For example, the active construction "I remember" shifts to "I am remembered" in the passive. Because "am" is present, the construction "am remembered" is present, even though "remembered" is a past participle.

Mood

7.8 Mood refers to the relationship between the verb and reality.

7.9 **Indicative**. A verb in the indicative describes something that *is*, as opposed to something that *may* or *might* be, or something that is commanded. We say that it is the mood of reality. The indicative includes statements and questions. For example, "I am rich." "Are you rich?" Most of the verbs we will meet for some time are in the indicative mood.

> Greek *is* fun.
>
> Hebrew *requires* more study.
>
> Why *am* I procrastinating?

7.10 The **subjunctive** does not describe what *is* but what *may* (or *might*) be. In other words, it is the mood not of reality but of possibility (or probability). In a sense, it describes an action that is one step removed from reality.

> I *might learn* Hebrew.

7.11 A common use of the subjunctive is in an "if" clause.

> If I *were* a rich man, I would hire a Greek tutor.

If in fact the speaker were rich, he would not have used the subjunctive "were" but the indicative: "I *am* rich and therefore I will hire a tutor." This would be a statement of fact, the mood being one of reality. However, if he were not rich, the speaker would use the subjunctive form "were": "If I *were* rich ...."

7.12   **Imperative**. The verb is in the imperative mood when it is making a command. In English, the subject is always second person ("you"), whether implicit or expressed, sometimes with an exclamation mark as the sentence's punctuation.

> *Watch* the basketball game!

The English imperative is usually not inflected, but we do add words to strengthen or further define the intent of the imperative.

> Go *quickly*!

7.13   **Infintive**. An infinitive is a verbal noun. It is most easily recognized as a verb preceded by the word "to."

> *To study* is my highest aspiration.

In this case, the infinitive "to study" is the subject of the sentence.

> I began *to sweat* when I realized finals were three weeks away.

In this sentence, the infinitive "to sweat" is completing the action of the verb "began."

7.14   **Participles** are "verbal adjectives." They can be formed by adding "-ing" to a verb.[6]

> The man, *eating* by the window, is my Greek teacher.

> After *eating,* I will go to bed.

7.15   A participle can have an *adverbial* function.

> After *eating,* my Greek teacher gave us the final.

In this sentence, "eating" is a participle that tells us something relative to the verb "gave." The teacher gave us the final after he was done eating. ("After" is an adverb that emphasizes when the action of the participle occurred.)

7.16   A participle can also have an *adjectival* function.

> The woman, *sitting* by the window, is my Greek teacher.

In this example, "sitting" tells us something about the noun "woman."

_____

[6]   There are other ways to form a participle. For example, in the following sentence, "eaten" is a past participle: "The food, eaten by the class, was delicious."

7.17 In English we also have **gerunds**. They are identical in form to a participle, but instead of functioning as an adjective they function as a noun.

> *Living well* is a goal of our culture.

We will see that Greek does not have gerunds because a Greek participle can function as an adjective or a noun.

Aspect

7.18 Aspect is perhaps the most difficult concept to grasp in Greek verbs, and yet it is the most important and most misunderstood. The basic genius of the Greek verb is not its ability to indicate *when* the action of the verb occurs (time), but what *type of action* it describes, or what we call "aspect." So let's first learn about aspect in English.

7.19 What is the difference between saying "I studied last night" and "I was studying last night"? The first merely says that an event occurred last night; it describes a simple event. It does not give you a clue as to the precise nature of your study time. The second pictures the action of studying as an ongoing action, a process, something that took place over a period of time. This difference between a simple event ("studied") and a process ("was studying") is what I mean by "aspect."

In Galatians 2:12 the RSV reads,

> For before certain men came from James, he *ate* with the Gentiles; but when they came he drew back and separated himself, fearing the circumcision party.

What does Paul mean by "ate"? Did Peter eat one meal or did he eat often with the Gentiles? Is Paul confronting Peter for doing just one thing wrong? I always thought so, until I learned that this particular Greek verb indicates an ongoing action. Peter *ate often* with the Gentiles before he pulled back under pressure from some of the Jewish Christians. This is why the NIV uses "used to" in their translation.

> Before certain men came from James, he *used to eat* with the Gentiles. But when they arrived, he began to draw back and separate himself from the Gentiles because he was afraid of those who belonged to the circumcision group.

Another example is Jesus' words to his disciples in Mark 8:34:

> If anyone wishes to come after me, let him *deny* himself and *take up* his cross and *follow* me.

"Deny" and "take up" in the Greek are described as simple events while the aspect of the verb "follow" is a process. The aspect of "deny" and "take up" does not tell us anything about the nature of those actions. They do not tell us whether the "deny and take up" occur only once in your life, or if you are to do this every day. But the aspect of "follow" emphasizes that the commitment to discipleship involves a day-to-day following, as you might assume from the meaning of the word.

7.20 There are three aspects. The **continuous** aspect means that the action of the verb is thought of as an ongoing process.

> In pointing out these things to the brethren, you will be a good servant of Christ Jesus, *constantly nourished* on the words of the faith and of the sound doctrine which you have been following (1 Tim 4:6; NASB).

7.21 The **undefined** aspect means that the action of the verb is thought of as a simple event, without commenting on whether or not it is a process.

> For God so *loved* the world that he *gave* his only Son, that whoever believes in him should not perish but have eternal life (John 3:16; RSV).

7.22 The **perfective** aspect describes an action that was brought to completion and its results are felt in the present. (Of course, the time of the verb is from the viewpoint of the writer/speaker, not the reader.) In one sense, it is the combination of the undefined (completed act in the past) and the continuous (ongoing effects of that act).

> For the one who *has died* has been set free from sin (Rom 6:7).

> For *it is written* that Abraham had two sons (Gal 4:22).

> That which *is born* of the flesh is flesh, and that which *is born* of the Spirit is spirit (John 3:6).

Chapter 8

Greek Grammar: Verbs (Indicative)

Verbs have a linkage to their subject not by word order but because the verb "agrees" with its subject in person and number (along with the subject being in the nominative). There are, for the most part, five Greek tenses, and they convey a mixture of time and aspect.

Inflection

8.1 **Agreement**. A Greek verb must agree with its subject in person and number. If the subject is singular, the verb must be singular. If the subject is first, second, or third person, then so must the verb.

8.2 **Personal endings**. Greek verbs indicate their person and number by adding different suffixes to the end of the word. These suffixes are called *personal endings*. This is somewhat like adding an "s" to an English verb when its subject is third person singular present. "I walk Rufio," becomes, "She walk*s* Rufio." (Rufio is our German Shepherd.)

The word "morphology" is an important term. Morphology is the study of how a language uses small pieces of information (called "morphemes") to construct a word. A personal ending is a morpheme.

The stem of a word is another morpheme; it carries the basic meaning of the word. So technically, you can form a verb by starting with its stem, adding another morpheme called a "connecting vowel" (to help pronounce the verb), and then adding the personal ending (the final morpheme).

So, for example, if you want to say "we hear," you join three morphemes: ἀκου (stem) + ο (connecting vowel) + μεν (personal ending) → ἀκούομεν.

8.3 **Paradigm**. Here is a Greek paradigm of the verb ἀκούω, which means "I hear." Notice how the endings change depending on the subject's person and number. (You do not have to memorize these endings; just be aware of how they function.)

person and number	Greek	Translation
first person singular	ἀκούω	I hear
second person singular	ἀκούεις	You hear
third person singular	ἀκούει	He/she/it hears
first person plural	ἀκούομεν	We hear
second person plural	ἀκούετε	You hear
third person plural	ἀκούουσι	They hear

8.4 **Parsing**. The software will simply "parse" this information for you, i.e., tell you the verb's person and number (along with other information about the verb). Here is an example from Accordance when I hover the mouse over ἠγάπησεν in John 3:16.

> **ἠγάπησεν** ēgapēsen **ἀγαπάω** (**ἀγάπη**) agapaō
> (agapē) **Verb** third singular aorist active indicative **to love**
> (Predicate)

Lexical form

8.5 **Lexical form**. The lexical form of a verb is the first person singular, present indicative. In the traditional language approach, you would have to be able to figure out the lexical form from an inflected form. But in our approach, the tools will tell us the lexical form. If you did a mouse over the inflected form κόσμον ("world"), you would see that the lexical form is κόσμος.[7]

> **world** GK **G3180 κόσμος** kosmos
> [GNT-T] **κόσμον** kosmon Noun masculine singular
> accusative **world, mankind, earth; adornment, decoration**

8.6 **GK Numbers**. For many years we have used what are called "Strong's numbers." Each Greek and Hebrew word was tagged with a unique number by Dr. James Strong. This way, no matter what inflected form a word took, it could always be identified by the same number. κόσμον and κόσμος are both #3180.

Because Strong's numbers originally omitted many Greek and Hebrew words, Zondervan introduced a new set of numbers (done by Ed Goodrick and John Kohlenberger; hence, "GK"), and it is these numbers that I am using in this text and

---

[7] Some of the older grammars and some modern commentaries list the infinitive form (λέγειν, "to say") as the lexical form, but lexicons are consistent now in listing verbs in the first person singular, present indicative (λέγω, "I say").

my databases. At the online class you will find a conversion chart to move between the two numbering systems. κόσμος in the Strong system is #2889.

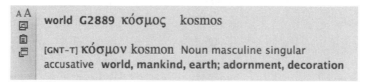

However, if you are using my translation (*MOUNCE-NT*), it will show the GK number (#3180).

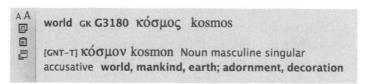

Aspect

8.7   In English, "time" is more important than "aspect." It is just the reverse in Greek; aspect is more important than time.

In other words, what is at the heart of the Greek verbal system is not so much telling the reader *when* something happens but rather what *kind of action* occurrs. I wish we could put off discussing aspect until Church Greek, but you need to have some basic idea of what is going on in order to achieve our goals for Foundational Greek.

8.8   The **continuous** aspect describes an action as ongoing.

1 Tim 2:4   πάντας   ἀνθρώπους   θέλει   σωθῆναι
               all   people   *he wishes*   to be saved
               He [God] ... *wishes* all people to be saved.

God's salvific plans are not a one-time thought but his ongoing preoccupation.

8.9   The **undefined** aspect tell us nothing about the kind of action.

1 Tim 1:12   Χάριν   ἔχω   τῷ   ἐνδυναμώσαντί   με   Χριστῷ   Ἰησοῦ   τῷ κυρίῳ   ἡμῶν
              thanks   I have   to the   *one who strengthens*   me   Christ   Jesus   Lord   our
              I thank Christ Jesus our Lord, who *has given* me *strength*.

Paul isn't telling Timothy anything more, other than that Jesus strengthened him. He doesn't comment about this being a one-time enablement, or a daily strengthing. For whatever reason, it was not important for Paul to be more specific, so he uses the undefined aspect.

8.10 The **perfective** aspect describes an action that was brought to completion (and hence is usually in the past) but has effects felt in the speaker's present.

> *1 Tim 4:2*   ἐν ὑποκρίσει ψευδολόγων, κεκαυστηριασμένων τὴν ἰδίαν συνείδησιν
> in   hypocrisy   of liars   *having been seared*   their own   conscience
> NIV: Such teachings come through hypocritical liars, whose consciences *have been seared* as with a hot iron.
>
> Because the opponents' consciences have been seared (completed past event), they are liars (present effects).

Tense

8.11 In Greek, a tense carries two connotations: aspect and time. For example, the aorist (tense) describes an undefined action (aspect) that normally occurs in the past (time). In this text, I use the term "tense" to refer only to the *form* of a verb (e.g., present tense, future tense, aorist tense); I do not use "tense" to designate *when* an action of a verb occurs. I always use the term "time" to describe *when* the action of that verb occurs. Please do not confuse "tense" and "time."

8.12 There are five tenses in Greek. The key is to see the combination of aspect and time conveyed by each tense.

tense	time (normally)	aspect
present	present	continuous
future	future	undefined
imperfect	past	continuous
aorist	past	undefined
perfect	completed, effects felt in present	perfective (undefined and continuous)

Present Indicative

8.13 The present indicative describes an action that generally occurs in the present. The word "generally" is important. As we learn more about Greek verbs, you will discover that they are not tied to time. For example, a present tense verb can describe a past action. But more about that later.

The present tense can convey any form of undefined or continuous action, which at times can make translation hard and interpretive. For example, a translator can choose either "I study" or "I am studying" based on which fits the context best.

Phil 1:15 τινὲς δὲ καὶ δι᾿ εὐδοκίαν τὸν Χριστὸν κηρύσσουσιν
some but indeed through goodwill the Christ *preach*
ESV: Some indeed *preach* Christ from good will.
NASB: Some … *are preaching* Christ … from good will.

Future Indicative

8.14 The future indicative describes an action that will occur in the future (*predictive*).

1 Tim 4:1 Τὸ δὲ πνεῦμα ῥητῶς λέγει ὅτι ἐν ὑστέροις καιροῖς ἀποστήσονταί τινες
the but Spirit expressly he says that in later times *will fall away* some
ESV: Now the Spirit expressly says that in later times some *will depart* from the faith.

Futures are generally translated with a simple form (i.e., undefined aspect), "will fall away," rather than "will be falling away."

Two Past Tenses (Imperfect and Aorist Indicative)

8.15 Greek has two tenses that indicate past time. The difference between the two is aspect.

8.16 The imperfect describes a *continuous* action that normally occurs in the past (*progressive, durative*).

Mark 1:21 εἰσελθὼν εἰς τὴν συναγωγὴν ἐδίδασκεν.
after entering into the synagogue *he was teaching*
He entered the synagogue and *was teaching*.

8.17 The aorist tense describes an *undefined* action that normally occurs in the past (*constative*).

Mark 1:4 ἐγένετο Ἰωάννης [ὁ] βαπτίζων ἐν τῇ ἐρήμῳ
he appeared John the Baptizer in the desert
John the baptizer *appeared* in the desert.

8.18 This distinction between the aorist and imperfect can be important for exegesis. The ESV translates John 19:3 as,

John 19:3	ἤρχοντο		πρὸς	αὐτὸν	καὶ	ἔλεγον·	χαῖρε	ὁ βασιλεὺς	τῶν	Ἰουδαίων·
	they were coming up		*to*	*him*	*and*	*said*	*Hail*	*King*	*of the*	*Jews*

	καὶ	ἐδίδοσαν		αὐτῷ	ῥαπίσματα.
	and	*they were striking*		*him*	*hands*

ESV: They *came up* to him, saying, "Hail, King of the Jews!" and *struck* him with their hands.

But how often did the soldiers approach Jesus, and how often did they strike him? Only once? The NET and NRSV make the English as clear as the Greek.

> They came up to him *again and again* and said, "Hail, King of the Jews!" And they *struck* him *repeatedly* in the face. (NET)

> They *kept coming up* to him, saying, "Hail, King of the Jews!" and *striking* him on the face. (NRSV)

Having said this, recognize that the aorist is kind of like the default past tense. If you want to say something occurred in the past and don't want to say anything else, then you use the aorist. What this means for exegesis is that you have to be careful attributing too much significance to an aorist verb. There may not be much.

Perfect Indicative

8.19   The Greek perfect describes an action that was brought to completion and whose effects are felt in the present from the standpoint of the speaker. Because it describes a completed action, the action described by the perfect verb normally occurred in the past.

For example, "Jesus died" is a simple statement of an event that happened in the past. In Greek this would be in the aorist. But if we used the Greek perfect to say, "Jesus has died," then we would expect the verse to continue by spelling out the present significance of that past action. "Jesus has died *for my sins*."

Another example is the verb "to write." When the Bible says, "It is written," this is usually in the perfect tense. Scripture was written in the past but is applicable in the present. That is why some translations choose the present "It is written," instead of "It has been written." This emphasizes its abiding significance.

Mark 9:13	ἐποίησαν	αὐτῷ	ὅσα	ἤθελον,	καθὼς	γέγραπται	ἐπ᾽	αὐτόν
	they did	*to him*	*whatever*	*they wished*	*just as*	*it had been written*	*about*	*him*

NRSV: They did to him whatever they pleased, as *it is written* about him.

NLT: They chose to abuse him, just as the Scriptures *predicted*.

8.20 In English, using "have" or "has" has somewhat the same meaning as the Greek perfect. They describe an action that was completed in the recent past but as having implications in the immediate present.

> I *ate* last night.

> I *have eaten* and am still full.

The English present tense can also describe a past action with current consequences.

> It *is written.*

Indicative mood

8.21 In the next chapter we are going to learn the different moods. However, you already know one, the indicative mood. Most of the examples we have seen so far are indicative verbs.

8.22 A verb in the indicative describes something that *is*, as opposed to something that *may* or *might* be, or something that is *ought* to be. Statements, questions, and even lies are in the indicative.

1 Tim 2:7   ἀλήθειαν λέγω οὐ ψεύδομαι
              truth   *I speak* not *I lie*
              I am speaking the truth; *I am* not *lying*.

Rom 3:31   νόμον οὖν   καταργοῦμεν διὰ   τῆς πίστεως;
             law   therefore *we nullify*   through the faith
             Do we therefore *nullify* the law through faith?

Vocabulary

8.23 There is vocabulary for this chapter in the online class.

Chapter 9

Greek Grammar: Verbs (Nonindicative)

In this chapter we will see a quick overview of the different moods, and how aspect shows itself in each. We will also look at the middle voice and deponent verbs

Aspect

9.1 Once you are out of the Indicative, the Greek verbal system has no time significance; it is all about aspect.[8]

- Verbal forms built on a *present* tense stem indicate a *continuous* action.

- Verbal forms built on an *aorist* tense stem indicte an *undefined* action

- Verbal forms built on a *perfect* tense stem indicate a *completed* action with *ongoing effects*.

This is a significant switch from English, and you have to watch yourself carefully. Just because a nonindicative verb is formed from the present tense does not mean it describes an event happening in the present; it only means it is continuous.

9.2 You remember that "mood" is the verb's relationship to reality.

Subjunctive

9.3 Because the subjunctive is one step removed from reality, it is appropriate for purpose statements (*purpose*) and "if" clauses (*conditional*).

1 Tim 5:7   ταῦτα   παράγγελλε,   ἵνα   ἀνεπίλημπτοι   ὦσιν
these things   command   in order that   above reproach   *they might be*
Command these things so that *they may be* above reproach.

---

[8]   There is something called "relative time," and we will discuss that in Church Greek. Technically, there is no *absolute* time outside of the indicative.

2 Tim 2:21	ἐὰν	οὖν	τις	ἐκκαθάρῃ	ἑαυτὸν	ἀπὸ τούτων,	ἔσται	σκεῦος εἰς	τιμήν
	if	therefore	someone	*might cleanse*	himself	from these things	he will be	vessel for	honor

ESV: Therefore, if anyone *cleanses* himself from what is dishonorable, he will be a vessel for honorable use.

Imperative

9.4 The basic function of the imperative is to state a command.

1 Tim 4:4 Γύμναζε δὲ σεαυτὸν πρὸς εὐσέβειαν.
train but yourself for godliness
Rather, *train* yourself for godliness.

9.5 **Person**. In English all imperatives are second person; in Greek there are second and third person imperatives. Because there is no English equivalent to a third person imperative, the translation must be a little idiomatic. βλέπε (second person singular) means "(You) look!" βλεπέτω (third person singular) means "Let him look!" or "He must look!" The words "let" or "must," and a pronoun supplied from the person of the verb ("him"), can be added to convey the correct meaning.

9.6 It is difficult to bring out the significance of the present continuous in an imperative.

1 Tim 3:10 οὗτοι δὲ δοκιμαζέσθωσαν πρῶτον, εἶτα διακονείτωσαν ἀνέγκλητοι ὄντες.
they but *let them be tested* first then *let them serve* blameless being
NIV: They *must* first *be tested*; and then if there is nothing against them, *let them serve as deacons*.

1 Tim 6:20 Ὦ Τιμόθεε, τὴν παραθήκην φύλαξον
O Timothy the deposit guard
O Timothy, *guard* the deposit.

Matt 6:10 ἐλθέτω ἡ βασιλεία σου· γενηθήτω τὸ θέλημά σου.
let it come the kingdom your *let it be* the will your
HCSB: Your kingdom *come*. Your will *be done*.
NET: *May* your kingdom *come*, *may* your will *be done*.

Infinitive

9.7 The infinitive can complete the thought of the verb (*complementary*).

| *Matt 4:17* | ἤρξατο ὁ Ἰησοῦς κηρύσσειν καὶ λέγειν· μετανοεῖτε· |
| | began Jesus *to preach* and *to say* repent. |

NASB: Jesus began *to preach* and *say*, "Repent".

ESV: Jesus began *to preach*, *saying*, "Repent".

| *1 Tim 1:15* | Χριστὸς Ἰησοῦς ἦλθεν εἰς τὸν κόσμον ἁμαρτωλοὺς σῶσαι. |
| | Christ Jesus he came into the world sinners *to save* |

Christ Jesus came into the world *to save* sinners.

Participle

9.8 As a verbal adjective, a participle can function adjectivally or adverbially; and as an adjective, it can function both as a normal adjective (*attributive*) and also as a noun (*substantival*). This gives us three basic uses.

| *1 Tim 3:15* | ἥτις ἐστὶν ἐκκλησία θεοῦ ζῶντος |
| | which is church of God *living* |

which is the church of the *living* God

| *1 Tim 1:12* | Χάριν ἔχω τῷ ἐνδυναμώσαντί με Χριστῷ Ἰησοῦ τῷ κυρίῳ ἡμῶν |
| | thanks I have to the *one who strengthened* me Christ Jesus Lord our |

I thank Christ Jesus our Lord, who *has given me strength*.

| *1 Tim 1:13* | ἠλεήθην, ὅτι ἀγνοῶν ἐποίησα ἐν ἀπιστίᾳ |
| | I was shown mercy because *being ignorant* I acted in unbelief |

ESV: I received mercy because I had acted *ignorantly* in unbelief.

NIV: I was shown mercy because I acted *in ignorance* and unbelief.

Middle Voice

9.9 Greek has the active and passive voices. It, however, also has a third voice called the "middle." It is a tad complicated to understand at first, but if we are going to understand our Strong's Bibles, this needs to be learned.

9.10 If a verb is in the active voice, it means the subject does the action of the verb. If a verb is in the passive voice, it means the subject receives the action of the verb. "Bill *hit* (active) the ball." "Bill *was hit* (passive) by the ball."

9.11 If a verb is in the middle voice, it means the subject still does the action of the verb but in some way in which the subject is emphasized in the action of the verb. I know; it's complicated. In a sense, the verb in the middle voice is pointing a finger back at the subject and saying that the subject has some special interest in the action of the verb other than just doing the action of the verb.

9.12 We don't need to go into this in detail now; that is reserved for Church Greek. But here is what you do need to know now.

- The middle often has a meaning that sounds active to us. When you do your mouse-over, don't be surprised to see the software parse the verb as a middle even though the translation is active.

- In the present, imperfect, and perfect tenses, the middle is identical in form to the passive. λύομαι could be either passive ("I am loosed") or middle ("I am loosed for myself"). The "for myself" is a standard way grammars identify the middle voice, even though it sounds strange. Most software doesn't differentiate middle from passive since they are telling you the form, not the meaning.

- In the future and aorist, the middle is distinctly different from the passive. ἐλύθην means "I was loosed" (aorist passive), and ἐλυσάμην means "I loosed for myself" (aorist middle).

  For example, ἔρχομαι is middle in the present. It always has an active meaning, "to come" or "to go." Your software may parse it as a middle, or a middle/passive.

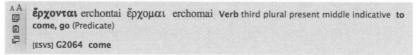

Voice and Deponent Verbs

9.13 Greek has a category of verbs called "deponent" verbs. A deponent verb is one that is middle or passive in its *form* but active in its *meaning*. Its form is always middle or passive but its meaning is always active. It can never have a passive meaning. For example, ἐλεύσομαι means "I will come."

9.14 Most tools will list these forms as "middle" or "passive" and not "deponent." In Matt 2:9, ἐπορεύθησαν is translated, "they continued their journey"; the verb is deponent.

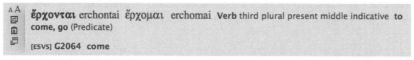

9.15 How then will you know how these deponents are to be translated? The translators know which verbs are deponent, and they have translated these words with active meanings. Nondeponent verbs have lexical forms ending in ω or μι (λύω, δίδωμι). If the lexical form of the verb ends in ομαι, it is deponent in the present tense (e.g., πορεύομαι).

Chapter 10

Word Studies

Words have a "semantic range." "Semantic" refers to a word's meaning; "semantic range" refers to the range of possible meanings a word possesses. Think of all the ways we use the word "run."

> I scored six runs today.
> Could you run that by me again?
> My computer runs faster than yours!
> He runs off at the mouth.
> I left the water running all night.
> He ran to the store.
> The car ran out of gas.

> The clock ran down.
> Duane ran for senate.
> Her nose ran.
> I ran up the bill.

I prefer the phrase "bundle of meanings." A word usually does not possess just one meaning; a word has different meanings, hence "bundle." This is true in any language.

For example, the semantic range of the preposition ἐν is quite large. Look at how it is used in the following verses. (All translations are from the ESV.)

Matt 1:20   τὸ γὰρ ἐν αὐτῇ γεννηθὲν ἐκ πνεύματός ἐστιν ἁγίου.
the for *in* her conceived of spirit is holy
for that which is conceived *in* her is of the Holy Spirit

Matt 2:1   Τοῦ ... Ἰησοῦ γεννηθέντος ἐν Βηθλέεμ ... ἐν ἡμέραις Ἡρῴδου
the Jesus was born *in* Bethlehem *in* days of Herod
Jesus was born *in* Bethlehem ... *in* the days of Herod.

Matt 3:9   καὶ μὴ δόξητε λέγειν ἐν ἑαυτοῖς
and not presume to say *in* yourselves
and do not presume to say *to* yourselves

Matt 3:11   Ἐγὼ ... ὑμᾶς βαπτίζω ἐν ὕδατι
I you baptize *in* water
I baptize you *with* water.

Matt 4:23   θεραπεύων πᾶσαν νόσον καὶ πᾶσαν μαλακίαν ἐν τῷ λαῷ.
healing every disease and every infirmity *in* the people
healing every disease and every affliction *among* the people

Matt 5:34   μὴ ὀμόσαι ὅλως· μήτε ἐν τῷ οὐρανῷ, ὅτι θρόνος ἐστὶν τοῦ θεοῦ
not swear at all either *in* the heaven for throne it is of God
Do not take an oath at all, either *by* heaven, for it is the throne of God.

Languages are not codes. There is not a one–to–one correspondence between languages, especially vocabulary. Rarely if ever can you find one word in one language that corresponds exactly to another word in another language, especially in its semantic range. English has no single word that matches the range of meanings for ἐν. The semantic domains of a Greek and English word may overlap, but they are not identical.

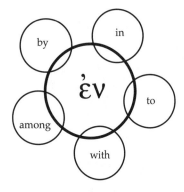

So how do we translate when we do not have English words that correspond exactly to the Greek? We have to interpret. All translation is interpretive. For example, in 1 Timothy 6:13-14 Paul writes,

> In the presence of God who gives life to all things, and of Christ Jesus who in his testimony before Pontius Pilate made the good confession, I *charge* you to keep the commandment unstained and free from reproach until the appearing of our Lord Jesus Christ. (RSV)

The Greek word behind "charge" is παραγγέλλω, which means "to command, insist, instruct, urge," a wide range of meanings for which there is no single counterpart in English. The translator must decide whether Paul is "commanding" Timothy (who is a member of his inner circle, fully trusted, and probably his best friend) or

"urging" him. This is an interpretive decision that must be made by the translator. The RSV chose "charge," the NLT "command," and the NKJV rightly (in my opinion) selected "urge."

But let's say that you want to discover for yourself what Paul means when he "charges" Timothy to keep the commandment unstained. It makes no sense to look up the English word "charge," because "charge" can't mean "urge," and "urge" can't mean "charge." If you want to decide for yourself what Paul is saying, you have to know the Greek word behind the English, learn its semantic range, and then make a decision.

How do you do this? There are four steps.

- Decide what word to study.

- Identify the Greek word.

- Discover its semantic range.

- Look for something in the context that helps determine what the biblical author meant by this word in this particular verse.

Step 1. Choose the English Word

I annoyed many people for many years asking what I think is an extremely important question: "What is the minimum it takes to become a Christian?" You are at the dorm in college and a freshman walks up to you and says, "You're a graduate student in divinity, aren't you?" ("Divinity" is the word they use in Scotland for Biblical Studies.) You say, "Yes." She says, "What is a Christian anyway?" Go! You have two minutes to tell her. What are you going to say? You want to tell her enough of the gospel, so that if she responds, she will truly have become a Christian. If you don't tell her enough and she responds, will she really have become a Christian? If you add to the basic gospel message, will it drive her away unnecessarily?

Sound hypothetical? No, it happened to me, and I didn't have an answer. I promised myself that would never happen again, so I started searching out all the short and succinct statements about becoming a Christian, because I wanted to have a two-minute answer the next time I was asked that question.

Romans 10:9-10 is one of those succinct and crucial passages on the nature of salvation.

> If you confess with your mouth that Jesus is Lord and believe in your heart that God raised him from the dead, you will be saved. For with the heart one believes and is justified, and with the mouth one confesses and is saved (ESV).

The key term in the entire passage is what? It's "Lord," isn't it. The essence of salvation is the confession, "Jesus is Lord," accompanied with the acceptance of the resurrection. So what does "Lord" mean? Its meaning is crucial to our salvation.

This is actually the first step in doing a Greek word study: you've decided on a significant word. If you try to do word studies on every word you read, not only will you run out of time but you'll get bored. So how do you pick the right words? There is not a clear-cut answer to this question, but here are some suggestions.

1. Look for the hub. Think of a paragraph or verse as a bicycle wheel. If you pull one spoke off here and another off there, the wheel still functions. However, if you remove the hub, the entire wheel falls apart. Likewise, the most important words to study are the ones that form the hub, the center of

a paragraph or verse; these are the words that, if removed, cause the passage to fall apart.

For example, in the Beatitudes Jesus pronounces a blessing on the "poor" (which means, those who know they have nothing and therefore turn to God), the "hungry" (whose spiritual appetites are satisfied only by God), and those who "weep" (over their spiritual bankruptcy). If any of those words are removed from the verse, it loses its meaning.

Jesus' answers to Satan's temptations are built around the words "bread" (all that sustains us, physically and spiritually), "worship" (offering all that we are before God), and "test" (unnecessarily questioning God's promise to care).

When Jesus called Levi as a disciple, he says, "I have not come to call the righteous but sinners to repentance" (Luke 5:32). The "righteous" are those who mistakenly think they are right with God, and the "sinners" are those who perhaps do not follow Jewish ritual but understand their lack of righteousness before God.

To say it another way, does a verse "hang" on a word? It will be a word that is central to the meaning of the verse, and without it the sentence will not make sense. In Romans 10:9, this word is "Lord."

2. Does a word sound like a theological term? You cannot get far especially in Paul's letters without coming across terms that describe theological truths, which carry the weight of the passage. Consider Romans 3:22-24, one of the most condensed theological passages in the Bible. (The words in parentheses are my explanatory additions.)

> "This righteousness (being declared innocent of sin) from God comes through faith (trusting that God did on the cross for us what we

could not do for ourselves) in Jesus Christ to all (Jew and Gentile alike) who believe. There is no difference, for all have sinned (broken the rules that govern our relationship with Gold) and fall short of the glory of God (the praise and honor God intended for his creation), and are justified (made righteous; same word group as the previous "righteousness") freely by his grace (God's goodness extended to those who do not deserve it) through the redemption (the freedom from sin gained through Christ's work on the cross) that came by Christ Jesus."

You can see that every word I explained is a key theological term.

3. Is the word repeated? When a word weaves its way through a paragraph, it may be an important word. In the prologue to John (1:1-18), "grace" plays an important role. Jesus was full of grace and truth (vv 14, 16b), and we have received from him "grace upon grace" (v 16).

Sometimes a theme may weave its way through the passage but uses different words. Again, in John's prologue, many words are used to describe Jesus: word; life; light; flesh; only Son; only God. All would make for good word studies.

When repeated words are used with different meanings in different verses, you have a ripe candidate for word studies. Jesus ends his sermon with the words, "Why do you call me 'Lord, Lord,' and not do what I tell you" (Luke 6:46). In the next chapter the centurion addresses Jesus as "Lord" (7:6). Paul tells us that a confession of Jesus as "Lord" is a necessary part of salvation (Romans 10:9). "Lord" can't mean the same thing in all three passages. The centurion addresses Jesus as "Sir," the disciples as "Master" (in the sense of, Rabbi), and salvation requires submission to Jesus as "God." This is the range of mean-

ings for the same Greek word translated "lord."

4. Sometimes passages contain words that don't make sense. These may even be common English words, but the common meaning doesn't fit in a particular verse. This may be a clue that a particular word is worth investigating. What is an "unclean" spirit? One that doesn't bathe properly? No. In this context, "unclean" means that which cannot be brought into contact with what is holy, and carries the idea of moral and spiritual corruptness.

What does it mean for a "word" to become "flesh"? (John 1:14). In everyday discourse we do not speak of a "word" becoming "flesh." "Word" in this passage has Old Testament and philosophical roots that John adapts to define Jesus; "flesh" doesn't mean something sinful but that Jesus, the Word, actually became a human being.

5. Verbs can be especially important. For example, what does it mean that the Word "dwelt among us?" (John 1:14). In what sense? The Greek σκηνόω means "to pitch, live in a tent." The dictionary points out that the related noun (σκηνή) was used of the tabernacle in the wilderness. So the idea of Jesus' incarnation reflects the Old Testament dwelling of God with his people.

6. Compare translations. Sometimes a word or phrase will be translated quite differently from translation to translation. The translators are obviously struggling with what is probably an important word.

Matthew 6:13 contains the most difficult phrase in the Lord's Prayer to understand. The NIV writes, "And *lead us not* into temptation," but the NLT says, "And *don't let us yield* to temptation." Which is it?

When Jesus calms the wind and the waves (Mark 4:38), most translations say something like, "Teacher, do you not care that we *are perishing*?" The NIV writes, "Teacher, don't you care *if we drown*?" Which is it? Were the disciples actually in the process of drowning, or were they afraid they might? Think of the historical situation; the difference is significant and affects how we understand Jesus' rebuttal. "Why are you so fearful? Have you still no faith?"

Word studies are generally fun and informative. They give us good preaching and teaching illustrations and help to fill out the meaning of a passage. But most importantly, these are God's words and it is worth hanging on to them.

What do you think "Lord" means in Romans 10:9? Let's find out.

2. Identify the Greek Word

Your next step is to find the Greek word behind the English. You can use your software program or one of my interlinears. Here is the phrase in *IRU*.

"Jesus	is	Lord,
Ἰησοῦν		κύριον
n.asm		*n.asm*
2652		*3261*

The inflected form is κύριον, it is a noun, and its GK number is *#3261*. The conversion chart at the back of *IRU* tells you its Strong's number is *#2962*.

If you prefer to work with software, and if you have purchased the correct modules, finding the Greek behind the English is easy. Because software is always changing, I hesitate to show you how to do this; so I will keep the video on the class' website updated so you can see how the different software programs work. But here is how you do this in Accordance.

1. Be sure you are using an English text that is connected to the Greek; they are called "Strong's Bibles"). Not surprisingly, I will be using the *Mounce Reverse-Interlinear New Testament* translation from Accordance.

2. Go to Romans 10:9 and mouse over the word "Lord."

3. If you have the tagged Greek New Testament, Accordance will highlight κύριον, which is the inflected form. In the Instant Details window (see page 46), you can see that this lexical form is GK number 3261, and its lexical form is κύριος (transliterated *kurios*). The other information showing will become important later on. Examples of other Bible search software are on pages 46–47.

Since this is the first time I have used the *IRU* format for showing you a verse, I need to stop and explain it to you.

- ■ The first line is the English (in English word order).

- ■ The second line is the Greek, with the word order altered to match the English.

- ■ The third is the parsing. Ἰησοῦν is a noun, accusative singular masculine. There is a key in the front of *IRU* as to what the codes mean.

- ■ The fourth is the word's GK number. There is a conversion guide to strong's numbers at the online class.

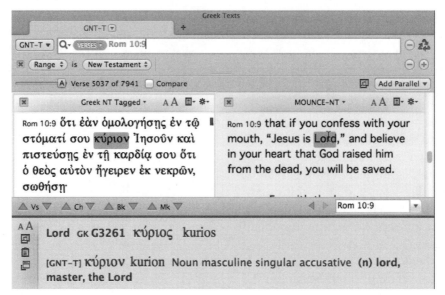

Accordance

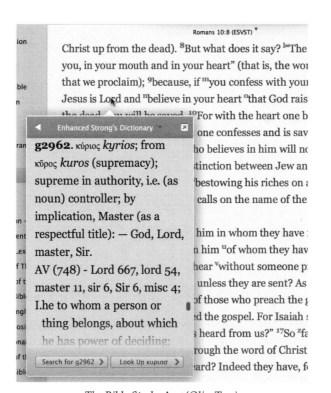

The Bible Study App (OliveTree)

Romans 10:9 (Mounce Reverse-Interlinear New Testament)

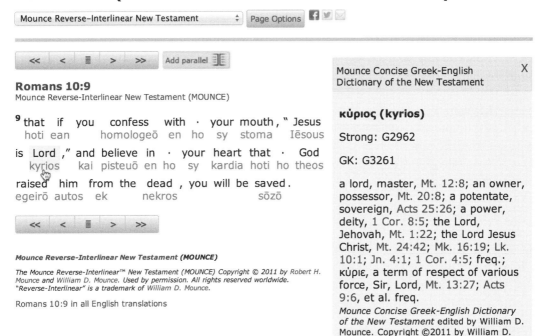

Mounce Reverse–Interlinear New Testament ⇳   Page Options

Romans 10:9
Mounce Reverse-Interlinear New Testament (MOUNCE)

9 that   if   you   confess   with   ·   your   mouth ," Jesus
hoti   ean   homologeō   en   ho   sy   stoma   Iēsous

is   Lord ," and   believe   in   ·   your   heart   that   ·   God
kyrios   kai   pisteuō   en ho   sy   kardia   hoti   ho   theos

raised   him   from   the   dead ,   you   will be   saved .
egeirō   autos   ek   nekros   sōzō

Mounce Reverse-Interlinear New Testament (MOUNCE)

The Mounce Reverse-Interlinear™ New Testament (MOUNCE) Copyright © 2011 by Robert H. Mounce and William D. Mounce. Used by permission. All rights reserved worldwide. "Reverse-Interlinear" is a trademark of William D. Mounce.

Romans 10:9 in all English translations

Mounce Concise Greek-English Dictionary of the New Testament   X

κύριος (kyrios)

Strong: G2962

GK: G3261

a lord, master, Mt. 12:8; an owner, possessor, Mt. 20:8; a potentate, sovereign, Acts 25:26; a power, deity, 1 Cor. 8:5; the Lord, Jehovah, Mt. 1:22; the Lord Jesus Christ, Mt. 24:42; Mk. 16:19; Lk. 10:1; Jn. 4:1; 1 Cor. 4:5; freq.; κύριε, a term of respect of various force, Sir, Lord, Mt. 13:27; Acts 9:6, et al. freq.
Mounce Concise Greek-English Dictionary of the New Testament edited by William D. Mounce. Copyright ©2011 by William D. Mounce. All rights reserved. Free Greek dictionary.

BibleGateway.com

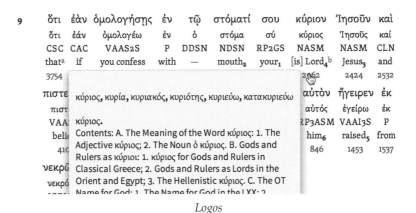

Logos

Step 3. Discover Its Semantic Range

Before you can discover what the word means in a particular context, you have to learn its range of meaning, its "semantic range." As I have been saying, we are looking for the semantic range of the Greek, not the English, since they are almost always (if not always) different. So we are going to learn the semantic range of the Greek word κύριος. (If you like to use paper resources to do this, check out the website class for instructions.)

1. The easiest way is to have the right software and the right text modules. If you double click on "Lord" in my translation, the default Greek dictionary shows (which here is mine). It will give you a feel for the semantic range.

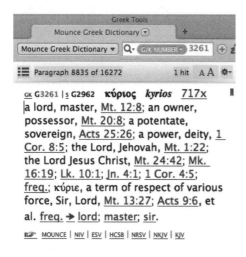

If you have purchased another Greek dictionary, you can access that as well.

2. Another way to see the word's semantic range is to consult what used to be called an "Englishman's concordance," which is now called a "Greek-English concordance." There is a considerable difference between this type of concordance and others. In a regular

concordance, if you look up "Lord," the entries list all the places where the English word "Lord" occurs. However, there may be several different Greek words that are translated "Lord," and κύριος may not always be translated with "Lord"; these are the limitations of a regular concordance. For example, σάρξ is translated in Galatians by the NIV (1984) as "body" (1 time), "flesh" (1), "human effort" (1), "illness" (2), "man" (1), "no one" (1), "ordinary way" (2), "outwardly" (1), "sinful nature" (7), and "that nature" (1). (In some of these occurrences, σάρξ was combined with another word when translated.)

But with a Greek-English concordance, you know you are looking at every place the same Greek word occurs, regardless of how it is translated. In contrast to a Greek concordance, the verses are listed in English and not Greek. As you scan through the entries, you can see how the NIV has translated κύριος.

There are several ways to do this in Accordance (and the other software; see the online course for videos), but one is to go to my dictionary and click on the link to your favorite translation. (You need to have

> Lord, Mt. 13:27; Acts 9:6, et al. freq. ➔ lord; master; sir.
> ☞ MOUNCE | 🔍 | ESV | HCSB | NRSV | NKJV | KJV

purchased that translation as well.) If you want to see how the NIV translates all the verses where κύριος occurs, click on NIV (see illustration on page 49, where I displayed a parallel Greek text so I can confirm the Greek behind the English).

Clicking on the frequency (e.g., 717x) in my dictionary will also display a Greek-English concordance listing.

Another way is to right click on "lord," and choose "Search for :: Key Number."

Mt	1: 20	an angel *of* the **Lord** appeared to him in a dream and said,
	1: 22	All this took place to fulfill what the **Lord** had said through the
	1: 24	he did what the angel *of* the **Lord** had commanded him and took
	2: 13	they had gone, an angel *of* the **Lord** appeared to Joseph in a dream.
	2: 15	so was fulfilled what the **Lord** had said through the prophet:
	2: 19	an angel *of* the **Lord** appeared in a dream to Joseph in Egypt
	3: 3	'Prepare the way *for* the **Lord**, make straight paths for him.' "
	4: 7	"It is also written: 'Do not put the **Lord** your God to the test.' "
	4: 10	it is written: 'Worship the **Lord** your God, and serve him only.' "
	5: 33	break your oath, but keep the oaths you have made *to* the **Lord**.'
	6: 24	"No one can serve two **masters**. Either he will hate the one
	7: 21	"Not everyone who says to me, '**Lord**, Lord,' will enter the
	7: 21	"Not everyone who says to me, 'Lord, **Lord**,' will enter the
	7: 22	Many will say to me on that day, '**Lord**, Lord, did we not prophesy
	7: 22	Many will say to me on that day, 'Lord, **Lord**, did we not prophesy
	8: 2	A man with leprosy came and knelt before him and said, "**Lord**,
	8: 6	"**Lord**," he said, "my servant lies at home paralyzed and in terrible
	8: 8	The centurion replied, "**Lord**, I do not deserve to have you come
	8: 21	disciple said to him, "**Lord**, first let me go and bury my father."
	8: 25	The disciples went and woke him, saying, "**Lord**, save us!
	9: 28	you believe that I am able to do this?" "Yes, **Lord**," they replied.
	9: 38	Ask the **Lord** of the harvest, therefore, to send out workers into his

. . . . .

18: 25	the **master** ordered that he and his wife and his children and all
18: 27	The servant's **master** took pity on him, canceled the debt
18: 31	and went and told their **master** everything that had happened.
18: 32	"Then the **master** called the servant in. 'You wicked servant,'
18: 34	In anger his **master** turned him over to the jailers to be tortured,
20: 8	the **owner** of the vineyard said to his foreman, 'Call the workers
20: 30	going by, they shouted, "**Lord**, Son of David, have mercy on us!"
20: 31	shouted all the louder, "**Lord**, Son of David, have mercy on us!"
20: 33	"**Lord**," they answered, "we want our sight."
21: 3	If anyone says anything to you, tell him that the **Lord** needs them,
21: 9	"Blessed is he who comes in the name *of* the **Lord**!" "Hosanna in
21: 30	to the other son and said the same thing. He answered, 'I will, **sir**,'
21: 40	"Therefore, when the **owner** of the vineyard comes, what will he do
21: 42	the **Lord** has done this, and it is marvelous in our eyes'?
22: 37	" 'Love the **Lord** your God with all your heart and with all your
22: 43	then that David, speaking by the Spirit, calls him '**Lord**'?
22: 44	" 'The **Lord** said to my Lord: "Sit at my right hand until I put your
22: 44	" 'The Lord said *to* my **Lord**: "Sit at my right hand until I put your
22: 45	If then David calls him '**Lord**,' how can he be his son?"
23: 39	until you say, 'Blessed is he who comes in the name *of* the **Lord**.' "
24: 42	because you do not know on what day your **Lord** will come.
24: 45	whom the **master** has put in charge of the servants in his
24: 46	It will be good for that servant whose **master** finds him doing

The Greek-English Concordance to the New Testament

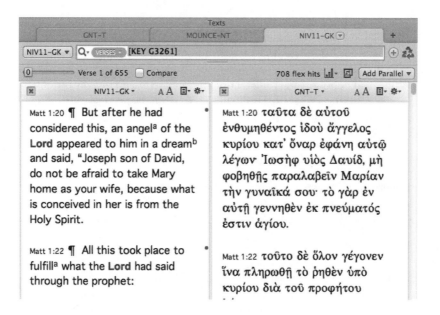

And once you have done a Key number search, you can have the Analysis function show you what words were used to translate κύριος (page 51).

3. You could also access my *Expository Dictionary* and look at especially the first paragraph, which is where we spell out the semantic range (see right column).

Quite a wide range of meanings, isn't it? "Sir" to "master" to God's name.

4. You can also check other translations to see how they translate the term. For our case, they all use "Lord." But if we were looking up another word, you might see more variety.

For example, the RSV translates 1 Corinthians 7:1 as, "It is well for a man not to *touch* a woman." (The Greek word behind "touch" is ἅπτω, #721.) But the NIV (1984) translates, "It is good for a man not to *marry*," and the NLT writes, "Yes, it is good to *live a celibate life*." The NIV (2011) says,

Noun: κύριος (*kyrios*), GK G3261 (S G2962), 717x. *kyrios* means "master, lord, sir" as well as "Lord." Most of its occurrences are in Luke's two works (210x) and Paul's letters (275x). The most plausible reason for this is that Luke wrote for, and Paul wrote to, people whose lives were dominated by Greek culture and language. *kyrios* occurs over 9,000x in the LXX, 6,000 of which replace the Hebrew proper name for God, Yahweh.

Mounces Expository Dictionary

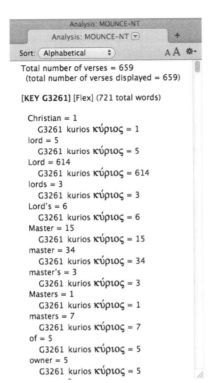

"Yes, 'It is good for a man not to have sexual contact with a woman.'" (The use of "Yes" and the quotation marks shows the NIV translators think Paul is quoting what is being said in Corinth.) The point is that you can see the range of the word's meaning. If you use different translations to discover the word's semantic range, be sure to chose different types of translations, both formal and dynamic.

5. If you want to learn more about the semantic range, you can always go to a Greek lexicon. The standard one is *A Greek-English Lexicon of the New Testament and Other Early Christian Literature*, third edition edited by Frederick Danker (University of Chicago Press, 2000, see next page). The entries are listed alphabetically (based on Greek, of course), and on pp.

576-579 you will find the entries for κύριος (see page 52).

A two-volume set that is more affordable and supplements Danker's work is *The Greek-English Lexicon of the New Testament Based on Semantic Domains* by Louw and Nida (United Bible Society). Look up your word in their index first; the words are not listed alphabetically but by their basic meanings. Logos shows these entries in a simple mouse-over (see below).

There are some older Greek lexicons that, in their day, were helpful and often groundbreaking, but because of their age you should not use them now. *The Vocabulary of the Greek New Testament,* by Moulton & Milligan (Eerdmans); *Biblico-Theological Lexicon of New Testament Greek,* by Cremer (T. & T. Clark); *A Greek-English Lexicon of the New Testament,* by Thayer (Harper).

6. There are specific books that help you see the semantic range of a word and, to a

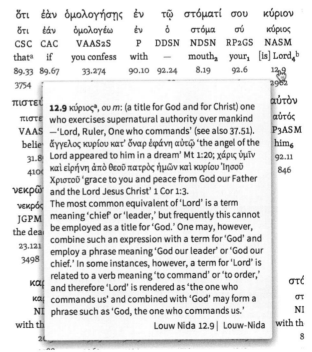

ὅτι	ἐὰν	ὁμολογήσῃς	ἐν	τῷ	στόματί	σου	κύριον
ὅτι	ἐάν	ὁμολογέω	ἐν	ὁ	στόμα	σύ	κύριος
CSC	CAC	VAAS2S	P	DDSN	NDSN	RP2GS	NASM
that[a]	if	you confess	with	—	mouth₂	your₁	[is] Lord₄[b]
89.33	89.67	33.274	90.10	92.24	8.19	92.6	12.9
3754							2962

12.9 κύριος[a], ου *m*: (a title for God and for Christ) one who exercises supernatural authority over mankind —'Lord, Ruler, One who commands' (see also 37.51). ἄγγελος κυρίου κατ' ὄναρ ἐφάνη αὐτῷ 'the angel of the Lord appeared to him in a dream' Mt 1:20; χάρις ὑμῖν καὶ εἰρήνη ἀπὸ θεοῦ πατρὸς ἡμῶν καὶ κυρίου Ἰησοῦ Χριστοῦ 'grace to you and peace from God our Father and the Lord Jesus Christ' 1 Cor 1:3.
The most common equivalent of 'Lord' is a term meaning 'chief' or 'leader,' but frequently this cannot be employed as a title for 'God.' One may, however, combine such an expression with a term for 'God' and employ a phrase meaning 'God our leader' or 'God our chief.' In some instances, however, a term for 'Lord' is related to a verb meaning 'to command' or 'to order,' and therefore 'Lord' is rendered as 'the one who commands us' and combined with 'God' may form a phrase such as 'God, the one who commands us.'

Louw Nida 12.9 | Louw-Nida

1. one who is in charge by virtue of possession, *owner*
2. one who is in a position of authority, *lord, master*
   a. of earthly beings, as a designation of any pers. of high position
   b. of transcendent beings
      a. as a designation of God
      b. Closely connected w. the custom of applying the term κ. to deities is that of honoring (deified) rulers with the same title
      g. κύριος is also used in ref. to Jesus:
         א in OT quotations, where it is understood of the Lord of the new community
         ב Apart from OT quots., Mt and Mk speak of Jesus as κύριος only in one pass.... but they record that he was addressed as 'Lord' (κύριε), once in Mk (7:28) and more oft. in Mt.... Lk refers to Jesus much more frequently as ὁ κ.
         ג Even in the passages already mentioned the use of the word κ. raises Jesus above the human level
      d. In some places it is not clear whether God or Christ is meant
      e. of other transcendent beings

A Greek-English Lexicon of the New Testament and Other Early Christian Literature

greater or lesser degree, will tell you more about the word, especially its usage throughout the Bible and other ancient writings. But be careful when using these books. Up to this point you have been reading and studying the Bible and learning for yourself what the word means. It is a lot more fun and rewarding to discover this information by yourself. The minute you turn to one of these books, much of the fun of self-exploration is gone; but more importantly, realize that you are reading a person's opinion about the word. The word study books, while good, are not inspired like Scripture.

You will excuse me, but my favorite is my own, *Mounce's Complete Expository Dictionary of Old and New Testament Words* (Zondervan). I included the entry on κύριος at the end of this chapter (pp. 60–63). This book was specifically written for people who have not learned Greek in the traditional way (or for-

got what they did learn) and yet want to know what the Greek and Hebrew words of the Bible mean. It avoids many of the pitfalls and limitations of previous word study books. I prefer to use the electronic version of my *Expository Dictionary*; it is so easy to access the correct article.

My second favorite one-volume word study book is Verlyn D. Verbrugge's *New International Dictionary of New Testament Theology (Abridged)* (Zondervan). It lists words alphabetically and by their GK number, and the discussion is excellent. I've also included Verbrugge's article on κύριος at the end of this chapter (pp. 64–68). His work is an abridgment of the three-volume set, *New International Dictionary of New Testament Theology,* edited by Colin Brown (Zondervan). This too is an excellent discussion of the words in the New Testament that often moves, as the name implies, into the word's theological significance; however, it is generally too advanced for most people at the Foundational Greek level. Zondervan publishes a fourth volume that contains all the indexes. Be sure to find the word here first; the indexes in the individual volumes are indexed just to that single volume and not to the set. Also, words are often listed with similar words, so it can be hard to find a word if you try to look it up alphabetically.

Geoffrey W. Bromiley's one volume *Theological Dictionary of the New Testament: Abridged in One Volume* (Eerdmans) is, as the name says, an abridgment of the multivolume *Theological Dictionary of the New Testament*, edited by G. Kittel and G. Friedrich (Eerdmans). We affectionately call Bromiley's abridgment *Little Kittel* or *Kittelbits.* Whatever its name, Bromiley did a masterful job of cutting out discussion that is mostly irrelevant for you at the Foundational level. It lists words alphabetically based on their transliteration. But be sure to use the index; it doesn't discuss every Greek word, and you could spend a long time looking for an entry that isn't included. The full multivolume series of *TDNT*, while looking good on your shelf, is of little value for you at your stage.

Vine's Expository Dictionary of Old and New Testament Words has been widely used since its publication in 1939. But there have been many advances in our understanding of Greek words since then, and I know of no Greek teacher who will recommend this work. There are also multivolume word studies by Wuest (*Word Studies in the Greek New Testament*), Vincent (*Word Studies in the New Testament*), and Robertson (*Word Pictures in the New Testament*), but my preferences are for

my own dictionary, Verbrugge, and Bromiley.

7. You could look up your passage in a good commentary, and it might discuss the word's meaning.

8. If the word is an important theological term, it may be discussed in reference works like the *Evangelical Dictionary of Theology,* edited by Walter A. Elwell (Baker). This is a marvelous book, and everyone ought to have a copy of it for their study. (I don't say that often.)

4. Explore the Context

It's time to make a decision. Once you have located the Greek word and learned its semantic range, it is time to decide what it means in the particular verse you are studying. The question is, how do you decide?

In short, the answer is "context." You look for something in the immediate context that gives a clue as to the precise meaning of the word. I like to think in terms of a series of concentric circles. The word you are studying is the center of the circle. The next circle out is the verse, then the paragraph, the book, etc.

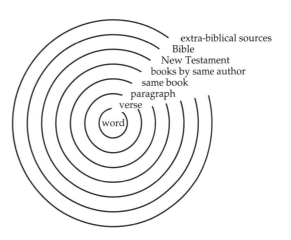

The point is that you first look for something in the verse that will define the word. If there isn't anything, then look at the paragraph. If there is nothing to help you in the paragraph, go to the book as a whole. But you want to stop as soon as you can. The further you go out from the center, the less assuredness you have that you are defining the word properly. But if you have to keep going out from the center, then you have to.

Why do you want to stop as soon as possible? Because different people can use the same word differently. Even the same person can use the same word differently in different contexts, as our previous example of σάρξ in Paul shows. Paul and James use "justify" in significantly different ways, even though they both mention Abraham and the same verse in Habakkuk (discussed later).

I saw this sign the other day: "GO CHILDREN SLOW." One of the sillier signs I

have ever seen, it seemed to me. What does it mean? Does it mean, "Go, the children are slow," or, "Go children, but slowly," or, "Go slow, there are children." Obviously, it is the latter, but why is it obvious? Because we understand the sign within its *context* of

being a road sign, and we probably notice that we are driving through a neighborhood full of children. And yet, in order to get to this understanding, we had to alter the word order and recognize that there is a grammatical error in the sign ("slow" should be "slowly" since it is an adverb).

Another good one is, "Speed radar controlled." Silly sign #2. The radar doesn't control my speed. My foot does. (Of course, it could be argued that the threat of a ticket proven by a radar gun is the ultimate cause of my speed.) How about these signs? "Stop." Shouldn't it be "Stop and then go"? "No parking here," when the sign is not in the parking

lot but on the curb. And my other favorites from New England: "Lightly salted"; "Blind drive"; "Thickly settled."

The point is that common sense tells us these signs are to be understood within their context. The same is true for word studies. How does the context help us decide what a word means? Let's look at some examples as we move out from the center of the concentric circles.

Verse. 1 Thess 4:3. "For this is the *will* of God, your sanctification." What is God's will for your life? To be sanctified; to be holy.

Paragraph. 1 Tim 2:14-15. "and Adam was not deceived, but the woman was deceived

("Justify" and "righteous" are the same concept.) What does "justification" mean? How are we justified? If you look at James 2:21-24 you will see that James says,

> Was not Abraham our father justified by works when he offered up his son Isaac upon the altar? You see that faith was active along with his works, and faith was completed by his works; and the Scripture was fulfilled that says, "Abraham believed God, and it was counted to him as righteousness"—and he was called a friend of God. You see that a person is justified by works and not by faith alone. (ESV)

As you look at the whole of the New Testament a fuller picture emerges as to the meaning of "justification." Paul is discussing how justification is granted; James is discussing how justification is shown to have occurred. What at first appears to be a contradiction are actually complementary teachings.

Bible. Acts 4:8. "Then Peter, *filled* with the Holy Spirit, said to them, 'Rulers of the people and elders....'" But I thought Peter was filled at Pentecost (Acts 2:4)? What does "filled" mean in v 8? If you look through Acts you will see this statement of "filling" repeated, always followed by mention of what the person said or did. But if you look at the book of Judges in the Old Testament, you will see the same metaphor used the same way for the Spirit possessing the person in a powerful but temporary way in order to accomplish a specific task. While the Holy Spirit comes in his fullness at a believer's conversion, Luke uses the terminology of Judges to describe a work of the Holy Spirit in which he grips a person in a special way to enable him or her to say or do something special.

and became a transgressor. Yet woman will be *saved* through bearing children, if she continues in faith and love and holiness, with modesty" (RSV). What does "saved" mean? V 14 suggests we are dealing with spiritual salvation ("transgression") and not physical safety.

Book. 1 Tim 1:10. At the end of a list of sins, Paul states that these are "contrary to *sound* doctrine." What is "*sound* doctrine"? Most translations miss the fact that the word is a medical metaphor meaning "healthy," and that it contrasts with the heresy being spread in Ephesus, which Paul elsewhere describes as sick and morbid (1 Tim 6:4), infectious abrasions (1 Tim 6:5) spreading like gangrene (2 Tim 2:17). Sound doctrine is that which is opposed to the false teaching.

New Testament. In Romans 4:2-3 (ESV) Paul says,

> For if Abraham was justified by works, he has something to boast about, but not before God. For what does the Scripture say? "Abraham believed God, and it was counted to him as righteousness."

As you continue out to the outer circles, be careful. Once you get out of the Bible and are looking at how the word is used in secular thought, it becomes more and more possible that the words are going to be used differently. And especially if you are looking at how the word was used 500 years before the writing of the New Testament, you must recognize that words can totally change their meaning over this time span. For example, a century ago, if you were to "skim" a book, this meant you would read it carefully. "To prevent" was "to go before," which obscures Paul's meaning in the KJV of 1 Thessalonians 4:15.

> For this we say unto you by the word of the Lord, that we which are alive and remain unto the coming of the Lord shall not *prevent* them which are asleep.

The dead in Christ will go *first*.

These extrabiblical references can sometimes give us helpful *illustrations*. For example, Paul tells Timothy not to become "entangled" in civilian affairs (2 Tim 2:4). The verb ἐμπλέκω (#1861) can mean much more than "to be involved" (contra the NIV 1984; corrected to "entangled" in 2011), and this unfortunate translation has caused unnecessary grief for many pastors who were forced by their churches to have little or no contact with secular society, including a second job. (The blame for this does not lie with the NIV but with the unfortunate and unbiblical notion that a church must keep its pastor poor—but I digress.) ἐμπλέκω means "to be involuntarily interlaced to the point of immobility, be entangled; to become involved in an activity to the point of interference with other activity or objective" (BDAG, 324). The word is used by Hermes (*Similitudes*, 6.2.6-7) of a sheep, and by Aesop

(74) of hares caught in thorns. These make great illustrations, but it is dangerous to define a biblical word based on them since they are so far removed from the biblical writer.

Frankly, for those pursuing Foundational Greek, it is probably too dangerous (exegetically) and too difficult to look at examples outside of the biblical canon. Extrabiblical texts may introduce problems with which you are not prepared to deal—best left alone at this stage I think.

So let's get back to our word study on "Lord" in Romans 10:9. Is there anything in the immediate context that will help us define the confession "Jesus is Lord" more precisely? The connection between the confession and belief in Jesus' resurrection suggests "Lord" means much more than "sir"; someone raised from the dead is more than a "sir."

As you move out into the paragraph, in v 12 Paul says that Jesus is "Lord of all," asserting his universal lordship. It is especially significant that in v 13 Paul quotes Joel 2:32, because in its Old Testament context Joel is speaking of Yahweh, God. Moo writes, "In the OT, of course, the one on whom people called for salvation was Yahweh; Paul reflects the high view of Christ common among the early church by identifying this one with Jesus Christ, the Lord" (*The Epistle to the Romans* [Eerdmans], p. 660).

In Romans 1:4 Paul states that Jesus "was declared to be the Son of God in power according to the Spirit of holiness by his resurrection from the dead, Jesus Christ our Lord," connecting Jesus' Lordship with his resurrection as in 10:9 and with his identification as the Son of God. As we see who Jesus is as Lord, we see that he is also God's

Son. As God's Son, the Old Testament references to God can be applicable to Jesus. It is a small step from this to agreeing with Thomas' confession: "My Lord and my God!" (John 20:28).

As you expand further out into the New Testament, we find similar confessions: "at the name of Jesus every knee should bow, in heaven and on earth and under the earth, and every tongue confess that Jesus Christ is Lord, to the glory of God the Father" (Phil 2:10-11; cf. 1 Cor 12:3).

The answer to the question with which I started this word study is much clearer. What is the minimum it takes to get into heaven? You must have a correct understanding of who Jesus is, and that understanding causes you to submit to his lordship. We must believe that Jesus was raised from the dead, that he was raised to a position of lordship over all, and in his lordship we see that he is in fact the Son of God, Yahweh himself. Christianity is grounded in the historical event of the incarnation, death, and resurrection of Jesus Christ. Who we are as disciples is intimately tied up with who he is as Lord, our Lord and our God.

Septuagint

As you get further into word studies, you will often see writers paying special attention to how a word is used in the Septuagint, often abbreviated LXX. This is the Greek translation of the Hebrew Scriptures that was probably started about 250 BC and finished somewhere around the time of Christ. There are certain words that are important in the Hebrew Old Testament, especially theological words. When the Septuagint was translated, the translators chose a Greek word for each of these Hebrew words. When

it comes to defining these Greek words in the New Testament, it is the word's background in the Old Testament via the Septuagint that is the most important background in defining the Greek word, not its general usage in the first century.

For example, how did the LXX to translate the Hebrew word חֶסֶד (ḥesed, "steadfast love," ESV), which describes God's love for his covenantal people, when there is no such word in Greek? When the LXX translators finally settled on ἔλεος, generally translated as "mercy," ἔλεος automatically carried the specific meaning of חֶסֶד into the New Testament.

Given the fact that κύριος is used by the LXX to translate יהוה, "Yahweh," it is hard for me to imagine that the Jewish Paul meant anything less than confessing the deity of Christ in Romans 10:9.

Cognates

A cognate is a word that is related to another and actually shares the same root. In English, the words "prince" and "princess" share the same root, although their specific forms are altered because they are masculine and feminine gender, respectively.

Most cognates have similar meanings. There may be differences in nuance, and perhaps in meaning, but for the most part cognates share the same basic meaning. The root ἀγαπ, "love," shows itself as a verb (ἀγαπάω), a noun (ἀγάπη), and an adjective (ἀγαπητός). Each of these words is called a "cognate," and each shares the same basic meaning.

Common Mistakes

Before ending this discussion of word studies, I must cover common mistakes made in doing word studies. For a more detailed discussion of these issues you can read *Exegetical Fallacies* by D. A. Carson (Baker).

Anachronism

The first is the bad habit of defining a Greek word using an English word derived from that Greek word. My favorite example is when someone talks about the "power" of God, and adds that this word "power" is δύναμις, from which we get our word "dynamite," and then to say God's power is dynamite. This is totally backwards and totally wrong. English wasn't a language until the second millennium AD. Regardless of where our words came from, the English definitions don't work backwards to the Greek definitions. Supposedly there was a reason why a specific Greek word was used as the basis of an English word, but especially as the years go by, that English word can take on a meaning totally different from its Greek origin. God's power is never pictured in Scripture as something that blows rocks apart.

Etymological Fallacy

"Etymology" refers to how the word was originally created. What would you say if a pastor or Bible study leader told you that the "butterfly" is an animal made of butter that can fly? Or perhaps that a pineapple is a type of apple grown on pine trees? After the laughter died down, and if the speaker were serious, you would point out that this is not what the word means. The etymology, the pieces ("morphemes") that were originally used to make up the word, does not define the word today, any more than a butterfly is a milk by-product.

The worse example I know of is the Greek word for "repent," μετανοέω, which some people define as, "to change your mind," but not necessarily your behavior. They often base their position on the meaning of the two morphemes that were used to create μετανοέω. "Repentance," they say, "involves an intellectual shift in understanding, but repentance does not require a change of action." This type of misuse of Greek etymology runs throughout Vine's *Expository Dictionary of Old and New Testament Words*, and why it is not recommended. Vine writes, "*meta*, 'after,' implying 'change,' ... *nous*, 'the mind,' ... hence signifies 'to change one's mind or purpose'" (Nelson, 1985, p. 525). Certainly, the word can mean "to regret" (cf. Luke 17:3-4; 2 Cor 7:9-10), but the New Testament's understanding of repentance is not drawn from the etymology of one morpheme but from the biblical concept of repentance, especially from the background of conversion in the Old Testament. See the article on *metanoeō* in Bromiley's *Theological Dictionary of the New Testament: Abridged*, where he writes, "the concept of conversion stresses positively the fact that real penitence involves a new relation to God that embraces all spheres of life and claims the will in a way that no external rites can replace.... It means turning aside from everything that is ungodly" (pp. 640, 641). Besides, I am not convinced that μετά can actually mean "change."

(BDAG lists a meaning of μετανοέω as, "change one's mind," but wisely does not list any biblical examples. The noun μεταοία also has a meaning, "a change of mind," but all biblical references are under the gloss, "with the nuance of 'remorse," and later on adds, "in our lit[erature] w[ith] focus on the need to change in view of responsibility to deity." And nowhere in BDAG's entry do you find the definition "after.")

Is it ever the case that a word carries the meaning of its parts? Sure. εἰσέρχομαι is made up of the preposition εἰς, meaning "into," and ἔρχομαι, meaning "to go." εἰσέρχομαι means "to go into." But it is not the word's etymology that determines its meaning. It is the use of this verb when Jesus and his disciples entered a house or a city. In other words, through its use we can see it has retained the meaning of its morphemes.

It is also true that some prepositions (ἐκ, κατά, ἀπό, διά, σύν) have what is called a "perfective" function. When added to a word they can intensify its meaning. ἐσθίω means "I eat"; κατεσθίω means "I devour." Some perfective forms, however, have lost their intensified meaning, and the compound form has the same basic meaning as the simple word. For example, Paul tells Timothy that the teaching of the opponents in Ephesus produce only "speculations," ἐκζήτησις. It is difficult to determine whether Paul intended the intensified "extreme speculations" (or perhaps "useless speculations"), or just "speculations," which is the meaning of the simple ζήτησις ("investigation, controversy, debate"). As always, context is the guide as to whether or not the intensified meaning is present.

Greek does have the "alpha privative," which is a way to negate a word much like the English "un-" or "ir-." These words always carry the meaning of the initial morpheme. πίστις means "faithful"; ἀπιστία means "lack of belief, unbelief."

Connected to the etymological fallacy is the fact that words change their meaning over the years. Just think of the lyrics to the old song that ends, "We'll have a gay old time," or the KJV use of "prevent" in 1 Thessalonians 4:15 (cited above). What a word meant when it was first created, or what it meant 1,000 years ago, may be at best irrelevant today. A word's meaning today is seen in how it is used today, not in how it used to be used.

- "Hussy" is from the Middle English word "huswife," meaning "housewife."

- "Enthusiasm" meant to be inspired or possessed by a god.

- "Nice" originally meant "foolish" in Middle English (from the Latin *nescire*, "to be ignorant").

- "Gossip" is from *godsib*, a word that refered to godparents, and came to be used of the type of chatter that stereotypically occurs at christenings (see *God, Language and Scripture* by Moisés Silva, Zondervan). Today, when I preach about gossip, christenings are nowhere in my mind, and its etymology is irrelevent in an attempt to define the Bible's prohibition of slander.

Words have a range of meaning, but that range is not determined by the morphemes that made up the word or even by how it was used 1,000 years earlier.

Focus on the Larger Unit

Don't put too much weight on a word, thinking that the word, all by itself, is full of meaning. Granted, there are a few technical terms that have a specific meaning in almost any context. But for the most part, we do not communicate with individual words but with phrases, sentences, and paragraphs. Focus your study on the larger unit, hesitating to place too much emphasis on an individual word. (This is connected to the technical concept of semantic "minimalism.")

Tied to this is the fact that theological concepts are larger than a word. Regardless of how many times you have heard the word ἀγάπη defined as the sacrificial love for the unlovely, the kind of love that is bestowed on the undeserving, that simply is not what the word in and of itself means. (I talk more about this on the lecture on this chapter in the online class.) It is not the word that conveys this meaning, but it is the concept of biblical love as illustrated by God that infuses ἀγάπη with this particular meaning in the biblical context.

Mounce's Complete Expository Dictionary of Old and New Testament Words

Entry on "Lord" *(used with permission)*

Old Testament

Noun: אָדוֹן ('*ādôn*), GK 123 (S 113), 773x. '*ādôn* is used with reference to "the Lord" and to people of high rank (especially superiors and persons of authority). '*ādôn* was commonly pronounced in place of the covenant name of Israel's God, Yahweh (יהוה [GK 3378]). The specific form of that vocalization is '*ᵃdōnāy* ("my Lord"), a plural noun with a first person singular suffix. This practice became so well established that the Greek translators of the Heb. Bible rendered "Yahweh" with the Greek equivalent of Lord (*kyrios*). English translations usually signify Yahweh as "Lord" by placing the letters "Lord" in small caps: "Lord." The commandment not to take the Lord's name in vain, however, does not necessarily prohibit its pronunciation as Scripture is read, nor does the prohibition against blaspheming the name (Lev. 24:15–16) prevent any and every use of it.

(1) In addition to its use as the substitute pronunciation for the divine name Yahweh (GK 3378), '*ᵃdōnāy* also appears as a title for Yahweh approximately 442x (GK 151) in the Hebrew Bible. When it appears in this context, it is normally translated "Lord," but may also be understood as "Master" or "my Master."

(2) About 30x the word '*ādôn* addresses God as "Lord," as in Ps. 8:1, 9: "O Lord, our *Lord*, how majestic is your name in all the earth." Isaiah frequently calls God "The *Lord*, the Lord Almighty" (Isa. 3:1; 10:3). When Joshua sees the captain of the Lord's army, he addresses him as "my *Lord*" (Jos. 5:14; cf. Ps. 110:1).

(3) This word also refers to various human beings addressed as "lord" or "master." Joseph is the "master" of Pharaoh's household (Gen 45:8). A "husband" (even a wicked one) can be addressed with this word (Jdg. 19:26). Elijah the prophet is likewise called "lord" (1 Ki. 18:7). Uriah calls both King David and his army commander Joab 'ādôn ("master" and "lord" in NIV of 2 Sam. 11:11). In fact, anyone with a position of leadership or authority can be addressed by this term. At the same time, to call someone "my lord" is sometimes merely a title of respect for someone (e.g., Gen. 24:18; 32:5; 1 Ki. 18:7).

(4) Similar to other biblical names, 'ādôn appears in Heb. royal personal names: Adonijah, Adonikam, and Adoniram; it also appears in the names of some pagan rulers, such as Adoni-Zedek (Jos. 10:1, 3) and Adoni-Bezek (Jdg. 1:5–7, "lord of Bezek," the Canaanite king of Bezek).

Noun: אֲדֹנָי ('ªdōnāy), GK 151 (S 136), 442x. 'ªdōnāy means "Lord." In addition to its use as the substitute pronunciation for the divine name Yahweh (see discussion of GK 3378), 'ªdōnāy also appears as an independent title for Israel's God. When it appears in this context, it is normally translated "Lord," but it may also be understood as "Master" or "my Master."

Proper Noun: יְהוָה (yhwh), GK 3378 (S 3068/3069), 6829x.

Proper Noun: יָהּ (yāh), GK 3363 (S 3050), 49x. The Hebrew name yhwh or "Yahweh," commonly translated into English as "the LORD," is the most frequently appearing name for God in the OT (almost 7000x). It appears in every OT book except Ecclesiastes, Song of Songs, and Esther. This name is often referred to as the Tetragrammaton because of the four (tetra) letters (grammaton) used in its Hebrew spelling. There is also an alternate, short form of the divine name (yāh) that appears nearly 50x, mostly in the book of Psalms (43x); it is best known from the Hebrew expression "Hallelu-yah" (translated, "Praise the LORD").

The modern spelling and pronunciation "Yahweh" merely represents our best, educated guess as to what the original pronunciation might have been. This is due to the fact that biblical Hebrew was originally written without vowels, and in Hebrew the vowels would show us the precise pronunciation and meaning of the name. The problem is compounded by the fact that the pronunciation of this name ceased from the Hebrew (Masoretic) reading tradition in order to avoid misuse in connection with the third commandment (Exod. 20:7; Deut. 5:11). That is, when the Jews were reading the Hebrew text and came to yhwh, instead of saying "Yahweh" they would say the Hebrew word "Adonai" ('ªdōnāy, GK 151, which means "Lord").

In terms of the origin and significance of the divine name, three texts from Exodus are especially important. (1) The first is Exod. 3:13–15. Here, the divine name is given for the first time in the context of Israel's imminent deliverance from Egypt. The revelation of the name is related to the statement, "I AM WHO I AM" (v. 14), where Moses is commanded to tell the Israelites that "I AM has sent me." Then, in verse 15, the divine name "Yahweh" is connected to the God of the patriarchs where it is stated that this name, "Yahweh," is his "eternal name." The connection between "I AM" and "Yahweh" is one of verbal person. "I AM" is the first person form of the verb "to be" (hāyâ; GK 2118; see be), while "Yahweh" represents the third person form of the same verb, perhaps "HE IS" or "HE WILL BE."

(2) In Exod. 6:2–8, the significance of the divine name resurfaces. In verses 2–3 it is stated, "God also said to Moses, 'I am the LORD [Yahweh], I appeared to Abraham, to Isaac and to Jacob as God Almighty, but by my name the LORD [Yahweh] I did not make myself known to them.'" This text also connects the fulfillment of the patriarchal promises (vv. 4, 7–8) with the deliverance of the nation of Israel from Egypt (vv. 5–6) and concludes with the statement, in verse 8, "I am the LORD" or "I am Yahweh."

(3) The texts from Exodus 3 and 6 record the origin of the divine name and locate its significance in the fulfillment of the patriarchal promises through Israel's deliverance from Egypt. The third text is Exod. 34:5–7. Here, in a remarkable display of the divine glory, God *himself* "proclaimed his name" while passing in front of Moses. This proclamation is to be understood as an exposition of the significance or character of the divine name. What does the divine name mean? It is written, "The LORD [Yahweh], the LORD [Yahweh], the compassionate and gracious God, slow to anger, abounding in love and faithfulness, maintaining love to thousands, and forgiving wickedness, rebellion and sin. Yet he does not leave the guilty unpunished; he punishes the children and their children for the sin of the fathers to the third and fourth generation." According to these verses, the divine name is God's covenant name and represents his steadfast determination to maintain the covenant relationship with his people.

In subsequent biblical history, the divine name, "Yahweh," is referred to as "the Name" (Lev. 24:11) or, more passionately, as "this glorious and awesome name" (Deut. 28:58). With reference to the eschatological city of God, the prophet Ezekiel records that its name will be, "THE LORD IS THERE" or "Yahweh is there." In light of the origin, significance, and use of the divine name in the OT, Jesus' statement in Jn. 8:58, "before Abraham was born, *I am*," clearly identifies Jesus as God, the God of the patriarchs and the deliverer of Israel, Yahweh himself (Exod. 3:14). See *I (am)*.

New Testament

Noun: δεσπότης (*despotēs*), GK *1305* (S *1203*), 10x. *despotēs* is similar in meaning to *kyrios* ("lord"), though it occurs far less often. The nuance of *despotēs* emphasizes the right and power to command. See *master*.

Noun: κύριος (*kyrios*), GK *3261* (S *2962*), 717x. *kyrios* means "master, lord, sir" as well as "Lord." Most of its occurrences are in Luke's two works (210x) and Paul's letters (275x). The most plausible reason for this is that Luke wrote for, and Paul wrote to, people whose lives were dominated by Greek culture and language. *kyrios* occurs over 9,000x in the LXX, 6,000 of which replace the Hebrew proper name for God, Yahweh.

In the secular sense, *kyrios* in the NT is translated as the "master" of a slave (Mt. 10:24–25; Eph. 6:5), "owner" (Mt. 15:27; Gal. 4:1), or "employer" (Lk. 16:3, 5). The husband is characterized as *kyrios* with respect to his wife (1 Pet. 3:6; cf. Gen. 18:12, where "master" is *kyrios* in the LXX). By this Peter makes his point that Sarah thought of her husband respectfully. *kyrios* may also communicate politeness as in Mt. 18:21–22; 25:20–26; Acts 16:30, translated with the term of address "sirs." This word is also used to address heavenly beings such as angels (Rev. 7:14).

God is consistently depicted as *kyrios*, especially when the NT author is quoting an OT passage that uses *kyrios* for Yahweh (Rom. 4:8; 9:28–29; 10:16). Many OT formulas surface in the phrases "the hand of the *Lord*" (Lk. 1:66), "the angel of the *Lord*" (Mt.

1:20), "the name of the *Lord*" (Jas. 5:10), "the Spirit of the *Lord*" (Acts 5:9), and "the word of the *Lord*" (Acts 8:25). The prophetic formula, "says the Lord," also emerges from the OT (Rom. 14:11; 1 Cor. 14:21; 2 Cor. 6:17). Jesus also reflects his adoption of OT patterns when he refers to his Father as the "*Lord* of heaven and earth" (Mt. 11:25) and as "the *Lord* of the harvest" (Mt. 9:38).

The earliest Christian confession is that "Jesus is Lord." This was the climax of Peter's speech on Pentecost (Acts 2:36); by making this confession a person is saved (Rom. 10:9–10). Jesus is Lord whether he is on earth (Mt. 7:21; 21:29–30) or exalted in heaven (1 Cor. 16:22; Rev. 22:20). By confessing Jesus as *Lord*, the Christian community was also recognizing that he has dominion over the world. As a result of Jesus' sovereignty, one day every created being will acknowledge what the insignificant, persecuted community at Philippi confesses in its worship: "Jesus Christ is *Lord*" (Phil. 2:11).

Presently, all powers on earth and in heaven are subject to Jesus and must serve him, for he has been elevated to the position of *kyrios* (Eph. 1:20–21; 1 Pet. 3:22). John envisions him as the ruler over all the kings of the earth—"King of kings and *Lord* of lords" (Rev. 17:14; 19:15–16). The Roman emperor was called "king of kings" because he presided over the vassal kings of the empire, but how puny and conceited in light of the absolute sovereignty of the Lamb, the true *Lord* of lords. NT writers found their evidence for Jesus' lordship in Ps. 110:1, the most quoted psalm in the NT (see Mt. 22:44; 26:64; Acts 2:34; Eph. 1:20; Heb. 1:3, 13). This royal psalm speaks of the *kyrios* being seated at Yahweh's right hand in a rank of power, as demonstrated by the subjugation of his enemies. This is where Jesus currently abides, for the benefit of the church. See *NIDNTT-A*, 323-25.

The New International Dictionary
of New Testament Theology: Abridged

by Verlyn D. Verbrugge *(used with permission)*

3261	κύριος

κύριος (*kyrios*), lord, master, owner, Lord (3261); κυρία (*kyria*), lady, mistress (3257); κυριότης (*kyriotēs*), lordship, dominion (3262); κυριεύω (*kyrieuō*), be lord, master, rule (3259); κατακυριεύω (*katakyrieuō*), rule over, conquer, be master of (2894).

CL & OT 1. (a) In cl. Gk. *kyrios* is an adj., having power, authoritative, derived from the noun *to kyros*, power, might. As a subst. *kyrios* meant lord, ruler, one who has control. *kyrios* always contains the idea of legality and authority. Anyone occupying a superior position can be referred to as *kyrios* and be addressed as *kyrie* (fem. *kyria*).

(b) In early Gk. *kyrios* was not used as a divine title. Although the term was applied to the gods, there was no general belief in a personal creator Lord. The gods were not creators and lords of fate but were, like human beings, subject to fate. The Gks. of this period did not feel dependent on a god or personally responsible to the gods. Only insofar as the gods ruled over particular spheres in the world could they be called *kyrioi*.

(c) The situation was different in the East. The gods created humans who were personally answerable to them. They could intervene in human lives to save, punish, or judge. They also established justice and law, which they communicated to human beings, e.g., through the king. Therefore they were called lords.

(d) Instances of the title *kyrios* in Hel. times with reference to gods or rulers do not occur until the 1st cent. BC *kyrios basileus*,

"lord and king," is found often between 64 and 50 BC. In 12 BC Emperor Augustus was called *theos kai kyrios*, "god and lord," in Egypt. *kyrios* was also used of Herod the Great (ca. 73 – 4 BC), Agrippa I (ca. 10 BC – AD 44), and Agrippa II (AD 27 – ca. 100). Other high officials also received this title. *kyrios* was used of the gods who, in contemporary popular thought, were referred to as lords. Where *kyrios* was used of a god, the servant (→ *doulos*, 1528) using the term stood in a personal relationship of responsibility to the god. Individual gods were worshiped as lords of their cultic communities and of the separate members of the fellowship. The worship of other lords was not excluded, however, for no god was worshiped as universal lord.

(e) The Roman emperors Augustus (31 BC – AD 14) and Tiberius (AD 14 – 37) rejected the title *kyrios* and all that it meant. But Caligula (AD 37 – 41) found the title attractive. During and after the time of Nero (AD 54 – 68), who was described in an inscription as "lord of all the world," the title *kyrios* occurs more frequently (one of the oldest instances is Acts 25:26). In and of itself the title *kyrios* does not call the emperor god, but when he is worshiped as divine, the title *lord* also counts as a divine predicate. It was against such religious claims that the early Christians rejected the totalitarian attitudes of the state.

2. (a) *kyrios* occurs over 9,000x in the LXX. It translates '*ādôn*, lord, which refers 190x to men as the responsible heads of groups (e.g., 1 Sam. 25:10). It is used only 15x for *ba'al*, which means the owner of a wife or a piece of land (e.g., Jdg. 19:22 – 23). Yahweh

is rarely called owner (Hos. 2:16), but more frequently Lord of the community belonging to him (cf. Ps. 123:2). *kyrios* can also mean commander or ruler.

(b) In over 6,000 instances, however, *kyrios* replaces the Heb. proper name of God, the tetragrammaton *YHWH* (Yahweh). The LXX thus strengthened the tendency to avoid the utterance of God's name and finally to avoid its use altogether. Where *kyrios* stands for *'ādôn* or *'adōnāy* as a word relating to God, there is genuine translation; but where it stands for Yahweh, it is an interpretative circumlocution for all that the Heb. text implied by the use of the divine name: Yahweh is Creator and Lord of the whole universe, of humans, Lord of life and death. Above all he is the Lord God of Israel, his covenant people. By choosing *kyrios* for Yahweh the LXX also emphasizes legal authority. Because Yahweh saved his people from Egypt and chose them as his possession, he is the legitimate Lord of Israel. As Creator Yahweh is also the legitimate Lord of the entire universe, with unlimited control over it.

(c) *kyrieuō* occurs more than 50x in the LXX, generally with the meaning to rule.

3. In post-OT Jewish lit. *kyrios* appears as a term for God in Wis. (27x; e.g., 1:1, 7, 9; 2:13), then esp. often in Philo and Josephus. Philo seems to have been unaware that *kyrios* stood for the tetragrammaton, for he used *theos* ("God") to indicate the gracious power of God, while *kyrios* describes God's kingly power.

NT Of the 717x in which *kyrios* occurs in the NT, the majority are found in Luke's writings (210x) and Paul's letters (275x). This one-sidedness can be explained by the fact that Luke wrote for, and Paul wrote to, people who lived in areas dominated by Gk. culture and language. On the other hand, Mk., more firmly based in Jewish Christian tradition, uses the *kyrios* title only 18x, and these mostly in quotations. The remaining occurrences of *kyrios* are spread over the other NT books. The uses of *kyrios* accords with its varied use in the LXX.

1. *The secular use of kyrios.* The *kyrios* stands over against the slave (Matt. 10:24 – 25; 18:25, 27; 25:19; Lk. 12:36 – 37, 46; Eph. 6:5, 9; Col. 3:22). *kyrios* means owner (Matt. 15:27; Mk. 12:9; Lk. 19:33; Gal. 4:1) or employer (Lk. 16:3, 5). The husband faces his wife as *kyrios*, i.e., as superior (1 Pet. 3:6). *kyrios* used as a form of address can emphasize the power of a superior over an inferior, but it can also simply be politeness (Matt. 18:21 – 22; 25:20 – 26; 27:63; Lk. 13:8; Jn. 12:21; 20:15; Acts 16:30). The term is also used to address angels (10:4; Rev. 7:14) and the unknown in the heavenly vision outside Damascus (Acts 9:5; 22:8, 10; 26:15). A twice-repeated *kyrios* corresponds to Palestinian usage (Matt. 7:21 – 22; 25:11; Lk. 6:46).

2. *God as the kyrios.* God is frequently called *kyrios*, esp. in the many quotations from the OT in which *kyrios* stands for Yahweh, corresponding to the custom of pronouncing the title *kyrios* instead of the tetragrammaton in public reading (e.g., Rom. 4:8 = Ps. 32:2; Rom. 9:28 – 29 = Isa. 10:22 and 1:9; Rom. 10:16 = Isa. 53:1). In Lk.'s birth narratives *kyrios* frequently denotes God (e.g., 1:32; 2:9). In the gen. accompanying another word it corresponds to OT usage: e.g., the hand of the *kyrios* (1:66); the angel of the *kyrios* (Matt. 1:20); the name of the *kyrios* (Jas. 5:10); the Spirit of the *kyrios* (Acts 5:9); the word of the *kyrios* (Acts 8:25). The formula "says the *kyrios*" (e.g., Rom. 12:19 = Deut. 32:35) also comes from OT. The formula "our Lord and God" (Rev. 4:11) is reminiscent of the title adopted by Domitian.

Jesus is adopting Jewish forms of speech when he addresses God the Father as "*kyrios* of heaven and earth" (Matt. 11:25; Lk. 10:21). God is "the Lord of the harvest" (Matt. 9:38). He is the only ruler, the King of kings and the *kyrios* of lords (cf. Dan. 2:47), who will cause our *kyrios* Jesus Christ to appear (1 Tim. 6:15).

God is the Creator and as such Lord of all (Acts 17:24). By acknowledging God as *kyrios*, the NT esp. confesses him as Creator—his power revealed in history and his just dominion over the universe.

3. *Jesus as the kyrios.* (a) The earthly Jesus as *kyrios*. This word applied to the earthly Jesus is first of all a polite form of address. This no doubt goes back to the title *Rabbi* (cf. Mk. 9:5 with Matt. 17:4; see also "sir" in Jn. 4:15; 5:7; 6:34). This address also implies recognition of Jesus as a leader and willingness to obey him (Matt. 7:21; 21:29 – 30). As Son of Man Jesus is also *kyrios* of the Sabbath; he has control over the holy day of God's people (Mk. 2:28 – 29). Even after his death and resurrection the words of the earthly Jesus have authority for the Christian community. Paul appeals to words of the *kyrios* to decide a question (1 Cor. 7:10, cf. 25; 1 Thess. 4:15; cf. Acts 20:35).

(b) The exalted Jesus as *kyrios*. The confessional cry used in worship, *kyrios Iēsous* ("Jesus [is] Lord"), originated early in the Christian community. This confession is one of the oldest Christian creeds, if not the oldest. Note the Aramaic formula *Marana tha* (see 1 Cor. 16:22, NIV text note), which means "Lord, come," "Our Lord has come," or "The Lord will come"(cf. Rev. 22:20).

With this confession the NT community submitted itself to its Lord, but at the same time it also confessed him as ruler of the world (Rom. 10:9a; 1 Cor. 12:3; Phil. 2:11). God raised Jesus from the dead and "gave him the name that is above every name" (Phil. 2:9; cf. Isa. 45:23 – 24), i.e., the name *kyrios*, and with it the position corresponding to the name. The exalted *kyrios* rules over humanity (Rom. 14:9, *kyrieuō*). All powers and beings in the universe must bow before him. When that happens, God the Father will be worshiped (cf. Eph. 1:20 – 21; 1 Pet. 3:22).

Jesus Christ is called the ruler over all the kings of the earth, King of kings and Lord of lords (Rev. 17:14; 19:15 – 16). In this way he has received the same titles of honor as God himself (1 Tim. 6:15; cf. Dan. 2:47). According to contemporary Jewish thought, the different spheres of the world in nature and history were ruled by angelic powers. Since Christ has now been raised to the position of *kyrios*, all powers have been subjected to him and must serve him (Eph. 1:20 – 21; Col. 2:6, 10). When Christ has overcome every power (1 Cor. 15:25), he will submit himself to God the Father. Thus his lordship will have achieved its goal and God will be all in all (15:28). The one God and the one *kyrios* Jesus stand in opposition to the many gods and lords of the pagan world (8:5 – 6; Eph. 4:5 – 6).

Scriptural evidence for the exaltation of Jesus and for his installation as Lord was found in Ps. 110:1, the most quoted Ps. in the NT (cf., e.g., Matt. 22:44; 26:64; Acts 2:34; Eph. 1:20; Heb. 1:3, 13). The Jewish interpretation of this passage looked forward to the messianic future, but in the faith of the Christians this hope was transferred to the present. The lordship of the Messiah, Jesus, is a present reality. He is exercising in a hidden way God's authority and lordship over the world and will bring it to completion in the future. This faith was articulated in Thomas's confession (Jn. 20:28): "My Lord and my God." Early Christianity saw no infringement of monotheism in the installation of Jesus as Lord, but rather its confirmation (1 Cor. 8:6; Eph. 4:5; Phil. 2:11). It is God who exalted the Lord Jesus (Acts 2:36) and made him Lord of all things.

As far as we can establish, the NT church did not formally reflect on the relationship of the exalted Christ to God the Father as the church did later. Perhaps we can say that there is no developed doctrine of the Trinity in the NT, but that the writers thought in Trinitarian forms.

(c) *kyrios* and the Lord's Supper. *kyrios* figures frequently in expressions connected with the Lord's Supper. Note the phrases that are partly pre-Pauline: "the Lord's table"

(1 Cor. 10:21), "the Lord's death" (11:26), "the cup of the Lord" (10:21; 11:27), "arouse the Lord's jealousy" (10:22), "the Lord's Supper" (11:20; → *kyriakos, 3258*), "judged by the Lord" (11:32), and "guilty of sinning against the body and blood of the Lord" (11:27). These expressions indicate that the Lord's Supper is the place where the Christian community submits itself in a special way to the saving work of the *kyrios* and receives a share in his body and power (see also *deipnon, 1270*).

(d) *kyrios* and Spirit. Paul taught the Christian community to distinguish between the one who is speaking in the Holy Spirit and the one who is not (1 Cor. 12:3). A person can only say "Jesus is Lord" if he or she is filled with the Holy Spirit. Anyone who, by acknowledging allegiance to Jesus as *kyrios*, belongs to the new covenant, belongs to the sphere of the Spirit and no longer to that of the old covenant and of the letter. Such a one stands in freedom: "Where the Spirit of the Lord is, there is freedom" (2 Cor. 3:17).

(e) *kyrios* in epistolary greetings. In the opening greetings of Paul's letters the "Lord Jesus Christ" is frequently mentioned beside God the Father (e.g., Rom. 1:7; 1 Cor. 1:3). The concluding greeting, with the phrase "the grace of the *kyrios* Jesus be with you," continued the pre-Pauline tradition that may have had its origin in the Lord's Supper (cf. 1 Cor. 16:23; 2 Cor. 13:14; Phlm. 25). The description of God as the "Father of our *kyrios* Jesus Christ" goes back to the early Christian community (Rom. 15:6; 2 Cor. 1:3; 11:31; cf. 1 Pet. 1:3). The formula was introduced into an originally Jewish context (the praise of God). Christian missionaries did not just call people to faith in God the Father but also to faith in the *kyrios* Jesus (Acts 5:14; 18:8).

4. *The lordship of the kyrios.* (a) The activity of the church before the *kyrios* Jesus. In every expression of its life the Christian community stands before the *kyrios* who has authority and exercises it over the community (1 Cor. 4:19; 14:37; 16:7). He causes the community to grow (1 Thess. 3:12 – 13), bestows authority on the apostles (2 Cor. 10:8; 13:10), and gives different ministries to the members of his body, the church (1 Cor. 3:5; 7:17; 12:5). The *kyrios* also gives visions and revelations (2 Cor. 12:1). The whole life of the Christian community is determined by its relationship to the *kyrios* (Rom. 14:8). The body, i.e., the complete earthly existence of the Christian, belongs to the *kyrios*; this precludes dealings with prostitutes (1 Cor. 6:13 – 17).

The *kyrios* gives to each one the measure of faith (1 Cor. 3:5; 7:17; Eph. 4:5). He is the *kyrios* of peace and gives peace (2 Thess. 3:16), mercy (2 Tim. 1:16), and insight (2:7). On the basis of faith in the *kyrios* Christ, even earthly relationships between masters and slaves take on a new aspect. Faithful service of earthly masters (*kyrioi*) is service of the *kyrios* of the church (Col. 3:22 – 24; cf. 1 Pet. 2:13).

(b) The formulae "through" and "in" the *kyrios*. The formula "through the [our] Lord Jesus [Christ]" occurs in the most varied contexts: e.g., thanksgiving (Rom. 7:25; 1 Cor. 15:57), praise (Rom. 5:11), and exhortation (15:30; 1 Thess. 4:2). In such phrases *kyrios* is used in order to claim the power of the exalted Lord for the life of the church and of the individual.

The phrase "in the Lord" occurs especially. in Paul and means the same as "in Jesus Christ," e.g., *in the Lord*: a door was opened for mission (2 Cor. 2:12), Paul affirms and exhorts (Eph. 4:17; 1 Thess. 4:1), Paul is convinced (Rom. 14:14), people are received (16:2; Phil. 2:29), and the church is to rejoice (3:1), stand firm (4:1), and greet one another (Rom. 16:22; 1 Cor. 16:19). Christians are to marry in the Lord (7:39), be strong in the Lord (Eph. 6:10), and walk in the Lord (Col. 2:6). People are chosen (Rom. 16:13) and loved (16:8; 1 Cor. 4:17) in the Lord; in him their work is not in vain (15:58). The whole of life, in both the present and the future, is determined by the fact of Christ expressed by this formula: Paul and his churches stand in the presence and under the power of the *kyrios*.

(c) Statements about the Parousia. At present Christians are separated from the *kyrios* and long to be with him (2 Cor. 5:6, 8). Those who are alive at the Second Coming will be caught up to meet the *kyrios* (1 Thess. 4:17). Thus, the NT church looks forward to the future, visible return of Christ and to a final union with the Lord of life and death. We read about the day of the Lord (1 Cor. 1:8; 5:5; 2 Cor. 1:14; 1 Thess. 5:2; 2 Thess. 2:2), "the coming [*parousia*] of our *kyrios*" (2 Thess. 2:1), and the "appearing [*epiphaneia*] of our *kyrios*" (1 Tim. 6:14). When he comes, the exalted *kyrios* is Judge (2 Thess. 1:9; 2:8) and Savior (Phil. 3:20).

5. *Derivatives of kyrios.* (a) *kyria* (fem. of *kyrios*) means lady, owner, mistress of the house. In the NT it occurs only in 2 Jn. 1, 5, where it refers to the church (cf. v. 13, where the churches are sisters and their members children). In addressing the church as "lady," the author is expressing his respect for it and honors it as a work of the *kyrios*.

(b) *kyriotēs*, lordly power or position, dominion. In the NT this word occurs in the pl. with reference to angelic powers (Eph. 1:20 – 21; Col. 1:16). The NT letters stress that the exalted Christ rules over these dominions. *kyrioteō* occurs in the sing. in Jude 8 and 2 Pet. 2:10, where the thought is not of angels but of God's dominion.

(c) *kyrieuō*, be a lord, act as master. In the NT this vb. occurs 7x. The rule of kings over their people is characterized by ambition (Lk. 22:25), because they misuse their power for selfish ends; the disciples are to seek rather to serve, as Jesus did (22:26 – 27). Paul uses *kyrieuō* to describe relationships of power. Because Christ has risen, death no longer has any power over him (Rom. 6:9). Christ died and rose in order that he might reign over the living and the dead (14:9). God is the ruler of those who rule (1 Tim. 6:15). Since Christians have been baptized into Jesus' death and have risen with him (Rom. 6:3 – 4), sin must not reign over them any longer (6:14). For they no longer stand under law but under grace (7:1, 6). Paul does not want to lord it over the faith of the Corinthians but to work with them for their joy (2 Cor. 1:24).

(d) *katakyrieuō*, rule over, conquer. The prefix *kata-* has a negative force. In the NT the word occurs 4x. It is a characteristic of Gentile rulers to exercise their rule to their own advantage and contrary to the interests and well-being of the people (Matt. 20:25; Mk. 10:42). The vb. also describes the man with an evil spirit who leaped on the seven sons of Sceva and "overpowered" them (Acts 19:16) as they attempted to imitate Christian exorcism. Finally, Peter exhorts elders not to exercise their office by lording it over the congregation, but to be examples to the flock (1 Pet. 5:2 – 3).

See also *theos*, God (2536); *Emmanouēl*, Immanuel (1842); *despotēs*, lord, master (of a house), owner (1305); *kyriakos*, belonging to the Lord, the Lord's (3258).

Part II

Church Greek

In our second pass through the Greek language, we will be delving much deeper into the grammar, enough so you can use a reverse interlinear. Conceptually, this section is not as difficult as all the new material in Foundational Greek, but it does require a deeper level of thinking and analyzing. Be sure to have purchased the laminated sheets for the book. In this section we will learn:

- Different uses of the case and verbal system

- Pronouns and how to modify an idea

- Conjunctions

- Phrasing, a new exegetical method that can revolutionize the way you study your Bible, and a method that will start to help you understand why commentaries do what they do.

Chapter 11

Cases

It is time to see how the Greek case system is more flexible than perhaps you have realized. Like vocabulary in word studies, cases are used in more intricate ways than I have shared to this point.

Nominative

11.1 We learned in Foundational Greek that the nominative can be used to indicate the *subject* of a verb.

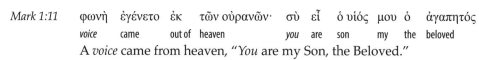

> *Mark 1:11*   φωνὴ ἐγένετο ἐκ τῶν οὐρανῶν· σὺ εἶ ὁ υἱός μου ὁ ἀγαπητός
> *voice* came out of heaven *you* are son my the beloved
> A *voice* came from heaven, "*You* are my Son, the Beloved."

> φωνὴ does the action of the verb ἐγένετο. σύ is the subject of the stative verb εἶ.

You remember that there are two sets of linkages indicating the subject of the verb.

- Subject is in the nominative

- Verb agrees with its subject in person and number.

What is the professor doing there? You have been learning a lot about Greek, and there is much more to go. Some of what you have been learning has to do with meaning, but other points have to do with the structure of the language, how it holds together, the different constructions that link the pieces together. These structural clues are especially important, so the professor is going to point at those items you need to take special note of.

I use two different drawings, but always with a hand pointing to the important information. Be sure to check out the downloadable summary (from the online class) and start referring to it, as well as the last page of the laminated sheets.

11.2   The nominative is also used for a *predicate nominative.* In correct English we would say, "It is I," not, "It is me." Why? Because the verb "I am" in all its forms (e.g., "is," "was") is not followed by a direct object but by a predicate nominative. This means that the following word is in the subjective case.

We have the same situation with the Greek verb εἰμί, which is always followed by a nominative.

Matt 24:5	ἐγώ	εἰμι	ὁ	χριστός
	I	am	*the*	*Christ*

I am *the Christ.*

χριστός is predicating something about ἐγώ.

11.3   A nominative can be in apposition to another substantive in the nominative (*simple apposition*). "Apposition" means that the second word refers to the same entity as the first and is telling us something more about that entity. The two substantives will be next to each other and in the same case.

Matt 3:1	παραγίνεται	Ἰωάννης	ὁ	βαπτιστὴς	κηρύσσων	ἐν	τῇ	ἐρήμῳ
	came	John	*the*	*Baptist*	preaching	in	the	desert

NIV: John *the Baptist* came, preaching in the wilderness.

ὁ βαπτιστὴς is referring to the same person as Ἰωάννης, and identifies this John as opposed to other Johns.

Eph 1:1	Παῦλος	ἀπόστολος	Χριστοῦ	Ἰησοῦ	διὰ	θελήματος	θεοῦ
	Paul	*apostle*	of Christ	Jesus	through	will	of God

Paul, an apostle of Christ Jesus through the will of God

As Wallace explains, "'Paul the apostle' could be unpacked as 'Paul is the apostle' or 'the apostle is Paul'" (53).

Simple apposition occurs in all four cases.

11.4   A Greek sentence does not require an expressed subject. A verb by itself can be a complete sentence. ἀκούω means, "I hear," which is a sentence. The subject is supplied by the personal ending on the verb.

1 Tim 1:8	Οἴδαμεν	δὲ	ὅτι	καλὸς	ὁ νόμος
	we know	but	that	good	the law

But *we know* that the law is good.

There is no expressed subject "we," so it is derived from the verb Οἴδαμεν.

Mark 1:16	εἶδεν	Σίμωνα	καὶ	Ἀνδρέαν	τὸν ἀδελφὸν	Σίμωνος
	he saw	Simon	and	Andrew	the brother	of Simon

He saw Simon and Andrew, the brother of Simon.

If a simple "he/she/it" or "they" from the verb might be confusing, translators will sometimes supply the actual subject. Take, for example, Hebrews 4:7-9.

> He again fixes a certain day, "Today," saying through David after so long a time just as has been said before, "Today if you hear His voice, Do not harden your hearts." For if Joshua had given them rest, *He* would not have spoken of another day after that. So there remains a Sabbath rest for the people of God (NASB).

Who is the "He" who "would not have spoken"? It may appear, initially, to be Joshua; that is what the normal rules of English grammar would require. However, the subject of the verb is God, who is alluded to in the context. That is why the NASB capitalizes "He," and why the NIV replaces "He" with "God."

Heb 4:8	οὐκ	ἂν	περὶ	ἄλλης	ἐλάλει	μετὰ	ταῦτα	ἡμέρας.
	not	would	concerning	another	*he was speaking*	after	these	days

NIV: *God* would not have spoken later about another day.
ESV: *God* would not have spoken of another day later on.

> The ESV supplies the antecedent "God" and adds a footnote, "Greek *he*," as is its custom in this situation.

Another example is Romans 3:9, where the ESV adds "Jews" and marks it with a footnote, "Greek *Are we*."

Rom 3:9	Τί	οὖν;	προεχόμεθα;	οὐ	πάντως·
	what	therefore	*we are better off*	not	at all

ESV: What then? Are we *Jews* any better off? No, not at all.

Accusative

11.5 We have seen how the accusative is used for the *direct object*.

Mark 8:7	καὶ	εἶχον	ἰχθύδια	ὀλίγα
	and	they had	*fish*	few

They also had a few small *fish*.

What did they have? They had ἰχθύδια.

By the way, remember that not only do indicative verbs have a direct object; most verbal forms like participles can also take a direct object.

11.6   We have seen the accusative used for the *object of certain prepositions.*

Matt 2:1   ἰδοὺ   μάγοι   ἀπὸ   ἀνατολῶν   παρεγένοντο   εἰς   Ἱεροσόλυμα
behold   wise men   from   East   came   to   Jerusalem
Magi from the east came to *Jerusalem.*

Ἱεροσόλυμα is the object of the preposition εἰς, which takes its object in the accusative.

11.7   The accusative can be in an appositional relationship to another substantive in the accusative (*simple apposition*).

Mark 1:16   εἶδεν   Σίμωνα   καὶ   Ἀνδρέαν   τὸν ἀδελφὸν   Σίμωνος
he saw   Simon   and   *Andrew*   *the brother*   of Simon
He saw Simon and Andrew, Simon's *brother.*

This Andrew was in fact Simon's brother.

11.8   Some verbs require two objects to complete their meaning (*double accusative*). This constructions falls into two categories.

Sometimes the two objects will be a personal (e.g., "you") and a non-personal (e.g., "thing") word (*person–thing*).

John 14:26   ἐκεῖνος   ὑμᾶς   διδάξει   πάντα
he   you   he will teach   *all things*
He will teach *you all things.*

The coming Holy Spirit will teach the disciples ("you"), and he will teach everything ("all things") Jesus taught them.

The other category is the *object–complement.* This means that one word will be the direct object and the second will predicate something about the direct object.

Matt 4:19   δεῦτε   ὀπίσω   μου,   καὶ   ποιήσω   ὑμᾶς   ἁλιεῖς   ἀνθρώπων.
follow   after   me   and   I will make   *you*   *fishermen*   of men
ESV: Follow me, and I will make *you fishers* of men.

Jesus is going to make the disciples (ὑμᾶς) into fishermen (ἁλιεῖς ἀνθρώπων).

Sometimes a translation will add a word like "as" or "to be" before the second accusative to help you understand its meaning.

1 John 4:10   ἀπέστειλεν   τὸν υἱὸν   αὐτοῦ   ἱλασμὸν
He sent   the son   of him   *propitiation*
NIV: he … sent his Son *as an atoning sacrifice.*
NASB: He … sent His Son *to be the propitiation.*

11.9 A word in the accusative can be functioning as if it were the *subject* of an infinitive. Infinitives are "in-finite" in that they are not limited by a subject, but a word in the accusative (usually following the infinitive) can act as if it were.

1 Cor 10:13 ὁ θεός … οὐκ ἐάσει ὑμᾶς πειρασθῆναι ὑπὲρ ὃ δύνασθε
God   not will allow *you* *to be tempted* beyond what you are able
NIV: God… will not let *you* be tempted beyond what you can bear.

ὑμᾶς is accusative and is functioning as the subject of the infinitive πειρασθῆναι.

Dative

11.10 Many of the times when English uses prepositions, Greek uses the dative case (often without prepositions).

Matt 5:24 ὕπαγε πρῶτον διαλλάγηθι τῷ ἀδελφῷ σου
go   first   be reconciled   to   brother   your
First, go be reconcilled *to* your *brother*.

Since English does not have a dative case, the translator will often use an extra word in the translation of the dative such as "to," "in," or "by." They are normally prepositions. In *IRU*, you will have seen these little words with arrows under them. The arrow is pointing to the word in the dative case (or one of the other cases) that requires this helping word, such as "by" in Ephesians 2:8.

For	it	is	by	grace		you	have	been	saved
γὰρ	→	ἐστε	→	⌞Τῇ	χάριτι⌟	→	→	→	σεσωσμένοι
cj		v.pai.2p		d.dsf	n.dsf				pt.rp.npm
1142		1639		3836	5921				5392

Logos uses arrows as well (illustration on page 75).

Is it wrong for a translator to "add" these words? Of course not. Because we do not have a dative case in English, we cannot say something in the same way as it is said in Greek. We have to use the tools our language gives us to say the same thing.

11.11 It is customary to break the dative down into three basic divisions: the dative proper ("to"), the locative ("in"), and the instrumental ("by").[1]

---

[1] Some people used to teach that there are eight cases, in which case these are three distinct cases although identical in form. I will discuss this in Functional Greek.

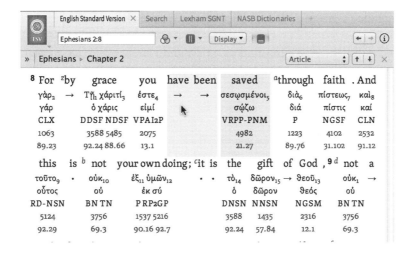

Dicative Proper

11.12 We have seen that the *indirect object* functions the same in Greek as it does in English, with the indirect object placed in the dative case.

John 5:27 καὶ ἐξουσίαν ἔδωκεν αὐτῷ κρίσιν ποιεῖν,
and authority he gave *to him* judgment to make
And he gave *him* authority to judge.

"He" did not give "him"; he gave "authority," and he gave it αὐτῷ, which is therefore dative.

11.13 We have also seen the dative used as the *object of a preposition*.

Matt 3:6 ἐβαπτίζοντο ἐν τῷ Ἰορδάνῃ ποταμῷ ὑπ' αὐτοῦ
they were being baptized in the *Jordan* river by him
They were being baptized by him in the *Jordan* River.

Ἰορδάνῃ is the object of the preposition ἐν, which takes the dative.

11.14 The dative can also express the idea of "for" (*dative of interest*).

Luke 1:13 ἡ γυνή σου Ἐλισάβετ γεννήσει υἱόν σοι
wife your Elizabeth she will bear son *to you*
Your wife Elizabeth will bear a son *for you*.
NET: Your wife Elizabeth will bear *you* a son.

Elizabeth did not bear a son "to" Zechariah; it was "for" him.

When the idea is for the person's advantage, as in Luke 1:13 above, we call it a *dative of advantage*. When context tells us that it is not for the person's advantage, we can call it a *dative of disadvantage* and often use a different preposition based on the meaning of the phrase.

Matt 23:31   μαρτυρεῖτε ἑαυτοῖς
you testify   *to yourselves*
NRSV: You testify *against yourselves*.
KJV: Ye be witnesses *unto yourselves*.

Here the testifying is not "for" the Pharisees in a positive sense but is rather hostile; in English we say this with the preposition "against."

11.15 The dative can indicate what in English is awkwardly expressed by the phrase "with respect to" (*reference, respect*).

Rom 6:11   λογίζεσθε ἑαυτοὺς εἶναι νεκροὺς τῇ ἁμαρτίᾳ
consider   yourselves to be   dead   *to the sin*
ESV: Consider yourselves to be dead *to sin*.
TEV: You are to think of yourselves as dead, *so far as sin is concerned*.

They were dead, but in what sense? Physical? No. Their death was with respect to sin. Sin had died in them.

11.16 Like in the other cases, a word in the dative can be used in *simple apposition*.

Luke 1:47   ἠγαλλίασεν τὸ πνεῦμά μου ἐπὶ τῷ θεῷ τῷ σωτῆρί μου
rejoices   spirit   my   in   God   savior   my
My spirit rejoices in God my *Savior*.

"God" is also our "Savior," and so σωτῆρί is in the dative as is θεῷ.

Locative

11.17 This is a little more nebulous use of the dative, indicating the sphere or realm in which something occurs (*sphere*).

Matt 5:8   μακάριοι οἱ καθαροὶ τῇ καρδίᾳ
Blessed   the pure   *in the heart*
NIV: Blessed are the pure *in heart*.
NLT: God blesses those *whose hearts* are pure.

What type of purity is Jesus talking about? Cultic purity? No, but purity within the sphere of a person's heart.

Instrumental

11.18 The dative can also show the means (or the instrument) by which an action is accomplished (*means, instrument*).

> *Eph 2:8*   Τῇ γὰρ χάριτί ἐστε σεσῳσμένοι
> the   for   *by grace* you are being saved
> For it is *by grace* you have been saved.
>
> The means by which we are saved is grace.

> *Jn 11:2*   Μαριὰμ ... ἐκμάξασα τοὺς πόδας αὐτοῦ ταῖς θριξὶν αὐτῆς
> Mary   wiped   feet   his   *with hair* her
> Mary wiped his feet *with* her *hair*.
>
> The instrument with which Mary wiped Jesus' feet was her hair.

Genitive

11.19 We have seen that the most generic use of the genitive is to establish a simple modifier relationship (*descriptive*).

> *Matt 5:9*   μακάριοι οἱ εἰρηνοποιοί, ὅτι αὐτοὶ υἱοὶ θεοῦ κληθήσονται.
> blessed   the peacemakers   for they sons *of God* will be called
> Blessed are the peacemakers, for they will be called the sons *of God*.
>
> They will not be called just anyone's sons, but God's sons.

11.20 We have seen that the head noun can be possessed by the word in the genitive (*possessive*). The word can be a personal pronoun or a noun.

> *Matt 19:21*   ὕπαγε πώλησόν σου τὰ ὑπάρχοντα
> Go   sell   *of you* the things belonging
> Go, sell *your* possessions.
>
> He was to sell his own possessions.

> *1 Tim 1:1*   Παῦλος ἀπόστολος Χριστοῦ Ἰησοῦ κατ' ἐπιταγὴν θεοῦ
> Paul   apostle   *of Christ* *Jesus* because of command *of God*
> Paul, an apostle *of Christ Jesus* because of the command *of God*.
>
> Paul's apostolic ministry was not due to a general command, but a specifc command from God.

11.21 We have also seen that the word in the genitive can be the *object of a preposition*.

Matt 23:9   πατέρα   μὴ   καλέσητε   ὑμῶν   ἐπὶ   τῆς γῆς
                father   not   call   your   on   *earth*
Do not call anyone on *earth* your "father."

γῆς is in the genitive because it is the object of the preposition ἐπὶ, which can take the genitive.

11.22 After comparative adjectives you will often find a word in the genitive (*comparison*). This is due primarily to the meaning of the adjective, and you generally find "than" used with the genitive.

Matt 6:25   οὐχὶ   ἡ ψυχὴ   πλεῖόν   ἐστιν   τῆς τροφῆς
                not   life   more   is   *than food*
Is not life worth more than *food*?

πλεῖόν is a comparative adjective meaning "more," and hence τροφῆς must be in the genitive.

11.23 A word in the genitive can be in a *simple appositional* relationship with another genitive.

Col 1:2   χάρις ὑμῖν   καὶ   εἰρήνη   ἀπὸ   θεοῦ   πατρὸς   ἡμῶν
              grace to you   and   peace   from   God   *father*   our
Grace to you and peace from God our *father*.

Paul's blessing comes from God, who is also our Father.

The word in the genitive is basically equivalent to its head noun.

11.24 A word in the genitive can be part of another type of appositional relationship (*genitive of apposition, epexegetical genitive*).

- In the case of the simple apposition (11.23), the head noun and the word in the genitive are roughly equivalent, and both words must be in the genitive.

- With the genitive of apposition, the head noun represents a larger group (often ambiguous), and the genitive is a smaller, perhaps more specific part of the larger group. The head noun does not have to be in the genitive.

In this case, the two words refer to the same thing, but they are not exactly the same.

Rom 4:11	σημεῖον	ἔλαβεν	περιτομῆς	σφραγῖδα	τῆς δικαιοσύνης	τῆς πίστεως
	sign	he received	of circumcision	seal	of righteousness	by faith

NIV: He received *circumcision* as a sign, a seal of the righteousness that he had by faith.

ESV: He received the sign *of circumcision* as a seal of the righteousness that he had by faith.

"Sign" is the head noun for "circumcision" and is the larger category; "circumcision" is the smaller, more specific concept.

John 2:21	ἐκεῖνος	δὲ	ἔλεγεν	περὶ	τοῦ ναοῦ	τοῦ σώματος	αὐτοῦ.
	he	but	was speaking	concerning	the temple	of body	his

NRSV: But he was speaking of the temple *of* his *body*.

NIV: But the temple he had spoken of was his *body*.

NLT: But when Jesus said "this temple," he meant his own *body*.

Jesus was speaking of the temple, and the specific temple was his body.

Acts 2:38	λήμψεσθε	τὴν δωρεὰν	τοῦ ἁγίου	πνεύματος.
	You will receive	the gift	of the Holy	Spirit

You will receive the gift, *which is the Holy Spirit.*

NIV: You will receive the gift *of the Holy Spirit.*

TEV: You will receive God's gift, *the Holy Spirit.*

Of all the gifts we can receive, the gift here is the Holy Spirit.

Exercises

11.25 Remember, all the exercises are available on the class' website, at:

www.teknia.com/churchgreek

Chapter 12

Pronouns

There are 16,245 pronouns in the Greek Testament. If you are going to study Functional Greek as well, these forms should be memorized.

English

12.1   A **pronoun** is a word that replaces a noun. In the sentence, "It is red," "It" is a pronoun referring back to something.

A **personal pronoun** is a pronoun that replaces a personal noun.[1] In the sentence, "My name is Bill; I will learn Greek as well as possible," "I" is a personal pronoun referring to me, Bill.

The word that a pronoun refers back to, "Bill," is the **antecedent**.

12.2   **Person**. Pronouns can be first, second, or third person. We saw this same basic thing with verbs and their personal endings.

- First person refers to the person speaking ("I," "we").

- Second person refers to the person being spoken to ("you").

- Third person refers to that which is spoken about ("he," "she," "it," "they"). All nouns are considered third person.

	first person	*second person*	*masculine*	*third person* *feminine*	*neuter*
subjective sg	I	you	he	she	it
possessive sg[2]	my	your	his	her	its
objective sg	me	you	him	her	it
subjective pl	we	you		they	
possessive pl	our	your		their	
objective pl	us	you		them	

---

[1]   A personal noun is a noun referring to a person.
[2]   If the possessive forms are used substantivally, they are translated "mine," "yours," and "ours."

Notice how highly inflected the English pronoun is. They are radically changed, depending on their function.

There is no easy way to distinguish between second person singular and plural ("you"). Sometimes I will use the southern American expression "y'all" for the plural (although technically it is not plural).[3]

12.3 The number and person of a pronoun are determined by its antecedent.

- The **number** of the pronoun is determined by the antecedent. Because "Bill" is singular, you would use "I" and not "we."

- The **person** of the pronoun is determined by the antecedent. If the antecedent was the person speaking (first person), you use "I," not "you."

- There is no **gender** in the first and second person. "I" or "you" can be either a woman or a man. The third person pronoun has gender, but only in the singular.

12.4 The **case** of a pronoun is determined by its function in the sentence. For example, if the pronoun is the subject of the sentence, you would use "I" and not "me" since "I" is in the subjective case. You would not say, "Me would like to eat now," because "me" is objective.

Greek

12.5 The Greek personal pronouns function as they do in English. Number and gender are determined by the antecedent, and case by function.

12.6 You should memorize the first and second person personal pronouns, especially if you are going to study Functional Greek. They are extremely common, occurring 11,170 times in the New Testament. The forms in parentheses are called the "emphatic" forms, but have the same basic meaning as the non-emphatic. (More about this in Functional Greek.)

	first person			*second person*		
nom sg	ἐγώ		I	σύ		you
gen sg	μου	(ἐμοῦ)	my	σου	(σοῦ)	your
dat sg	μοι	(ἐμοί)	to me	σοι	(σοί)	to you
acc sg	με	(ἐμέ)	me	σε	(σέ)	you

---

[3] In older English, "thou," "thee," and "thy, thine" were singular, and "ye," "you," and "your, yours" were plural.

nom pl	ἡμεῖς	we	ὑμεῖς	you
gen pl	ἡμῶν	our	ὑμῶν	your
dat pl	ἡμῖν	to us	ὑμῖν	to you
acc pl	ἡμᾶς	us	ὑμᾶς	you

As you can see, the Greek pronouns do not have gender in the first and second person, singular or plural, just like English.

12.7 The Greek third person pronoun has gender in both the singular and plural. If you are going to study Functional Greek, the third section in this grammar, you should memorize this paradigm as well. αὐτός is Strong's #846, GK #899.

	masc	*fem*	*neut*	*translation*		
nom sg	αὐτός	αὐτή	αὐτό	he	she	it
gen sg	αὐτοῦ	αὐτῆς	αὐτοῦ	his	her	its
dat sg	αὐτῷ	αὐτῇ	αὐτῷ	to him	to her	to it
acc sg	αὐτόν	αὐτήν	αὐτό	him	her	it
nom pl	αὐτοί	αὐταί	αὐτά		they	
gen pl	αὐτῶν	αὐτῶν	αὐτῶν		their	
dat pl	αὐτοῖς	αὐταῖς	αὐτοῖς		to them	
acc pl	αὐτούς	αὐτάς	αὐτά		them	

12.8 There is some confusion with the Strong's numbers for the personal pronouns. Strong assigned a different number for each inflected form. In the GK system, all first person pronouns are #1609, and all second person pronouns are #5148.

	first person				*second person*		
nom sg	ἐγώ		1473		σύ		4771
gen sg	μου	(ἐμοῦ)	3450	(1700)	σου	(σοῦ)	4675
dat sg	μοι	(ἐμοί)	3427	(1698)	σοι	(σοί)	4671
acc sg	με	(ἐμέ)	3165	(1691)	σε	(σέ)	4571
nom pl	ἡμεῖς		2249		ὑμεῖς		5210
gen pl	ἡμῶν		2257		ὑμῶν		5216
dat pl	ἡμῖν		2254		ὑμῖν		5213
acc pl	ἡμᾶς		2248		ὑμᾶς		5209

Software programs differ on how they handle this. Accordance connects all the first person forms to ἐγώ (GK 1609), and all the second person forms to σύ (GK 5148). Logos uses a different number for first and second person, and all forms of αὐτός are 846. Be sure to check your software to see how it handles this issue.

12.9 Don't forget about natural gender in the third person. If αὐτός is referring to a person, it will be masculine or feminine. If it is referring to something else, it will be masculine, feminine, or neuter depending on the gender of its antecedent.

This can give us the somewhat unusal situation (for the English reader) in which the grammatical gender of the pronoun does not match up with natural gender. For example, if the antecedent is πνεῦμα, which is grammatically neuter, the pronoun will be neuter (e.g., αὐτό). But if the πνεῦμα is the Holy Spirit, then we translate the neuter pronoun αὐτό as "he," not "it."

John 14:17   τὸ   πνεῦμα τῆς ἀληθείας, ὃ   ὁ   κόσμος οὐ δύναται λαβεῖν
                the   Spirit   of truth   who the world   not able   to receive
               ESV: The Spirit of truth, *whom* the world cannot receive.
               NIV: The Spirit of truth. The world cannot accept *him*.

Or how about ἀγάπη? The noun is feminine, so the pronoun referring back to it must be feminine (e.g., αὐτῇ), but in English you refer back to "love" as "it," not "she."

2 John 6   καὶ αὕτη ἐστὶν ἡ   ἀγάπη … ἵνα   ἐν αὐτῇ περιπατῆτε.
          and this   is   the love   in order that in *it*   walk.
          And this is love … that you should walk in *it*.

12.10 Translators sometimes replace a personal pronoun with its antecedent for the sake of clarity, as in Matthew 8:24.

> Suddenly, a furious storm came up on the lake, so that the waves swept over the boat. But *Jesus* was sleeping (NIV).

The Greek only has "he was sleeping." On Matthew 9:10 the ESV writes,

> And as *Jesus* reclined at table in the house, behold, many tax collectors and sinners came and were reclining with Jesus and his disciples.

The footnote on "Jesus" reads, "Greek *he*."

Vocabulary

12.11 There is vocabulary for this chapter in the online class.

Chapter 13

Modifiers

There are many ways to modify a basic idea. In fact, if we only had subjects, verbs, and objects, communication would be more difficult and certainly less colorful. In this chapter we will look at many different modifiers.

Article

13.1 ὁ is the single most important Greek word to memorize. Not only does it occur 19,867 times in the New Testament, but it will give you significant clues as to the overall structure of a sentence. You need to memorize every form. It is most commonly translated as "the."

	masculine	feminine	neuter
nom sg	ὁ	ἡ	τό
gen sg	τοῦ	τῆς	τοῦ
dat sg	τῷ	τῇ	τῷ
acc sg	τόν	τήν	τό
nom/voc pl	οἱ	αἱ	τά
gen pl	τῶν	τῶν	τῶν
dat pl	τοῖς	ταῖς	τοῖς
acc pl	τούς	τάς	τά

13.2 ὁ will be in the same case, number, and gender as the word it modifies ("agreement"). ὁ and λόγος are both nominative singular masculine.

> *1 Tim 4:9*   πιστὸς ὁ λόγος καὶ πάσης ἀποδοχῆς ἄξιος
> faithful *the word* and all acceptance worthy
> Trustworthy is *the word* and worthy of complete acceptance.

13.3 Nouns are only one gender (usually). Because words like ὁ and adjectives can modify any noun regardless of its gender, and because they must be the same gender as the word they are modifying, they themselves must be able to be in any gender. That's why the paradigm for the article and adjectives have 24 forms and not just 8.

13.4 The most common translation of ὁ is as "the" (*definite article*).

> *Rev 1:8*   Ἐγώ εἰμι τὸ ἄλφα καὶ τὸ ὦ, λέγει κύριος ὁ θεός
> I   am   the Alpha and the Omega says Lord   God
> I am *the* Alpha and *the* Omega, says the Lord God.

13.5 Greek uses ὁ when English does not use the definite article, such as before a personal name.

> *Matt 15:15*   ὁ Πέτρος εἶπεν αὐτῷ· φράσον ἡμῖν τὴν παραβολὴν [ταύτην]
> the Peter   he said to him Explain to us the parable   this
> Peter said to him, "Explain this parable to us."

This includes the word for "God," θεός.

> *Acts 10:15*   ἃ ὁ θεὸς ἐκαθάρισεν, σὺ μὴ κοίνου
> what the God   he cleansed   you not consider common
> What God has made clean, you must not consider common.

13.6 ὁ is not always used when English requires the definite article. If it fits the context and is required by English, it can be included. For example, the article is often dropped when inside a Greek prepositional phrase, and translators sometimes have to add it back in.

> *Matt 3:11*   αὐτὸς ὑμᾶς βαπτίσει ἐν πνεύματι ἁγίῳ καὶ πυρί
> he   you   he will baptize in Spirit   holy   and fire
> He will baptize you in *the* Holy Spirit and fire.

13.7 There are many other uses of ὁ other than as the article. You will also see ὁ not translated because it can function grammatically in ways that are not translatable. Don't be frustrated; we will discuss ὁ in much greater detail in Functional Greek.

Adjectives

13.8   An adjective is a word that modifies a noun or pronoun (or another adjective).

> Bill threw his *big black* book at the *strange* teacher.

13.9   Adjectives can function **adjectivally** (i.e., like a regular adjective, also called an **attributive** adjective).

Matt 4:5   Τότε   παραλαμβάνει   αὐτὸν   ὁ   διάβολος   εἰς   τὴν   ἁγίαν   πόλιν
              then   he took   him   the   devil   into   the   *holy*   city
   Then the devil took him into the *holy* city.

We will see in Functional Greek that adjectives can also function like nouns ("substantival").

13.10   **Agreement**. When an adjective modifies another word, it will agree with that word in case, number, and gender, just like the article. In other words, if the noun is genitive in case, singular in number, and feminine in gender, the modifying word will also be genitive singular feminine.

Matt 7:13   Εἰσέλθατε   διὰ   τῆς   στενῆς   πύλης
              enter   through   the   *narrow*   gate
   Enter through *the narrow gate*.

πύλης is genitive singular feminine, and so στενῆς must be genitive singular feminine.

We will learn in Functional Greek that adjectives can occur in different locations. For example, they can be in the position of article–adjective–noun (as above) or article–noun–article–adjective, but this issue has been smoothed out in reverse interlinears.

Matt 8:12   οἱ   δὲ   υἱοὶ   τῆς   βασιλείας   ἐκβληθήσονται   εἰς   τὸ   σκότος   τὸ   ἐξώτερον.
              the   but   sons   of the   kingdom   will be cast out   into   the   *darkness*   the   *outer*
   But the sons of the kingdom will be cast out into *the outer darkness*.

Phrases

13.11 A "phrase" is a group of related words that does not have a subject or a finite verb.

> *After going home,* the rain stopped.
>
> *Because of love,* I will serve God.

13.12 A phrase is often categorized by the type of word with which it begins, such as a preposition or participle. Sometimes a phrase is categorized by its function, such as "adverbial" or "temporal."

13.13 Because a phrase by definition does not have a subject and verb, all phrases are dependent constructions. Normally, the author's main thought is in the independent clause, and the dependent clause modifies a main thought. This distinction will be especially important for our exegetical method, "Phrasing" (chapter 14).

Prepositions

13.14 Prepositions that end in a vowel might change their form when the following word begins with a vowel. The final vowel of the preposition may be dropped and marked with an apostrophe. This is called **elision**.

> μετὰ αὐτόν → μετʼ αὐτόν

13.15 When a preposition ends in a vowel and the following word begins with a vowel and a rough breathing, the consonant before the final vowel in the preposition often changes as well. These changes were necessary in order to pronounce the combination of sounds more easily. In this example, the alpha drops out and τ becomes θ.

> μετὰ ἡμῶν → μετʼ ἡμῶν → μεθʼ ἡμῶν

13.16 Some prepositions are followed by an object that can be in one or two or even three cases. For example, διά can have an object in the genitive or accusative; ἐπί can take an object in all three cases. (The object of a preposition will never be in the nominative.)

If a preposition takes an object in more than one case, the preposition has a different set of meanings for each case. This is why a Greek lexicon divides its discussion of prepositions based on the case of its object. The translator must identify the case of the object before translating the preposition.

For example, the preposition διά means "through" if its object is in the genitive case, but it means "on account of" if its object is in the accusative.

Matt 2:5	οὕτως	γὰρ	γέγραπται	διὰ	τοῦ	προφήτου
	in this way	for	it is written	*through*	*the*	*prophet*

for this is what has been written *by the prophet*

Matt 10:22	ἔσεσθε	μισούμενοι	ὑπὸ	πάντων	διὰ	τὸ	ὄνομά	μου
	you will be	hated	by	all	*on account of*	*the*	*name*	*my*

NIV: You will be hated by everyone *because of me.*
RSV: You will be hated by all *for my name's sake.*

Prepositional Phrases

13.17 We have already learned that the preposition, its object, and any modifiers are called a "prepositional phrase." They always begin with the preposition, and they will have an object and possibly modifiers.

Rom 1:2	ὃ	προεπηγγείλατο	διὰ τῶν προφητῶν αὐτοῦ	ἐν γραφαῖς ἁγίαις
	which	he promised	*through his prophets*	*in the holy scriptures*

which he promised *through his prophets in the holy scriptures.*

When doing Bible study, it is important to identify the end of the prepositional phrase.

13.18 Prepositional phrases are generally *adverbial,* especially if the preposition takes an object in the dative, which means they are connected to the verb (or a verbal construction such as a participle). In some way the prepositional phrase will tell you something about the action of verbal form.

Rom 3:24	δικαιούμενοι	δωρεὰν	τῇ	αὐτοῦ	χάριτι	διὰ	τῆς	ἀπολυτρώσεως
	Being justified	freely	by	his	grace	*through*	*the*	*redemption*

Being justified freely by his grace *through* the redemption

In Chapter 14 you will be learning an exegetical process I call "phrasing." It lays out the text graphically so you can see the main thoughts, the modifying thoughts, and the author's flow of thought. Here is the phrasing of Rom 3:24.

δικαιούμενοι	being justified
δωρεὰν	freely
τῇ αὐτοῦ χάριτι	by his grace
διὰ τῆς ἀπολυτρώσεως	through the redemption

Our being justified was done freely (i.e., at not cost to ourselves), it was done by God's grace (not our works), and it was accomplished through the redemption, as Paul continues, that came from Christ Jesus. You can see how the prepositional phrase διὰ τῆς ἀπολυτρώσεως modifies the verbal form δικαιούμενοι.

13.19 But prepositions can also modify nouns (*attributive*).

Rom 3:25   ὃν   προέθετο ὁ θεὸς ἱλαστήριον διὰ   [τῆς] πίστεως ἐν τῷ αὐτοῦ αἵματι
Whom   he set forth   God   as a propitiation *through the*   faith   in   the   his   blood

HCSB: God presented Him as a propitiation through faith in His blood.

The prepositional phrase "through the faith" tells us the means by which we receive the benefits of the sacrifice. "In his blood" is the means by which God accomplished the propitiation.

ὃν προέθετο ὁ θεὸς ἱλαστήριον

     διὰ [τῆς] πίστεως

     ἐν τῷ αὐτοῦ αἵματι

whom God put forward as a propitiation

     through faith

     in his blood

13.20 We saw in 13.10 that Greek has a article–noun–article–adjective construction. Actually, the final "adjective" slot can be any modifier, including a prepositional phrase.

Rom 3:24   διὰ   τῆς ἀπολυτρώσεως τῆς   ἐν   Χριστῷ Ἰησοῦ
through   the   redemption   the   in   Christ   Jesus

Through the redemption *that is in Christ Jesus*

Because we do not have this contruction in English, you will find translators adding extra words to make it acceptable English.

Clauses

13.21 Clauses are like phrases except that they have a finite verb and its subject. One of the most common types of clause is a relative clause.

13.22 A **relative pronoun** is a noun substitute: who(m); whose; that; which; what(ever).

> The man *who* is sitting at the table is my pastor.

The **antecedent** is the word the pronoun is replacing. "Whoever" is the "indefinite relative pronoun" and it functions just like the relative pronoun.

> *Mark 9:40* ὃς γὰρ οὐκ ἔστιν καθ' ἡμῶν, ὑπὲρ ἡμῶν ἐστιν.
> *who for not is against us for us is*
> *For whoever is not against us is for us.*

The whole relative clause, "For whoever is not against us," is the subject of the verb ἐστιν.

13.23 **Relative clauses** are comprised of the relative pronoun, a verb and its subject, and possibly other modifiers. The clause always starts with a relative pronoun.

> *Mark 4:9* καὶ ἔλεγεν· ὃς ἔχει ὦτα ἀκούειν ἀκουέτω.
> *and he said who has ears to hear let him hear*
> And he said, *"Whoever has ears to hear,* let him hear."

13.24 The Greek **relative pronoun** is ὅς. Here is the paradigm of ὅς (compared to the article). Memorization is optional but recommended; if you plan on studying Functional Greek, memorization is required.[4]

	relative pronoun			article		
nom sg	ὅς	ἥ	ὅ	ὁ	ἡ	τό
gen sg	οὗ	ἧς	οὗ	τοῦ	τῆς	τοῦ
dat sg	ᾧ	ᾗ	ᾧ	τῷ	τῇ	τῷ
acc sg	ὅν	ἥν	ὅ	τόν	τήν	τό
n/v pl	οἵ	αἵ	ἅ	οἱ	αἱ	τά
gen pl	ὧν	ὧν	ὧν	τῶν	τῶν	τῶν
dat pl	οἷς	αἷς	οἷς	τοῖς	ταῖς	τοῖς
acc pl	οὕς	ἅς	ἅ	τούς	τάς	τά

---

[4] In Greek, the two words ὅς (58x) and ἄν, or ὅς and ἐάν (43x), or the word ὅστις (144x) are translated as the indefinite relative.

13.25 Two factors determine the form of the relative pronoun.

- Gender and number are determined by its antecedent; they will be the same. This is part of the linkage so you can find what the relative pronoun is referring to.

- Case is determined by its function inside the relative clause. This is an important difference from the adjective. What the relative clause may (or may not) be modifying does not affect the form of the relative pronoun. Its case is determined by how it is used *inside* the relative clause.

  Think of the relative clause as its own sentence. If necessary, replace the pronoun with its antecedent, and then ask yourself, what function is the relative pronoun playing inside the relative clause? If it is the direct object of the verb, then it will be accusative. If the relative pronoun is the subject of the verb, it will be nominative.

13.26 You can find a nominative functioning as the subject of a verb, but a verb that is inside a relative clause.

1 Tim 6:16   ὁ   μόνος ἔχων   ἀθανασίαν … ὃν   εἶδεν οὐδεὶς ἀνθρώπων
             the   only   having immortality   whom saw   no one of men
             who alone has immortality … whom *no one* has ever seen

13.27 Relative clauses can be adjectival (*attributive*).

Matt 2:16   κατὰ   τὸν χρόνον ὃν   ἠκρίβωσεν παρὰ τῶν μάγων.
            according to the time which he had learned from the wise men
            according to the time *he had learned from the wise men*

13.28 Relative clauses can also act as parts of speech, like a noun (*substantival*). What functions do the relative clauses perform in the following sentences?

Matt 5:19   ὃς δ᾽ ἂν ποιήσῃ καὶ διδάξῃ, οὗτος μέγας κληθήσεται
            who but ever he does and he teaches this   great   he will be called
            But whoever does them and teaches them will be called great in the kingdom of heaven.

Mark 3:13   προσκαλεῖται οὓς   ἤθελεν αὐτός
            he called   whom he wished himself
            He called those *whom he himself wanted*.

Dependent (or "Subordinate") and Independent

13.29 A **dependent** clause is a clause that cannot grammatically stand on its own. In other words, it doesn't make sense by itself. It isn't a sentence. Do any of the following form a sentence?

> after the rain stops
>
> because I am tired
>
> which I read to you

No they don't, and therefore they are "dependent" or "subordinate" clauses. All phrases are dependent, and clauses can be dependent.

13.30 An **independent** clause is a clause that can stand on its own as a sentence.

> After the rain stops, *I will dry the car.*
>
> Because I am tired, *I will go to sleep.*
>
> *Please give me the book,* which I read to you.

Vocabulary

13.31 There is vocabulary for this chapter in the online class.

Chapter 14

Phrasing 101

When I started studying the Bible, I remember looking at a paragraph and having difficulty locating the main idea(s). I am a visual person, and sometimes the words started to blend together.

So I started working on a new way to study my Bible. I would xerox a paragraph of the Bible, cut each verse into its phrases, and lay the pieces out in a way that made sense to me visually. I would put the main thought all the way to the left, and ideas that were related to that main point were placed under or over it. For example (Mark 8:34):

> If anyone wishes to come after Me,
> he must
> > deny himself, and
> > take up his cross and
> > follow Me.

In other words, those who want to be a disciple of Jesus must do three things: "deny," "take up," "follow."

When I was done, I would xerox my reconstructed text and have something that visually helped me see the flow of the author's discussion.

As the years passed, I became more sophisticated. I used color pencils! Eventually I used a software program to get the actual text; I would copy it into my word processor and lay out the passage.

This process has helped me more than almost anything else to study my Bible. It forced me to identify the main point (or points) and to see the flow of the author's thought—how he moved from one main point to the next, and how he clarified the main point(s) by adding modifiers.

I eventually named this process "phrasing" because I found that it wasn't normally helpful to break a sentence into every word (which is done in grammatical diagramming). I would break the sentence into its phrases (or clauses) and found that I rarely needed to divide the phrases further. So when you see the examples of phrasing on the following pages, and if you have "baggage" from high school grammar classes, don't freak out. This isn't grammatical diagramming, although it uses grammar.

When I then started teaching phrasing to college and graduate students, I found that they too enjoyed the process because it helped them learn, for themselves, what the Bible was saying.

I also discovered that other people were doing the same type of procedure. They called it by different names—"sentence flow," "discourse analysis"—but they too had learned how laying a passage out visually helped them see what the author meant.

Let me show you how it works.

> On the following pages, the text that is boxed is an illustration. Text that is not boxed is my discussion.

By the way, why am I talking about phrasing in a text designed to teach you the basics of Greek grammar? My assumption is that you want to learn to use the language tools in order to study your Bible. After trying many other methods, I discovered that the tools are best learned while you are actually doing Bible study, or what is called "exegesis."

Do you have to do phrasing in order to learn a little Greek? No. There are different methods of doing Bible study that are effective. But phrasing works best for me and for my students, and so it becomes the context within which I will teach you how to use the language tools.

Also, one of the goals for this textbook is to help you read good commentaries. While some good commentaries may not actually phrase the text, the essence of the commentary will be to discover the flow of the author's thought and his main points. The better you become at phrasing, the more familiar a good commentary will feel.

Imagine that you have been asked to teach a Bible study on 1 Peter 1:2. How are you going to do it? How will you start?

Phrasing starts with two steps: (1) finding the beginning and the end of the passage, (2) and then breaking the passage into manageable sections. Let's walk through the process.

Step 1: Find the Beginning and the End of the Passage

The biblical writers don't intend you to read a single verse in isolation from the verses around it. If you want to understand what one verse means, you have to see how it fits into its context. But which verses provide this context?

The key is to find the beginning and the end of the passage in which your verse occurs. If you are starting with the beginning of a book, the process is a little easier; you start with 1:1. But if you are studying a verse somewhere in the middle of a book, it means you must find the beginning of the passage. Then you find the end of the passage.

What is a "passage"? This is my word for the basic "story" that the author wants to tell us. For example, John 3:3 is part of the story of Jesus and Nicodemus, which is John 3:1-21. Romans 3:23 is part of the passage that summarizes justification by faith, which is Romans 3:21-26. In other words, a "passage" is all the verses that make up a complete idea. If your Bible has headings, a passage is probably the verses under one heading.

1:1   Peter, an apostle of Jesus Christ, To God's elect, strangers in the world, scattered throughout Pontus, Galatia, Cappadocia, Asia and Bithynia,

1:2   who have been chosen according to the foreknowledge of God the Father, through the sanctifying work of the Spirit, for obedience to Jesus Christ and sprinkling by his blood: Grace and peace be yours in abundance.

1:3   Praise be to the God and Father of our Lord Jesus Christ! In his great mercy he has given us new birth into a living hope through the resurrection of Jesus Christ from the dead,

1:4   and into an inheritance that can never perish, spoil or fade—kept in heaven for you,

1:5   who through faith are shielded by God's power until the coming of the salvation that is ready to be revealed in the last time.

1:6   In this you greatly rejoice, though now for a little while you may have had to suffer grief in all kinds of trials.

1:7   These have come so that your faith—of greater worth than gold, which perishes even though refined by fire—may be proved genuine and may result in praise, glory and honor when Jesus Christ is revealed.

1:8   Though you have not seen him, you love him; and even though you do not see him now, you believe in him and are filled with an inexpressible and glorious joy,

1:9   for you are receiving the goal of your faith, the salvation of your souls.

1:10   Concerning this salvation, the prophets, who spoke of the grace that was to come to you, searched intently and with the greatest care,

1:11   trying to find out the time and circumstances to which the Spirit of Christ in them was pointing when he predicted the sufferings of Christ and the glories that would follow.

1:12   It was revealed to them that they were not serving themselves but you, when they spoke of the things that have now been told you by those who have preached the gospel to you by the Holy Spirit sent from heaven. Even angels long to look into these things.

1:13   Therefore, prepare your minds for action; be self-controlled; set your hope fully on the grace to be given you when Jesus ...

(NIV 1984)

You find the limits of the passage by reading and rereading the surrounding verses until the limits become apparent. You are looking for the natural breaks in the passage, where the author changes topics, even slightly. To put it another way, you are looking for a unifying theme that ties the verses together. Let the Bible tell you when the author shifts topics. Here are a few of the indicators that the topic has changed.

- Major shifts in the topic of discussion (e.g., Paul has stopped making one point and has gone on to another).

- Shifts in audience (e.g., Jesus stops talking to the Pharisees and starts talking to the disciples).

- Shifts of other types, such as moving from describing what Jesus did to relating what he is teaching.

- Changes in key words and repeated themes.

- Transitional phrases (e.g., "the next day," "after this").

This can be trickier than you think, and the temptation is to trust the chapter, paragraph, and verse divisions of your Bible. But none of these were part of the original Bible, and while usually helpful they can often get in the way. They can also rob you of the joy of exploring and deciding for yourself, and sometimes they are wrong.

Read the first part of 1 Peter (on p. 96) starting at 1:1 over and over. Where is the break, the end of the first passage? Go ahead and discover it for yourself. (I am working from the NIV 1984 translation.)

You probably saw rather quickly that v 2 is part of the letter's salutation, which runs from v 1 to v 2. Once you have found the beginning and the end, write out your heading for 1:1-2. If you are not sure what to call it, make a guess; you can always change it later.

Writing out the heading is crucial: your goal is to get the main point out of each section and then to state that main point in the heading. I call this the "passage heading" as opposed to another type of heading we will meet in a few pages.

Salutation

1:1   Peter, an apostle of Jesus Christ, To God's elect, strangers in the world, scattered throughout Pontus, Galatia, Cappadocia, Asia and Bithynia,

1:2   who have been chosen according to the foreknowledge of God the Father, through the sanctifying work of the Spirit, for obedience to Jesus Christ and sprinkling by his blood: Grace and peace be yours in abundance.

Step 2: Identify the Sections

The next step is to break the passage into sections. You do this by reading and rereading the passage you identified in Step 1 until the natural sections of the passage suggest themselves to you. You then label each section with the main point being made in that section. Writing out the section heading is crucial, just like writing out the passage heading, since the initial goal of phrasing (and exegesis) is to identify the main point. If you are not sure what to write, write it in pencil so you can change it later if necessary.

Don't be in a hurry to get into the details of the passage but take the time to get the *big* picture. So many times when studying the Bible we want to jump right in and see what this word or that phrase "means to me." That's where we are headed, but don't be in a rush. Take your time. God's Word is worth it. Be content to sit back and let the overall picture develop.

During this part of the process you may notice words and phrases that seem important, but you don't know what they mean. Don't stop now to look them up; we are concentrating on the big picture and the day's own trouble is sufficient. Let's concentrate on getting the big picture.

Don't be so concerned with the *meaning* of the verses. Concentrate on seeing the *structure* of the passage, the flow of the author's thought. Ask yourself how the different parts are related to each other. As you read and reread the passage, thinking primarily about structure, you will be surprised at how the passage starts to show you its structure.

Try this now with 1 Peter 1:1-2, before turning the page and seeing what I have done with it.

This is a different approach than many Bible study methods that recommend getting into the details right away. But I think the big picture is more important; and if you run out of time and can't do all your preparation for your Bible study or Sunday School class, it is much better to know the big picture than lots of details.

Salutation

1:1   Peter, an apostle of Jesus Christ,

Recipients

To God's elect, strangers in the world, scattered throughout Pontus, Galatia, Cappadocia, Asia and Bithynia,

1:2   who have been chosen according to the foreknowledge of God the Father, through the sanctifying work of the Spirit, for obedience to Jesus Christ and sprinkling by his blood:

Greeting

Grace and peace be yours in abundance.

What did you find? You can see my suggestions on page 100. I decided that there are three main sections that identify the writer ("Peter"), the recipients ("To God's elect"), and the greeting ("Grace and peace be yours in abundance").

Let me say it again: what you are doing is learning to study your Bible by breaking up the passage into manageable sections. Of course, you can always cheat yourself out of the joy of discovering the Bible's meaning for yourself and look at a study Bible, or check out a commentary, or ask a friend. But along with losing the joy of discovery, what makes you think that the next time you need help there will be a friend nearby or a study Bible within reach?

One of the nice aspects of phrasing is that if you run out of time after Step 2, you at least have learned something that will help you teach the passage. You know the verses that make up the passage, the main point of the passage, the passage's sections, and the main thought of each section. This provides a great context within which to discuss the verse in question.

Step 3: Identify the Phrases

Now that you have identified the passage (Step 1) and its sections (Step 2), it is time to look at each individual section and divide it into its phrases.

What's a phrase? A phrase is an assertion, a proposition, something that means something. I am using the word "phrase" in a broader way than its grammatical usage. However, many phrases are grammatical phrases such as prepositional phrases, or adverbial phrases, or dependent and independent clauses. As you will see on the next page, many of the phrases I have identified are in fact grammatical phrases and clauses.

For example, if I said, "My mom, Jean, likes to eat chocolate ice cream and drink iced tea," how many assertions did I make? How many phrases are there? In one sense,

I only made one assertion. But can you break it down into smaller assertions that have meaning?

Is "Jean" by itself a phrase? Not really. While it may name my mother, it says nothing more. How about "to eat chocolate ice cream" and "drink iced tea"? Sure, these are two phrases that have meaning. They may not make complete sense all by themselves (they are dependent constructions), but they do mean something. What does my mother like? She likes (at least) two things: ice cream; iced tea.

Here is where phrasing and grammatical diagramming are different. In grammatical diagramming, every word is shown in its grammatical relationship, and you get something like what you see below. (I hope this doesn't brings back too many bad memories.) This is not what phrasing is, and if you subdivide your phrases too far, they lose their effectiveness.

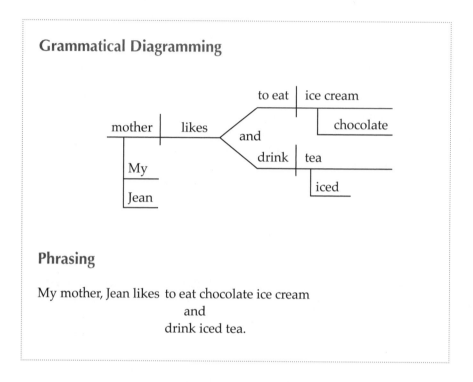

Grammatical Diagramming

Phrasing

My mother, Jean likes to eat chocolate ice cream
                            and
                    drink iced tea.

Let me explain it another way. In the sentence, "I want to go to the park but I must study first," how many words does it take until you have a phrase that has real meaning?

1. I
2. I want
3. I want to
4. I want to go
5. I want to go to
6. I want to go to the
7. I want to go to the park
8   I want to go to the park but
9. I want to go to the park but I
10. I want to go to the park but I must
11. I want to go to the park but I must study
12. I want to go to the park but I must study first.

While individual words have meaning, you don't really have a phrase that makes any sense until line 7. When you get to line 12, you realize that you have two phrases joined with the conjunction "but": "I want …" and "I must …."

Okay, back to 1 Peter. You have identified 1 Peter 1:1-2 as a passage and have seen that it has three sections. Now, break the two verses into its phrases. When done, check my work on the next page.

This fifth-century uncial manuscript, labeled 0301, contains John 17:1-4. It is located in Münster, Germany. The photo is provided by the Center for the Study of New Testament Manuscripts (Daniel Wallace, director). Used by permission of Institut für neutestamentliche Textforschung.

Salutation

Writer

1:1   Peter,

an apostle of Jesus Christ,

Recipients

To God's elect,

strangers in the world,

scattered throughout Pontus, Galatia, Cappadocia, Asia and Bithynia,

1:2   who have been chosen

according to the foreknowledge of God the Father,

through the sanctifying work of the Spirit,

for obedience to Jesus Christ and

sprinkling by his blood:

Greeting

Grace and peace be yours in abundance.

In "Section 1" ("writer"), Peter identifies himself by name and by office. In "Section 2" ("recipients") Peter addresses them as "God's elect" and follows with a series of descriptions. "Section 3" ("greeting") contains the letter's greeting.

Step 4: Identify the Main Phrase(s) and Modifying Phrases

Now comes the real fun. You have established the limits of the passage and its sections, and have broken it down into its phrases. As you have been reading and rereading the passage, you have started to identify the main points and the secondary points, and have seen how those secondary points relate to the main one. Now it is time to make a commitment as to what is the main point (or points).

Identify the main point(s) in each section and place its phrase furthest to the left. These "main" phrases will be stating the main points the author is making. Most likely a main phrase will have a subject and a verb, and in many cases the verb will be in the indicative mood (and not a subjunctive or a participle).

Indent the other phrases under or over the word they modify. Use extra spacing to separate subsections of thought. If you find it helpful, underline or highlight words or themes that run throughout the discussion. When done, recheck your passage and section headings to be sure they are right. You can see my work on the next page.

Many signs in modern Greece are written in both Greek and English. See if you can pronounce the Greek words on this sign in Corinth.

Salutation

Writer

1:1   <u>Peter</u>,

        an apostle of Jesus Christ,

Recipients

        <u>To God's elect</u>,

            strangers in the world,

                scattered throughout Pontus, Galatia, Cappadocia, Asia and Bithynia,

1:2   who have been chosen

                according to the foreknowledge of God the Father,

                through the sanctifying work of the Spirit,

                for   obedience to Jesus Christ and

                     sprinkling by his blood:

Greeting

        <u>Grace and peace</u> be yours in abundance.

Recipients

        <u>To God's elect</u>,

            strangers in the world,

                scattered throughout Pontus, Galatia, Cappadocia, Asia and Bithynia,

1:2   who have been chosen

                according to the foreknowledge of God the Father,

                through the sanctifying work of the Spirit,

                for   obedience to Jesus Christ and

                     sprinkling by his blood:

Here is how I phrase 1 Peter 1:1-2. Are there other ways this passage could have been laid out? Sure. Since "elect" and "chosen" are the same thing, it would have been nice to align the phrase "strangers …," "according …," "through …," and "for …" in a straight column so you could see that Peter is giving us four descriptions of who the elect are, as in the bottom example on page 106. (Actually, there is no Greek behind the phrase "who have been chosen." The NIV inserted it because they wanted the reader to understand that the following prepositional phrases modify the idea of "elect.")

The two phrases "obedience to Jesus Christ" and "sprinkling by his blood" could have been placed under the preposition "for" (see bottom example to the left), but when a word has multiple objects, I like to add the extra space to the right of the word (e.g., "for") so you can see that the following phrases are parallel (see top example).

I also could have listed the five place names ("Pontus, Galatia …") in a column, and often I will do this for a series. It didn't seem to make that much difference here.

Walk through 1 Peter 1:1-2

Now that we have 1 Peter 1:1-2 laid out, let's walk through the passage to see what Peter has to tell us. Here is your Bible study lesson.

Peter begins his letter with a three-part salutation. He first identifies himself by name and adds the qualifier that he is Jesus' apostle.

Peter then identifies to whom he is writing. His primary description is that they are the elect, Christians. He continues by explaining that this means they are strangers, scattered throughout five different areas in modern-day Turkey. (Although they still live on the earth, they are strangers to this land because they are elect.) But what is perhaps more significant is the following theological description of the elect. Their election was "according to the foreknowledge of God," an election accomplished "through the sanctifying work of the Spirit," and an election that has as its goal "obedience to Jesus Christ" and made possible by the "sprinkling by his blood," Christ's death on the cross.

Peter then concludes with the actual greeting.

Can you see how much help phrasing can be? It helps you get started, rewards you with some understanding of the passage if you are short of time (after Steps 1 and 2), and helps you dig deeper into the passage and discover its primary and secondary points.

Let's try the process again with another passage. Try to do the work on your own before seeing how I do it. We might as well check out the verses following Peter's salutation. (1 Peter 1:3-21 is on the next page.)

1:3	Praise be to the God and Father of our Lord Jesus Christ! In his great mercy he has given us new birth into a living hope through the resurrection of Jesus Christ from the dead,
1:4	and into an inheritance that can never perish, spoil or fade—kept in heaven for you,
1:5	who through faith are shielded by God's power until the coming of the salvation that is ready to be revealed in the last time.
1:6	In this you greatly rejoice, though now for a little while you may have had to suffer grief in all kinds of trials.
1:7	These have come so that your faith—of greater worth than gold, which perishes even though refined by fire—may be proved genuine and may result in praise, glory and honor when Jesus Christ is revealed.
1:8	Though you have not seen him, you love him; and even though you do not see him now, you believe in him and are filled with an inexpressible and glorious joy,
1:9	for you are receiving the goal of your faith, the salvation of your souls.
1:10	Concerning this salvation, the prophets, who spoke of the grace that was to come to you, searched intently and with the greatest care,
1:11	trying to find out the time and circumstances to which the Spirit of Christ in them was pointing when he predicted the sufferings of Christ and the glories that would follow.
1:12	It was revealed to them that they were not serving themselves but you, when they spoke of the things that have now been told you by those who have preached the gospel to you by the Holy Spirit sent from heaven. Even angels long to look into these things.
1:13	Therefore, prepare your minds for action; be self-controlled; set your hope fully on the grace to be given you when Jesus Christ is revealed.
1:14	As obedient children, do not conform to the evil desires you had when you lived in ignorance.
1:15	But just as he who called you is holy, so be holy in all you do;
1:16	for it is written: "Be holy, because I am holy."
1:17	Since you call on a Father who judges each man's work impartially, live your lives as strangers here in reverent fear.
1:18	For you know that it was not with perishable things such as silver or gold that you were redeemed from the empty way of life handed down to you from your forefathers,
1:19	but with the precious blood of Christ, a lamb without blemish or defect.
1:20	He was chosen before the creation of the world, but was revealed in these last times for your sake.
1:21	Through him you believe in God, who raised him from the dead …

Step 1: Find the Beginning and the End of the Passage

Read through the verses on page 108 until you decide where Peter stops his discussion.

_____

It is a little difficult isn't it? Peter changes his topic several times, and yet each time the new subject is explicitly connected to the previous. Peter starts by describing our salvation, our new birth. Then he moves from rejoicing in that salvation to suffering because of that salvation (vv 6-9), to how the prophets wanted to see the salvation (vv 10-12), and into how we should live in light of all this (vv 13-17).

The "therefore" that starts v 13 shows Peter is not starting a totally new topic, and yet Peter changes from discussing salvation (vv 3-12) to specifics on how that salvation is to show itself, so perhaps v 13 is a good place to mark the end of the passage.

Step 2: Identify the Sections

While you were working on Step 1, you were also getting ready for Step 2. How many basic sections do you find in vv 3-12? Break the passage into its sections and put a heading with each.

_____

See if you can figure out what this poster is advertising.

Salvation

1:3   Praise be to the God and Father of our Lord Jesus Christ! In his great mercy he has given us new birth into a living hope through the resurrection of Jesus Christ from the dead,

1:4   and into an inheritance that can never perish, spoil or fade—kept in heaven for you,

1:5   who through faith are shielded by God's power until the coming of the salvation that is ready to be revealed in the last time.

Salvation and Suffering

1:6   In this you greatly rejoice, though now for a little while you may have had to suffer grief in all kinds of trials.

1:7   These have come so that your faith—of greater worth than gold, which perishes even though refined by fire—may be proved genuine and may result in praise, glory and honor when Jesus Christ is revealed.

1:8   Though you have not seen him, you love him; and even though you do not see him now, you believe in him and are filled with an inexpressible and glorious joy,

1:9   for you are receiving the goal of your faith, the salvation of your souls.

Salvation and the Prophets

1:10   Concerning this salvation, the prophets, who spoke of the grace that was to come to you, searched intently and with the greatest care,

1:11   trying to find out the time and circumstances to which the Spirit of Christ in them was pointing when he predicted the sufferings of Christ and the glories that would follow.

1:12   It was revealed to them that they were not serving themselves but you, when they spoke of the things that have now been told you by those who have preached the gospel to you by the Holy Spirit sent from heaven. Even angels long to look into these things.

Step 3: Identify the Phrases

There is still too much in vv 3-12 for one Bible study (but just the right amount for a three-part series). Let's work with just the first section, vv 3-5. Go through the passage and break it down into its phrases.

_____

It looks as if v 3 begins with the theme statement, and then Peter follows with a series of prepositional phrases and a few relative clauses. As you are dividing these three verses into phrases, you will be starting to get a feel for the main assertions of the section.

1:3	Praise be to the God and Father of our Lord Jesus Christ!
	In his great mercy he has given us new birth
	into a living hope
	through the resurrection of Jesus Christ from the dead,
1:4	and into an inheritance
	that can never perish, spoil or fade—
	kept in heaven for you,
1:5	who through faith are shielded by God's power
	until the coming of the salvation
	that is ready to be revealed in the last time.

Step 4: Identify the Main Phrase(s) and Modifying Phrases

Now it is time to identify the main point (or points). Move those phrases to the left, and the modifying phrases under the word they modify. Keep parallel phrases equally indented from the left margin.

_____

1:3 <u>Praise</u> be to the God and Father of our Lord Jesus Christ!

    In his great mercy
  <u>he has given us new birth</u>
        {1} into a living hope
     through the resurrection of Jesus Christ from the dead,

1:4   {2} and into an inheritance

        that can never perish, spoil or fade—
        kept in heaven for you,

1:5 who through faith are shielded by God's power
        until the coming of the salvation

  that is ready to be revealed in the last time.

By the way, this is great biblical theology. Saying "Praise God" is not praising him. That is not the biblical pattern. To praise God is to give him glory, to describe his character and proclaim his deeds.

The main affirmation of the passage is that we are to praise God. The reason for praising God is that he has given us new birth, and he did this because he is merciful.

Peter then specifies that this new birth has two results. The first is that we now have a living hope. But how was that hope made available? The answer is Jesus' resurrection. Notice from my placement that the prepositional phrase ("through …") modifies the verb "given," telling us how it was given. But I wanted to show that "into a living hope" and "and into an inheritance" are parallel, both telling us something about our new birth. But they are separated by the prepositional phrase "through…." This illustrates one of the problems with phrasing—words can get in the way. One solution is to number them as I have. (I always use curly brackets when I insert something into the phrasing that is not in the text. I don't want to confuse my words with God's!)

The second result of our new birth is that we have an inheritance. But it is not just any inheritance. It is an inheritance that can never perish. Why? Because it is kept in heaven for you. This illustrates another problem of phrasing, but one easily remedied. Due to the nature of how we construct discussions, the visual representation of the flow of thought keeps moving to the right.

But eventually you will run out of paper, so I use a line to pull the discussion back to the left. The line should connect a word with what it is modifying. It is especially good to connect pronouns to their antecedents.

"Kept in heaven for you" isn't parallel with "that can never perish, spoil, or fade." It is telling you why our inheritance can never "perish, spoil, or fade." If I wanted to indicate this, I could have placed "kept …" under "never," or I could have drawn a line under the phrase "perish, spoil, or fade" and drawn a second line from it to "kept." In other words, you can make your phrasing more or less specific, depending upon what you need to do in order to understand the passage.

Peter adds one last note to his description of "you." While we look forward to our inheritance in heaven, we live out our lives here and now shielded by God's power. How long will this shielding last? Until our salvation comes in its fullness. When will that be? "In the last time." It is ready right now and waits for the end of time.

Can you see how this simple process of working through the text, seeing its sections, and identifying the main affirmations can make such a significant difference in your Bible study? I hope so.

1 Peter 1:3-5

[3] Praise be to the God and Father of our Lord Jesus Christ! In his great mercy he has given us new birth into a living hope through the resurrection of Jesus Christ from the dead, [4] and into an inheritance that can never perish, spoil or fade—kept in heaven for you, [5] who through faith are shielded by God's power until the coming of the salvation that is ready to be revealed in the last time.

---

[g] <u>Praise be to the God</u> and Father of our Lord Jesus Christ! // In his great mercy he has given us <u>new birth</u> / into a living hope through the resurrection of Jesus Christ from the dead, / [4] and into an inheritance that can never perish, spoil or fade—kept in heaven for you, // [5] who through faith are shielded by God's power / until the coming of the salvation // that is ready to be revealed in the last time

Another Method

If you do not like working on a computer, you can always write out the phrasing by hand. This has the advantage of slowing you down, which is always a good idea in Bible study.

But what if you want to mark your Bible? Well, we can still follow the basics of phrasing, although you lose the advantage of visually seeing the passage. Here is a suggested procedure.

- Divide the passage into sections (if necessary) by writing letters (for major sections) and numbers (for subsections) in the margin.

- Underline or highlight the main clause(s).

- Draw double slashes to separate the main phrases, and single slashes to separate secondary phrases.

- Underline (in different colors) the repeated themes and words. Circle the major conjunctions.

Hopefully this gives you a brief look at how phrasing can help you take a portion of Scripture and begin to understand what it says.

Phrasing has a minimum number of rules because it is a personal exercise. What helps one person see the structure of a passage may not help another. What is important is that you adopt the basic approach and then modify it to suit your own tastes and needs.

One of the neat things about phrasing is that you can stop almost anywhere along the process and still have learned your Bible a little better. For example, if all you do is break a larger passage down into its sections, you are well along to learning the passage better even if you don't do the actual phrasing. If all you do is find the main point, it will keep you from emphasizing the details of the passage, which in itself is a significant step forward.

Chapter 15

Verbal Aspect

Before we get into the different tenses, we need to spend some time talking about aspect. I introduced this topic in Foundational Greek, but I want to give you more detail of how it works.

15.1　In the Greek indicative, aspect is primary over time. When the writer chooses a certain tense, the aspect of the tense is more important than its time. There are three aspects: undefined; continuous; perfective.

I am going to draw the examples in this chapter from various tenses. Much of what I have to say is going to feel commonplace; but please trust me, it needs to be understood. It would be good for you to read Wallace's discussion of all this as well (*BNTS*, 213–18).

Three aspects

15.2　**Undefined**. The verb tells you nothing about whether the action stated in the verb was instantaneous, occurred over a period of time, or even was repeated a number of times. It views the action from the outside, as a whole, without interest in the internal makeup of the action. The aorist and future tenses express undefined actions.

1 Tim 1:13　ἠλεήθην,　ὅτι　ἀγνοῶν　ἐποίησα ἐν ἀπιστίᾳ.
I was shown mercy　because　being ignorant　*I acted*　in　unbelief
I was shown mercy since, being ignorant, *I had acted* in unbelief.

Paul's acts of unbelief were many, but that is not what he wants to emphasize here. He uses the aorist ἐποίησα to simply state what was.

15.3　**Continuous**. The verb is describing a continuous action. It looks at the action from the inside and focuses on the progress of the action, not concerned about the beginning or the end. The present and imperfect tenses usually describe continuous actions.

Matt 21:9　οἱ ἀκολουθοῦντες ἔκραζον　λέγοντες·　ὡσαννὰ τῷ υἱῷ Δαυίδ·
Those following　*were crying out*　saying　Hosanna　to the Son　of David
Those that followed *were shouting,* "Hosanna to the Son of David!"

As you would suspect from the meaning of the verb ἔκραζον (imperfect), they were shouting over and over.

15.4   **Perfective**. The verb describes a completed action whose ongoing effects are felt in the present (of the speaker). In a sense, it is the combination of the two prior aspects. The action is completed (undefined) and the state resulting from the action is ongoing (continuous). The perfect tense describes perfective actions.

> *1 Tim 4:10*   ἠλπίκαμεν ἐπὶ θεῷ ζῶντι, ὅς ἐστιν σωτὴρ πάντων ἀνθρώπων
> *we have hoped* in God living who is savior of all people
> *We have placed our hope* in the living God, who is the Savior of all people.

Paul and Timothy had already placed their hope in God, and as a result they were able to daily toil and strive.

Time frame of the speaker

15.5   While the following may seem obvious, it is amazing how many times it is forgotten: *the time frame of the verb is from the perspective of the speaker/writer, not the hearer/reader.* Of course, what was presently true for Paul may still be presently true for you, but this is a function of theology and not grammar. This is especially important for the perfect tense.

> *2 Tim 4:7*   τὸν καλὸν ἀγῶνα ἠγώνισμαι, τὸν δρόμον τετέλεκα, τὴν πίστιν τετήρηκα
> the good fight *I have fought* the race *I have finished* the faith *I have kept.*
> *I have fought* the good fight, *I have finished* the race, *I have kept* the faith.

These statements were true for Paul, and the effects of the actions are felt by Paul, but not necessarily by others (unless, by implication, they too have fought, finished, and kept).

Portrayal of reality

15.6   Language does not describe what necessarily is. We define the indicative mood as the mood of fact, of what *is,* but that is a simplification. The indicative mood is used when the speaker wants to express something as reality, as fact; but we still lie in the indicative. It is an issue of what the speaker wants to express. There is not a necessary link between reality and my description of that reality.

15.7   This issue of "portrayal of reality" is related to aspect as well. If I chose to use a continuous verbal form, it is saying that I want to emphasize its continuous nature. I want to look at the action from the inside, as if we were part of the action itself.

Mark 12:41	πολλοὶ	πλούσιοι	ἔβαλλον	πολλά
	Many	rich	*were putting in*	much.

NET: Many rich people *were throwing in* large amounts.

ESV: Many rich people *put in* large sums.

ἔβαλλον is an imperfect, emphasizing the continual action of putting money in.

What is interesting is that a few verses later, Jesus uses the aorist to describe the same event because in this context he is looking at the action as a whole, from the outside.

Mark 12:44	πάντες	γὰρ	ἐκ	τοῦ περισσεύοντος	αὐτοῖς	ἔβαλον
	all	for	out of	abundance	to them	*they put*

NRSV: For all of them *have contributed* out of their abundance.

Jesus says they "put" (ἔβαλον is an aorist), summing up all their actions.

It is not that one is right and one is wrong; it is a matter of what the speaker wants to emphasize. Language is a portrayal of reality.

Narrow-Band

15.8 "Narrow-band" means that the action of the verb occurs over a relatively short period of time, relative, that is, to the context and the point that the speaker is making.

15.9 **Instantaneous**. The action occurs relatively instantly.

Acts 9:34	Αἰνέα,	ἰᾶταί	σε	Ἰησοῦς	Χριστός.....καὶ	εὐθέως	ἀνέστη.
	Aeneas	*heals*	you	Jesus	Christ and	immediately	he got up

Aeneas, Jesus Christ *heals* you.... And immediately he got up.

Peter uses a present tense verb to describe something that happened immediately.

Acts 9:40	ἡ	δὲ	ἤνοιξεν	τοὺς	ὀφθαλμοὺς	αὐτῆς,	καὶ	ἰδοῦσα	τὸν Πέτρον	ἀνεκάθισεν.
	she	and	*opened*		eyes	her,	and	*seeing*	Peter,	*sat up.*

Then she *opened* her eyes, and *seeing* Peter, she *sat up*.

The three verbal forms are all aorist, indicating what happened instantly: she opened her eyes, saw Peter, and sat up.

15.10 **Progressive**. The action occurs over a period of time. The length of the time is determined by context and the emphasis of the speaker.

> *1 Tim 4:10*   εἰς τοῦτο γὰρ κοπιῶμεν καὶ ἀγωνιζόμεθα
> into this for *we are toiling* and *we are struggling*
> for with respect to this reason *we are toiling* and *struggling*
>
> Paul and his team continually toiled and struggled for the gospel.

15.11 **Ingressive** means that the emphasis is on the beginning of an action. Sometimes the meaning of the verb or the context is enough to show that the action was begun; other times the translators will add in a word like "began" to make it clear.

> Acts 3:8   ἐξαλλόμενος ἔστη καὶ περιεπάτει καὶ εἰσῆλθεν σὺν αὐτοῖς εἰς τὸ ἱερὸν
> jumping up he stood and *walk around* and entered with them into the temple
> NRSV: Jumping up, he stood and *began to walk*, and he entered the temple with them.
>
> The point is not that he jumped, stood, walked, and entered. It is that he jumped up to a standing position, and began to walk (showing his full recovery), and then entered the temple.

Broad-Band

15.12 "Broad-band" is used of actions occurring over a longer period of time, including actions that have nothing to do with time.

15.13 **Iterative**. This type of action is continual in that it happens over a period of time; however, it does not happen continually but rather repeatedly.

> *Matt 3:11*   Ἐγὼ μὲν ὑμᾶς βαπτίζω ἐν ὕδατι εἰς μετάνοιαν.
> I — you *baptize* in water for repentance
> I *baptize* you in water for repentance.
>
> John was not constantly baptizing, but he baptized (βαπτίζω is present) people one at a time, over and over.

15.14 **Customary**. These actions occur on a regular basis.

> *Mark 4:33*   τοιαύταις παραβολαῖς πολλαῖς ἐλάλει αὐτοῖς τὸν λόγον
> such parables many *he was speaking* to them the word
> NIV: With many similar parables *Jesus spoke* the word to them
>
> It was Jesus' custom to speak in parables.

15.15 Gnomic. This action is timeless (gnomic denotes a general aphorism). The speaker is not thinking of any specific event, but of an action that is always true.

1 John 2:23 πᾶς   ὁ ἀρνούμενος   τὸν υἱὸν   οὐδὲ   τὸν πατέρα   ἔχει
Each   one who denies   the Son   not   the Father   has

No one who denies the Son *has* the Father.

It is always true that anyone who denies allegiance to Jesus does not have (ἔχει is present tense) the Father. John is not thinking of any one particular act of denial; he is stating an axiomatic truth.

15.16 In the following chapters, you will see how this issue of aspect plays itself out in the different tenses and moods.

Aktionsart

15.17 Aktionsart is an important concept but too advanced for Foundational Greek. Meaning is not conveyed just by aspect. There are many different parts that make up the whole, so to speak. Aktionsart (yes, it is a German word) is a way of discussing all these different parts.

15.18 Aktionsart is the full meaning of a word in context, made up of these and perhaps other considerations.

- Lexical meaning of the word

- Tense (present, future, imperfect, aorist, perfect)

- Aspect (undefined, continuous, perfective)

- Grammar

- Context (e.g., narrative, poetry)

15.19 When you are exegeting a verse and studying a particular verb, that verb will always have a context that affects its meaning in that particular verse, and aspect will only be part of it and will rarely convey meaning all by itself.

For example, if you saw the verb "weeping," does the fact that the author might use a continuous verbal form surprise you? No. The author could have used a continuous or an undefined form since the meaning of the word is inherently continuous. However, the continuous aspect fits the actual meaning of the verb, assuming of course that the speaker wants to emphasize the ongoing nature of this particular act of weeping.

So as you are studying a verb, don't look just for aspect. Language uses a plethora of tools to convey meaning, and aspect is just one part, albeit an important part.

Chapter 16

Verbs (Voice)

Along with aspect and tense, we need to be sure to understand voice. Voice is the relationship between the verb and its subject. We will also look at the issue of transitive and intransitive verbs.

Active

16.1 If the verb is active voice, it means the subject does the action of the verb.

16.2 **Simple**. The subject does the action of the verb. This is the normal use of the active voice.

> *1 Tim 1:15*   Χριστὸς Ἰησοῦς ἦλθεν εἰς τὸν κόσμον ἁμαρτωλοὺς σῶσαι
> Christ   Jesus   came   into the world   sinners   to save
> Christ Jesus *came* into the world to save sinners.

16.3 **Causative**. The subject is performing the action of the verb, not directly but through someone or something. You can often put "causes" before the verb and it will make sense, or you can make it passive.

> *John 19:1*   Τότε οὖν   ἔλαβεν ὁ Πιλᾶτος τὸν Ἰησοῦν καὶ ἐμαστίγωσεν.
> Then therefore he took Pilate   Jesus   and   flogged
> ESV: Then Pilate took Jesus and *flogged* him.
> HCSB: Then Pilate took Jesus and *had Him flogged*.
>
> Pilate did not actually flog Jesus; he had someone else do it, but he was the ultimate cause of the flogging.

16.4 **Stative**. This is the category for stative verbs (e.g., εἰμί) and for predicate adjectives where the verb "to be" is supplied.

> *1 Tim 1:5*   τὸ δὲ   τέλος τῆς παραγγελίας ἐστὶν ἀγάπη ἐκ καθαρᾶς καρδίας
> the but goal of this charge   is   love from clean   heart
> But the goal of this command *is* love from a clean heart.

1 Tim 1:8   Οἴδαμεν δὲ ὅτι καλὸς ὁ νόμος, ἐὰν τις   αὐτῷ νομίμως χρῆται
we know   and that good   the law   if   someone it   lawfully   uses
Now we know that the law *is* good if someone uses it lawfully.

Passive

16.5   **Simple**. If a verb is passive, it means that the subject receives the action of the verb. Sometimes the agent of the action is expressed, sometimes not.

1 Tim 2:13   Ἀδὰμ γὰρ πρῶτος ἐπλάσθη, εἶτα Εὕα.
Adam for first   *was created*   then Eve
For Adam *was created* first, then Eve.

Adam did not do the creating, but rather was the object of creation. The agent of the creating is left up to context, but it is generally not hard to determine.

Matt 3:6   ἐβαπτίζοντο   ἐν τῷ Ἰορδάνῃ ποταμῷ ὑπ᾽ αὐτοῦ
they were being baptized   in   the Jordan   River   by   him
They were being baptized in the Jordan River *by him.*

Here the agent of the baptism is stated—"him"—which the context makes clear is John.

16.6   **Deponent**. There are some verbs that have no active form. They are passive in form but always active in their meaning. We have seen in Foundational Greek that the software marks these as "passive," not deponent.

Mark 12:10   οὗτος ἐγενήθη εἰς κεφαλὴν γωνίας.
He   *has become*   into head   of corner
He *has become* the chief cornerstone.

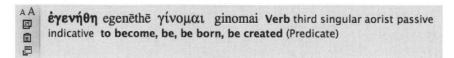

ἐγενήθη egenēthē γίνομαι ginomai **Verb** third singular aorist passive indicative **to become, be, be born, be created** (Predicate)

Middle

16.7   We saw in Foundational Greek that if a verb is in the middle voice, it means the subject still does the action of the verb but in some way in which the subject is emphasized. In a sense, the verb in the middle voice is pointing a finger back at the subject and saying that the subject has some special interest in the action of the verb.

"The active voice emphasizes the *action* of the verb; the middle emphasizes the *actor* [subject] of the verb" (*BNTS*, 182, who then gives the following examples).

Active		*Middle*	
■ αἱρέω	I take	αἱρέομαι	I choose, prefer
■ ἀναμιμνήσκω	I remind	ἀναμιμνήσκομαι	I remember
■ ἀποδίδωμι	I give away	ἀποδίδομαι	I sell
■ φυλάσσω	I guard	φιλάσσομαι	I am on my guard

16.8 We have also seen that the middle and passive are identical in the present, imperfect, and perfect. The middle and passive are distinctly different in the future and aorist.

16.9 **Direct**. This is the most basic use of the middle. In a direct middle, the subject performs the action of the verb on himself or herself. You may see it with verbs that are reflexive in meaning, such as "clothing yourself."

Matt 27:5   καὶ   ἀπελθὼν   ἀπήγξατο.
and   going away   *he hanged for himself*
And going away, *he hanged himself.*

Judas did the action to himself.

While common in Classical Greek, the direct middle is rare in Koine Greek. Some scholars argue that it does not even exist, being replaced by the active and the reflexive pronoun (e.g., σεαυτόν).

Matt 4:6   εἰ   υἱὸς   εἶ   τοῦ θεοῦ,   βάλε   σεαυτὸν   κάτω.
if   son   you are   of God   throw   yourself   down
If you are the Son of God, *throw yourself* down.

16.10 **Indirect**. In the indirect middle, "the subject acts *for* ... himself or herself, or in his or her *own interest*" (*BNTS*, 184). This is why you will often see something like "for myself" or "for yourself" in paradigms of the middle. This will sound almost active to your ears, but there is a slight emphasis on the subject.

Eph 1:4   ἐξελέξατο   ἡμᾶς   ἐν   αὐτῷ   πρὸ   καταβολῆς   κόσμου
He chose   us   in   him   before   foundation   of world
He chose us in him before the foundation of the world

God's election of his children was done, among other reason, for himself, for his glory.

16.11 Deponent. Just as there are passive deponents, so also are there middle deponents. These verbs do not have an active form, but use the middle form with an active meaning.

Luke 1:40	εἰσῆλθεν	εἰς	τὸν οἶκον	Ζαχαρίου	καὶ	ἠσπάσατο	τὴν Ἐλισάβετ.
	she entered	into	the house	of Zechariah	and	*greeted*	Elizabeth

She entered into the house of Zechariah and *greeted* Elizabeth,

2 Cor 7:15	μετὰ	φόβου	καὶ	τρόμου	ἐδέξασθε	αὐτόν.
	with	fear	and	trembling	*you received*	him

With fear and trembling *you welcomed* him.

16.12 Just to make things a little more challenging, you should know that merely because a verb is (or is not) deponent in the present tense does not mean it is deponent (or not deponent) in other tenses.

For example, here are the forms of ἔρχομαι, "I come, go," in different tenses.

- Present: ἔρχομαι (middle/passive deponent)

- Future: ἐλεύσομαι (middle deponent)

- Aorist: ἦλθον (not deponent)

- Perfect active: ἐλήλυθα (not deponent)

> **T**o be fair, you should know that this entire concept of deponent verbs is under question in the academy. Some argue that what we have traditionally called "deponent verbs" is just part of the range of meaning belonging to the middle. It is a technical debate and beyond what you are learning here.

Transitive and Intransitive

16.13 While you are filling in your knowledge of the verbal system, I need to make sure you understand the concept of a transitive verb. The issue of a verb being transitive or intransitive is a mattter of the relationship between the verb and its object (and not the verb and its subject, as in voice).

16.14 **Transitive** verbs require a direct object. The motion of the verb carries over to an object (think of the Latin preposition *trans*, "across"), whether that object is expressed or implied.

Titus 3:5   ἔσωσεν ἡμᾶς
            He saved   us
            He saved us.

John 19:1   ἔλαβεν ὁ Πιλᾶτος τὸν Ἰησοῦν καὶ ἐμαστίγωσεν.
            took   Pilate   Jesus   and   *flogged*
            ESV: Pilate *took* Jesus and *flogged* him.
            HCSB: Pilate *took* Jesus and *had* Him *flogged*.

            ἐμαστίγωσεν is a transitive verb and requires a direct object, but it was unnecessary in Greek since it is clear that the object of both verbs is τὸν Ἰησοῦν.

Transitive verbs can be active, middle, or passive.

Matt 1:21   αὐτὸς γὰρ σώσει τὸν λαὸν αὐτοῦ ἀπὸ τῶν ἁμαρτιῶν αὐτῶν.
            he   for   *will save*   people   his   from   sins   their
            For he *will save* his people from their sins.

1 Tim 2:15   σωθήσεται δὲ διὰ τῆς τεκνογονίας.
            She will be saved   but   through   the bearing of children
            But *she will be saved* through the bearing of children.

16.15 **Intransitive** verbs cannot have a direct object and cannot be passive.

2 Tim 2:19   στερεὸς θεμέλιος τοῦ θεοῦ ἕστηκεν, ἔχων τὴν σφραγῖδα ταύτην
            firm   foundation   of God   stands   having   seal   this
            The firm foundation of God *stands*, having this seal.

Vocabulary

16.16 There is no new vocabulary for this chapter in the online class, but there are some interesting things to look at.

Chapter 17

Verbs (Tense)

Now that you have a feel for aspect, we can delve into the tenses and see how they combine time and aspect. While a tense may have a general meaning, you will discover that it has many other nuances and variations.

tense	time	aspect	example
Present	present	any	λύω
Future	future	undefined	λύσω
Imperfect	past	continuous	ἔλυον
Aorist	past	undefined	ἔλυσα
Perfect	past and present	undefined and continuous	λέλυκα

17.1 What follows are some of the more common ways in which the Greek tenses are used. The primary function of these examples is to give you a feel for the variety of usages and to see why so much of translation is interpretive and therefore why translations are often different.

- Does this mean you can look at a verb and decide for yourself what its nuance is? Probably not.

- Does this mean you can argue with a commentary or translation based on your knowledge of Greek. Absolutely not. You just don't know enough Greek.

- Will you be able to see why translations are different and be able to follow the discussion in commentaries? Yes.

I am not showing you all the usages, nor will I in the following chapters. There are too many. But I have picked the common usages to give you a feel for the tense. This means you will come across passages in the Bible that illustrate one of those omitted uses. There are Greek grammars that discuss all the uses (such as Daniel Wallace's *The Basics of New Testament Syntax,* and his fuller, *Greek Grammar Beyond the Basics*). We will deal with them more fully in Functional Greek.

> **T**he terms in parentheses at the end of each category are its technical names. As you will see, Greek grammarians have not settled on one name per category. These are the terms the commentators will use.

17.2 How do translators decide which of these usages is correct in any one instance? It is easier than you may think, but it does involve some "linguistic sensitivity," otherwise known as "interpretation." We look at the context and especially the meaning of the word, and make a decision. But learning a language is both a science (i.e., there are rules to follow) and an art. It is the art side that takes years to develop, and it is the art side that enables the translator to make these types of decisions.

Present

17.3 The present tense describes an action normally occuring in the present time; its aspect covers the gamut from instantaneous to gnomic.

Narrow-Band

17.4 Sometimes a Greek present describes an action that happens immediately. In other words, it has no real continuous nature (*instantaneous, aoristic, punctiliar*).

Mark 2:5	τέκνον,	ἀφίενταί	σου	αἱ ἁμαρτίαι.
	child	*they are forgiven*	your	the sins

My son, your sins *are forgiven.*

Once Jesus made the pronouncement, the sins were instantly forgiven.

17.5 The Greek present can describe an ongoing action, even though in real time the action does not last very long (*progressive, descriptive*).

1 Cor 14:14	ἐὰν	προσεύχωμαι	γλώσσῃ,	τὸ πνεῦμά	μου	προσεύχεται
	if	I am praying	tongue,	the spirit	my	*is praying*

NLT: For if I am praying in a tongue, my spirit *is praying.*
ESV: For if I pray in a tongue, my spirit *prays.*

The prayer is an ongoing action, but probably for a short time.

Broad-Band

17.6 Some actions occur repeatedly (*iterative*).

> *Matt 17:15* πολλάκις γὰρ πίπτει εἰς τὸ πῦρ
> often for *he falls* into the fire
>
> For often *he falls* into the fire.
>
> The boy is not constantly falling into the fire (an impossible notion), but he falls in time and time again.

17.7 Actions can occur regularly but not necessarily constantly (*customary, habitual, general*).

> *Luke 18:12* νηστεύω δὶς τοῦ σαββάτου
> *I fast* twice the week
>
> I *customarily fast* twice a week.
> NIV: I *fast* twice a week.
>
> It is not that he fasts constantly, but that this is his regular habit.

17.8 The Greek present tense can express a timeless fact (*gnomic*).

> *2 Cor 9:7* ἱλαρὸν δότην ἀγαπᾷ ὁ θεός
> cheerful giver *he loves* the God
>
> God *loves* a cheerful giver.
>
> Paul is not thinking of any one specific response of love, but rather of God's constant response to cheerful giving.

17.9 Because the Greek verb system views time as secondary to aspect, it is possible for the Greek present tense to refer to an action that occurs in the past (*historical, dramatic*). The idea is to make the telling of the past event more vivid by using the present tense. We have the same construction in English, but the Greeks used it much more than we do, so this usage is often translated with the past tense.

> *John 1:29* βλέπει τὸν Ἰησοῦν ἐρχόμενον πρὸς αὐτόν
> *he sees* the Jesus coming to him
>
> The next day *he saw* Jesus coming toward him.
>
> As John (the author) is recounting the event, the time frame was past; but moving into the present βλέπει makes the story more vivid.

Future

17.10 Of all the Greek tenses, the future has the strongest emphasis on time, describing an action that will occur in the future (from the time frame of the speaker).

As a general rule, the future is translated with the undefined aspect ("I will eat") rather than the continuous ("I will be eating").

17.11 As we saw, the basic use of the future is to describe something that will happen in the future (*predictive*).

Phil 1:6   ὁ ἐναρξάμενος   ἐν   ὑμῖν   ἔργον   ἀγαθὸν   ἐπιτελέσει
         the one beginning   in   you   work   good   *will complete*
         He who began a good work in you *will bring it to completion.*

17.12 As in English, the Greek future can express a command (*imperatival*).

Matt 22:37   ἀγαπήσεις   κύριον   τὸν θεόν   σου
         you will love   Lord   the God   your
         ESV: *You shall love* the Lord your God.
         NET: *Love* the Lord your God.

         Because we use the future in English the same way, this is easy to understand.

Imperfect

17.13 The imperfect tense describes an action normally occuring in the past time; its aspect is always continuous.

Narrow-Band

17.14 Generally, the imperfect describes an ongoing action that happened in the past (*progressive, durative*).

Mark 9:31   ἐδίδασκεν   τοὺς μαθητὰς   αὐτοῦ
         He was teaching   the disciples   his
         NIV: *He was teaching* his disciples.
         KJV: *He taught* his disciples.

         "Teaching" (ἐδίδασκεν) is by definition an ongoing activity.

17.15 It can also place emphasis on the beginning of the action (*ingressive, inceptive*).

> *Matt 4:11* ἄγγελοι προσῆλθον καὶ διηκόνουν αὐτῷ
>   angels they came and *they were ministering* to him
>   NASB: Angels came and *began to minister* to Him.
>   NIV: Angels came and *attended* him.
>
>   It is an exegetical decision as to whether the angels ministered to Jesus over a period of time, or whether Matthew's emphasis is on the beginning of the action.

Broad-Band

17.16 Some continuous actions do not occur constantly but rather repetitively (*iterative*).

> *Luke 18:3* ἤρχετο πρὸς αὐτὸν
>   *she was coming* to him
>   NIV: A widow ... *kept coming* to [the judge].
>   KJV: *She came* unto him.
>   Remember: this is a shame-based culture. She came over and over, day after day, shaming him to do his job, and finally the unjust judge caved in.

> *John 19:3* ἤρχοντο πρὸς αὐτὸν καὶ ἔλεγον· χαῖρε
>   *They were coming* to him and *they were saying* Hail!
>   NRSV: *They kept coming* up to him, *saying*, "Hail."
>   NIV: (They) *went up* to him *again and again, saying*, "Hail."
>   NASB: *They began to come up* to Him and *say*, "Hail."
>
>   The imperfect makes it explicit that they taunted our Lord over and over. The NASB sees ἤρχοντο as inceptive, not iterative.

17.17 Other actions occur regularly, such as expressed by the English "used to" (*customary*).

> *Mark 15:6* Κατὰ δὲ ἑορτὴν ἀπέλυεν αὐτοῖς ἕνα δέσμιον
>   at now feast *he was releasing* for them one prisoner
>   NASB: Now at the feast *he used to release* for them any one prisoner.
>   NET: During the feast *it was customary to release* a prisoner to them.
>   NIV: Now *it was the custom* at the festival *to release* a prisoner.
>   KJV: Now at that feast *he released* unto them one prisoner.

Aorist

17.18 The aorist tense describes an action normally occuring in the past time; its aspect is always undefined. Remember that the aorist is, in a sense, the default past time tense; there may be no real significance in the fact that a particular verb is aorist.[1]

17.19 We have already seen that the aorist looks at an action as a whole and does not necessarily tell us anything about the precise nature of the action (*constative*).

Matt 15:39 ἐνέβη εἰς τὸ πλοῖον καὶ ἦλθεν εἰς τὰ ὅρια Μαγαδάν.
he got into the boat and *he went* into the region of Magadan
He got into the boat and *went* to the region of Magadan.

Even though getting into the boat and traveling across the Sea certainly was a continuous action (lots of rowing or working with the sails), it was not important for Matthew to make this emphasis, so he uses the aorist.

17.20 The aorist can place emphasis on the beginning of an action (*ingressive*).

Matt 22:7 ὁ δὲ βασιλεὺς ὠργίσθη
the but king *he was angry*
NLT: Then the king *became furious.*
RSV: The king *was angry.*

This is a matter of interpretation, but the NLT thinks that the emphasis was on the fact that he started to get angry, not the simple fact that he was angry.

17.21 Other times the aorist can emphasize the completion of an event (*consummative*). This usage is often tied to the actual meaning of the verb.

1 Cor 4:6 Ταῦτα δέ, ἀδελφοί, μετεσχημάτισα εἰς ἐμαυτὸν καὶ Ἀπολλῶν δι᾽ ὑμᾶς
these but brothers *I have applied* to myself and Apollos for you
I have applied all these things to myself and Apollos for your benefit, brothers.

As you would think from the meaning of μετεσχημάτισα, the emphasis is on the fact that he has completed the application of the truths he has been explaining.

---

[1] There is meaning in the fact that a verb is aorist, but it is often so subtle a nuance that for now you should view it as the default past tense and let it go at that.

17.22 The aorist can be used to describe a timeless truth (*gnomic*). These are often translated with the English present tense. This use of the aorist is rare; Greek tends to use the present tense to express the gnomic idea.

> *1 Pet 1:24*   ἐξηράνθη ὁ χόρτος, καὶ τὸ ἄνθος ἐξέπεσεν
> *withered*   *the grass*   *and*   *the flower*   *fell off*
> NET: The grass *withers* and the flower *falls off.*

> Peter is not thinking of any one event in which the grass and flowers die, but rather of the timeless truth that this is what happens.

Perfect

17.23 The perfect tense describes a completed action, with the results of that action felt in the present (of the speaker).

17.24 Sometimes the emphasis is on the fact that the action was completed (*consummative, extensive*).

> *Rom 5:5*   ἡ ἀγάπη τοῦ θεοῦ ἐκκέχυται   ἐν ταῖς καρδίαις ἡμῶν
> *the love*   *of the God*   *has been poured*   *in*   *the hearts*   *of us*
> ESV: God's love *has been poured* into our hearts.
> KJV: The love of God *is shed abroad* in our hearts.

> While the effects of that love are still felt by Paul, the context requires that the emphasis is on the accomplished fact that the love has in fact been poured out.

17.25 Other times the emphasis is on the continuing effect of the past action (*intensive*) and is generally translated with the English present.

> *Luke 5:20*   ἄνθρωπε, ἀφέωνταί   σοι   αἱ ἁμαρτίαι σου
> *man*   *have been forgiven*   *to you*   *the sins*   *your*
> Man, your sins *are forgiven* you.

> The forgiveness is an accomplished fact, but contextually the emphasis is on the man's ciurrent state of being forgiven, as evidenced by his getting up and walking out of the house.

Chapter 18

Verbs (Nonindicative)

Now it is time to look at the nonindicative moods as well as the infinitive. Participles are in chapter 19.

Time and Aspect

18.1   **Aspect**. A Greek verb has time significance only in the indicative. The only significance that a verb has in the other moods is one of aspect.

18.2   Remember:

- Forms built on the present tense stem indicate a continuous action
- Forms built on the aorist tense stem indicate an undefined action
- Forms built on the perfect tense stem indicate a perfective action: completed action with its effects felt in the present (of the speaker)

18.3   It is difficult to bring the sense of the continuous into the translation of a nonindicative mood. Sometimes translators might add in words like "continue" especially in the present subjunctive, but only rarely. As a result, the subjunctive is often under-translated.

Mood

18.4   You remember that the mood of a verb defines its relationship to reality. We have been looking primarily at the indicative mood. There are two other moods, the subjunctive and imperative.

Indicative

18.5 The indicative mood, which we have been studying, is the mood of reality. When you want to state what is—or at least what you want to project as being real—you use the indicative mood.

18.6 The simplest use of the indicative is to make a statement, a declaration (*declarative*).

> *1 Tim 1:14* ὑπερεπλεόνασεν δὲ ἡ χάρις τοῦ κυρίου ἡμῶν μετὰ πίστεως καὶ ἀγάπης
> *completely overflowed*   and the grace of Lord   our   with faith   and love
> And the grace of our Lord *completely overflowed* for me with faith and love.

18.7 The indicative is used to ask a question (*interrogative*). There is no difference in the form of the verb when asking a question; it is a matter of context, the editorial help of punctuation, and sometimes the presence of an interrogative word, such as "where," "why," who," etc.

> *Matt 2:2* ποῦ ἐστιν ὁ τεχθεὶς βασιλεὺς τῶν Ἰουδαίων;
> where *is*   the one born king   of the Jews
> Where is the one who is born king of the Jews?

18.8 The indicative is used in some forms of an "if ... then ..." sentence (*conditional sentence*). "If I were smart, I would have taken Hebrew." The "if" clause is called the "protasis," and the "then" clause is the "apodosis."

> *Rom 4:2* εἰ γὰρ Ἀβραὰμ ἐξ ἔργων ἐδικαιώθη, ἔχει καύχημα
> if for Abraham from law *was justified* he has boast
> For if Abraham *was justified* by works, he has something to boast about.

I will discuss conditional sentences in more detail in Functional Greek.

Subjunctive

18.9 Because the action described by a verb in the subjunctive is unfulfilled, it often refers to a future event.

> *Mark 2:20* ἐλεύσονται δὲ ἡμέραι ὅταν ἀπαρθῇ ἀπ᾽ αὐτῶν ὁ νυμφίος
> will come   but days   when *will be taken* from them   the bridegroom
> But the days will come when the bridegroom *will be taken* from them.

Jesus is referring to the future event of his ascension.

18.10 When the word ἄν (by itself or in combination with another word such as ἐάν) makes a statement more general, the verb will be in the subjunctive.

> *Mark 3:29* ὃ ἂν βλασφημήσῃ εἰς τὸ πνεῦμα τὸ ἅγιον, οὐκ ἔχει ἄφεσιν εἰς τὸν αἰῶνα
> whoever *blasphemes* against the spirit holy not he has forgiveness forever
> *Whoever blasphemes* against the Holy Spirit will never have forgiveness.
>
> Jesus is not thinking of any one person in particular, but rather is making a general statement that applies to anyone who blasphemes the Spirit.

18.11 As we have seen, the subjunctive is frequently used in statements of *purpose*. The purpose clause is often introduced with ἵνα.

> *Matt 12:10* ἐπηρώτησαν αὐτὸν ... ἵνα κατηγορήσωσιν αὐτοῦ
> they questioned him in order that *they might accuse* him
> NET: They asked him ... so that *they could accuse* him.
> NIV: *Looking for a reason to accuse* Jesus, they asked him.
>
> His enemies asked Jesus the question for the purpose of accusing him. It wasn't an honest question.

18.12 When a *conditional sentence* is introduced with ἐάν, the verb in the protasis will be in the subjunctive. This type of conditional sentence breaks down into two categories that are important for exegesis.

- The writer may be thinking of a *specific possible event in the future.*

> *Matt 4:9* ταῦτά σοι πάντα δώσω, ἐὰν πεσὼν προσκυνήσῃς μοι.
> these to you all I will give if falling down *you worship* me
> All these I will give you, if you will fall down and *worship* me.
>
> If Jesus might do this specific act (and did Satan really think he would?), then the promise is that he would give Jesus all the kingdoms of the world (which of course he never would).

- The writer may also be thinking not so much of a specific event but rather is stating a *general truth.*

> *John 11:9* ἐὰν τις περιπατῇ ἐν τῇ ἡμέρᾳ, οὐ προσκόπτει.
> if anyone *walks* in the day not he stumbles
> If anyone *walks* in the day, he does not stumble.
>
> John is not talking about any particular person's activity during any particular day; he is stating a general truth about how followers of Christ should walk, day in and day out.

18.13 A subjunctive in the first person (singular or plural) can be used as an exhortation (*hortatory*). The translator will usually have added words such as "let us."

Mark 4:35	Διέλθωμεν	εἰς	τὸ πέραν
	let us go across	*to*	*the other side*

Let us go across to the other side.

This has not yet happened, and hence the subjunctive is appropriate.

Imperative

18.14 As we have seen, the imperative mood is used when a verb expresses a command (*command*).

Mark 2:14	ἀκολούθει	μοι
	you follow	*me*

Follow me!

Mark 6:37	δότε	αὐτοῖς	ὑμεῖς	φαγεῖν
	you give	*to them*	*you*	*to eat*

You give them something to eat.

18.15 The imperative may also express a request, as is appropriate when addressing a superior, such as God (*request, entreaty*).

Luke 11:1	κύριε, δίδαξον	ἡμᾶς	προσεύχεσθαι
	Lord *you teach*	*us*	*to pray*

Lord, *teach* us to pray.

Obviously, the disciples were not able to command Jesus to do anything, but when you make a request of a superior, you still use the imperative form of the verb.

Matt 6:10	ἐλθέτω	ἡ βασιλεία	σοῦ	γενηθήτω	τὸ θέλημά	σου
	let come	*the kingdom*	*your*	*let be*	*the will*	*your*

NASB and most translations: Your kingdom *come*, your will *be done*.
NET: *May* your kingdom *come, may* your will *be done*.
NLT: *May* your Kingdom *come* soon. *May* your will *be done*.

This gives what I think is an unfortunate example of compromised translation. I would guess that virually no one who prays the Lord's Prayer with the traditional "Your kingdom come" knows that they are using an imperative to call on God to send his kingdom. The NET and NLT bravely make an attempt to convey the clear meaning of the Greek, placing clarity of translation above tradition.

18.16 The imperative (usually present tense) with the negation μή can prohibit an action (*prohibition*).

> *Mark 5:36* μὴ φοβοῦ, μόνον πίστευε.
>   *not* *fear*   *only*   *believe*
>   NIV: *Do not fear*; just believe.

> *Matt 5:34* ἐγὼ δὲ λέγω ὑμῖν μὴ ὀμόσαι ὅλως
>   *I*   *but* *say*   *to you* *not* *take an oath* *at all*
>   But I say to you, *do not take an oath* at all.

Infinitive

18.17 As we saw earlier, the infinitive is a verbal noun. It is formed with a verb but it functions as a noun, but with tense and voice. It can have a direct object and adverbial modifiers, but no person or number.

> *Matt 11:1* μετέβη ἐκεῖθεν τοῦ διδάσκειν καὶ κηρύσσειν ἐν ταῖς πόλεσιν αὐτῶν.
>   *he went on* *from there* *to teach*   *and* *to preach*   *in* *cities*   *their*
>   He went on from there *to teach* and *preach* in their cities.

18.18 **Subject**. Because an infinitive is not a finite verbal form (which have subjects), it technically cannot have a subject. However, we have seen that there is often a word in the accusative —often a pronoun—that acts as if it were the subject of the infinitive.

> *Acts 28:6* μεταβαλόμενοι ἔλεγον αὐτὸν εἶναι θεόν
>   *changing minds*   *they said* *he*   *to be*   *god*
>   They changed their minds and said that *he* was a god
>
>   αὐτὸν is accusative, acting as the subject of the infinitive εἶναι.

18.19 **Substantival**. Because the infinitive is a verbal noun, it can perform any function that a substantive can. When used as a substantive, it will usually be preceded by a neuter singular definite article, which will be declined according to its usage in the sentence. This construction can be translated with "to" and the verb, although normally the translators use another way to say it.

> *Phil 1:21* ἐμοὶ τὸ ζῆν Χριστὸς καὶ τὸ ἀποθανεῖν κέρδος.
>   *to me* *the* *to live* *Christ*   *and* *the* *to die*   *gain*
>   For to me, *to live* is Christ and *to die* is gain.
>
>   Both infinitives, ζῆν and ἀποθανεῖν, are the subject of the unexpressed verb "is," and each infinitive has a predicate nominative: Χριστὸς and κέρδος.

Phil 4:10 ἤδη ποτὲ ἀνεθάλετε   τὸ ὑπὲρ ἐμοῦ φρονεῖν
already at last you have revived *the* for me *concern*
NRSV: Now at last you have revived your *concern* for me.

The articular infinitive τὸ … φρονεῖν is the direct object of the verb ἀνεθάλετε.

18.20 We have already seen that an infinitive is often used to complete the meaning of a finite verb (*complementary*).

Acts 2:4 ἤρξαντο λαλεῖν ἑτέραις γλώσσαις
they began *to speak* other tongues
They began *to speak* in other tongues.

"Began" by itself does not make any sense; it needs "to speak" to complete its meaning.

18.21 Another function of the infinitive is to express *purpose*, "in order that." There are different ways the infinitive can express purpose, but one is the infinitive by itself.

Rev 13:7 ἐδόθη αὐτῷ ποιῆσαι πόλεμον μετὰ τῶν ἁγίων καὶ νικῆσαι αὐτούς
it was given to him *to make* war against the saints and to conquer them
He was given power *to make* war against the saints and to conquer them.

The dragon gave his authority to the beast for the purpose of making war against the saints.

18.22 A common way of indicating the *result* of some action is to use a clause introduced by ὥστε. In this case ὥστε will usually not be followed by a finite verb but by an infinitive. Because we do not have a similar use of the infinitive in English, we must translate this infinitive with a finite verb.

Luke 5:7 ἔπλησαν ἀμφότερα τὰ πλοῖα ὥστε βυθίζεσθαι αὐτά
they filled both the boats *so that* *to sink* them
NIV: They … filled both boats so full *that* they *began to sink*.
NASB: They … filled both of the boats, *so that* they *began to sink*.

The disciples filled the boat with fish, and the result was that the boats began to sink.

Chapter 19

Participles

Participles are special. We have already seen that they are "verbal adjectives." They exhibit most of the charactistics of adjectives; they can be attributive or substantival. They are also adverbial, which means they will be qualifying something about the indicative verb. These adverbial participles are especially fun to translate.

Introduction to English Participles

19.1   In Foundational Greek, we saw that the participle is a verbal adjective. This means it has characteristics of both a verb and an adjective. If you can keep this definition in your head, participles are easier to understand.

19.2   In English, a participle is formed by adding "-ing" to a verb.

The man, *eating* by the window, is my Greek teacher.

After *eating,* I will go to bed.

19.3   A participle can have an *adverbial* function.

After *reviewing the chapter,* my Greek teacher gave us the final.

In this sentence, "reviewing" is a participle that tells us something about the verb "gave." The teacher gave us the final *after* he was done reviewing. ("After" is an adverb that emphasizes *when* the action of the participle occurred.)

19.4   A participle can also have an *adjectival* function.

The woman, *sitting* by the window, is my sister.

In this example, "sitting" tells us something about the noun "woman." She is Teri, my sister.

19.5   The participle and its accompanying elements form a *participial phrase*. Participial phrases begin with a participle and can include a direct object and other modifiers.

> *After eating the cake,* I started *doing the dishes.*

> The dog *sitting in the road* is in real trouble.

In phrasing, it is important to identify the beginning and end of a participial phrase, much like you do with a relative clause. The participial phrase is always dependent.

19.6   In a sentence like, "While eating, he saw her." English requires that "he" is the one who is eating, not "her," since "he" is closer in word order to the participle. We will see that this is not the case in Greek, which uses inflection to link the participle to the word it is modifying.

Introduction to Greek Participles

19.7   **Aspect**. The key to understanding participles is to recognize that their significance is primarily one of aspect. This is the genius, the essence, of participles, as it is of all the nonindicative verbal forms (subjunctive, infinitive, imperative). Because there are three aspects, there are three types of participles.

- The *aorist* participle describes an action without commenting on the nature of the action (*undefined*).

- The *present* participle describes a *continuous* action.

- The *perfect* participle describes a completed action with present effects (*perfective*).

You will see that the translations often are not able to bring this significance of aspect into English.

The terms "present," "aorist," and "perfect" do not refer to the meaning but to the form of the participle. The present participle is built on the present tense stem of the verb, but it does not necessarily denote an event occurring in the present time.

Adjectival Participle

19.8   There are two kinds of participles, adjectival and adverbial. A participle is a "verbal adjective," and sometimes the adjectival side is emphaiszed and other times its verbal.

19.9 There is no difference in form between a participle functioning adjectivally or one functioning adverbially. οἰκοδομοῦντες, in and of itself, could be either adjectival or adverbial. However, there is a clue when you see a participle in context, and that is ὁ.

- Adjectival participles are usually preceded by ὁ; i.e., they are usually articular.

- Adverbial participles are always anarthrous.

To say it in reverse:

- If you see an articular participle, it must be adjectival.

- If you see an anarthrous participle, it is probably adverbial.

19.10 Attributive. The adjectival participle will modify some other noun or pronoun in the sentence and will agree with that word in case, number, and gender, just like an adjective.

1 John 3:3   πᾶς   ὁ ἔχων   τὴν ἐλπίδα   ταύτην   ἐπ᾽ αὐτῷ   ἁγνίζει   ἑαυτόν
         everyone *having*   hope   this   in him   purifies   himself
         Everyone who thus hopes in him purifies himself.

Both πᾶς and ὁ ἔχων are nominative singular masculine.

19.11 The translator may want to add the appropriate pronoun to make better English sense. Which pronoun is used is determined by the word the participle is modifying.

Matt 9:9   Καὶ   παράγων   ὁ Ἰησοῦς   ἐκεῖθεν   εἶδεν   ἄνθρωπον.
         And   *going along*   Jesus   from there   he saw   man
         And Jesus, as *he was passing on* from there, saw a man.

To show that it was Jesus who was passing on, I added "he."

19.12 Substantival. Since an adjective can also function as a noun, so can a participle.[2] Remember: a participle is a verbal adjective, and anything an adjective can do a participle can do, usually better. Just like with the adjective,

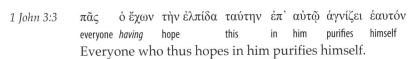

- a participle functioning substantivally gets its number and gender from the implied word it is referring to;

- its case will come from its function in the sentence.

---

[2] Technically, when an "-ing" word is used as a noun, in English it is called a "gerund." We don't use "gerund" in Greek grammar.

Mark 9:23   πάντα   δυνατὰ   τῷ   πιστεύοντι.

all things   possible   for the   *believing*

NIV: Everything is possible for *the one who believes.*

ESV: All things are possible for *one who believes.*

Notice that once again we had to add words —"the one who"; "one who" —to say the same thing in English as is said in Greek, just like we do with substantival adjectives. The translation of the Greek participle is often idiomatic, i.e., not word-for-word.

Adverbial Participle

19.13 Adverbial participles emphasize the verbal nature of the participle and modify some verb, usually the main verb of the clause. Because of this, most adverbial participles are nominative because the subject of the verb is doing the action of the participle.[3]

19.14 The aorist participle can describe an action occurring *before* the time of the finite verb, while the present participle can describe something happening *at the same time* as the action of the main verb (*temporal*). "After" and "when/while" are often added to this type of participle.[4] This use is frequent in narrative passages.

Matt 4:2   νηστεύσας ...   ὕστερον   ἐπείνασεν

fasting   then   he was hungry

ESV: *After fasting* … he was hungry.

NRSV: He *fasted* … and afterwards he was famished.

Acts 1:4   συναλιζόμενος   παρήγγειλεν   αὐτοῖς

staying with   he charged   them

RSV: *While staying with* them he charged them

NET: *While he was with* them, he ordered them

Eph 1:20   ἐνήργησεν   ἐν   τῷ Χριστῷ   ἐγείρας   αὐτὸν   ἐκ   νεκρῶν

he worked   in   Christ   *raising*   him   from   dead

NIV: which he exerted in Christ *when he raised* him from the dead

---

[3]   Wallace comments that about 70% of the adverbial participles in the Greek Testament are nominative, 14% accusative, 11% genitive, and 5% dative (*GGBB*, 623n28).

[4]   This is called "relative time" and will be discussed in more detail in Functional Greek.

19.15 The participle can indicate the means by which the action of the finite verb occurs (*means*).

> *1 Cor 4:12* κοπιῶμεν ἐργαζόμενοι ταῖς ἰδίαις χερσίν
> we toil   *working*   with the own   hands
> We toil *by working* with our own hands.
> NIV: We *work* hard with our own hands.
> ESV: We labor, *working* with our own hands.
>
> The means by which Paul toils is by working with his hands.

19.16 The participle can indicate the cause or reason or ground of the action of the finite verb (*cause*).

> *Acts 16:34* ἠγαλλιάσατο πανοικεὶ   πεπιστευκὼς τῷ θεῷ
> he rejoiced   with his whole house *having believed* in God
> NIV: He was filled with joy *because he had come to believe* in God.
> NASB: and rejoiced greatly, *having believed* in God
>
> The Philippian jailer rejoiced because he had believed.

19.17 The participle can indicate a condition that must be fulfilled if the action of the finite verb is to be accomplished (*conditional*).

> *Matt 21:22* πάντα ὅσα ἂν αἰτήσητε ... πιστεύοντες λήμψεσθε
> all   whatever you might ask *believing*   you will receive
> RSV: And whatever you ask in prayer, you will receive, *if you have faith.*
> NASB: And all things you ask in prayer, *believing,* you will receive.
>
> If the condition of faith is met, then you will have what you pray for.

19.18 The participle can indicate that the action of the finite verb is true despite the action of the participle (*concessive*).

> *Eph 2:1* Καὶ ὑμᾶς ὄντας νεκροὺς τοῖς παραπτώμασιν
> and you *being* dead   the tresspasses
> NET: And *although you were* dead in your transgressions
> NIV: You *were* dead in your transgressions.
> RSV: And you he made alive, *when you were* dead through the trespasses.
>
> The concessive idea is that even though we were dead in our sins, God made us alive. The RSV sees ὄντας as temporal.

Adverbial Participles and Relative Time

19.19 In the indicative, verbs indicate "absolute time." This means that if an aorist has temporal significance, it is in past time regardless of the other verbal forms around it. If the verb is present tense and it has temporal significance, then it indicates an action occurring in the present time.

19.20 Adverbial participles (not so much adjectival) indicate relative time.

- The participle built on the *present* tense stem indicates an action occurring at the *same time* as the time of the main verb.

- The participle built on the *aorist* tense stem indicates an action occurring *prior to* the time of the main verb.

main verb	participle	time
present	present	present continuous
present	aorist	past undefined
past	present	past continuous
past	aorist	past undefined

As you will see from the examples below, the relative time is not always expressed in translation, but the sequence of events should make the relative time clear.

19.21 For example, let's assume the main verb is aorist.

- The present participle is translated as *past* continuous.

Matt 4:18 Περιπατῶν δὲ παρὰ τὴν θάλασσαν τῆς Γαλιλαίας εἶδεν δύο ἀδελφούς.
   walking   *and alongside the sea*   *of Galilee,*   *he saw two   brothers*
   And *as he was walking* alongside the Sea of Galilee, he *saw* two brothers.

- The aorist participle is translated as *past* undefined.

Matt 2:7 Ἡρῴδης λάθρᾳ καλέσας τοὺς μάγους ἠκρίβωσεν παρ' αὐτῶν τὸν χρόνον
   Herod   *secretly* *calling*   *the magi*   *found out*   *from   them   the time*
   NASB: Herod secretly *called* the magi and *determined* from them the exact time.

19.22 But what if the main verb is present?

■ The present participle is translated as *present* continuous.

Matt 7:19   πᾶν δένδρον μὴ ποιοῦν καρπὸν καλὸν ἐκκόπτεται καὶ εἰς πῦρ βάλλεται
           Every tree   not *bearing*   fruit   good   *is cut down*   and   into   fire   *is thrown*
           Every tree *not bearing* good fruit *is cut down* and *thrown* into the fire.

■ The aorist participle is translated as *present* undefined.

Matt 2:11   ἐλθόντες εἰς τὴν οἰκίαν εἶδον τὸ παιδίον μετὰ Μαρίας τῆς μητρὸς αὐτοῦ
           after entering   into   the house   *they saw*   the child   with   Mary   mother   his
           After entering into the house, *they saw* the child with Mary, his mother.

Chapter 20

Conjunctions

Conjunctions are important words since they show us the flow of the author's thought. They are generally little words, but often quite difficult to translate, and some can be translated with punctuation.

20.1 Conjunctions are (normally) the little words that connect words, phrases, clauses, and sentences (e.g., and, but, for, or, so, yet). They are broken down into three basic categories.

- **Coordinating** conjunctions connect equal elements (*paratactic*).

  The Word was with God *and* the Word was God.

- **Subordinate** conjunctions begin a dependent clause and often link it to an independent clause (*hypotactic*).

  I studied *because* I want to pass this class.

- **Correlative** conjunctions work in pairs.

  Tyler has *both* strength *and* speed.

Significance

20.2 Conjunctions are linking words that connect thoughts. In exegesis (and phrasing), they are important because they tell us the specific relationship between different units of thought. By seeing this, we can better understand the author's flow of thought and therefore his meaning.

20.3 However, Greek can use conjunctions differently than we do in English. For example, almost every sentence in Greek narrative begins with a conjunction. One-third of all the sentences in John begin with καί, which generally means "and." It is poor English style to start so many sentences with conjunctions, so they are often dropped in translation. But they are there, and they might give us a clue as to the relationship between ideas.

20.4　Greek conjunctions, like all words, have a range of meanings. δέ can mean "but" or "and." How do translators decide which meaning to use in a specific instance? Context. In other words, they will use the meaning that makes the best sense in that sentence and paragraph. Sometimes it is obvious what a Greek conjunction means. Other times it is an issue of interpretation; when this is the case, translations differ.

20.5　In this chapter we will learn to identify these conjunctions and then use them to specify the relationship between the different phrases.

In what follows, I usually list two translations for most examples. The first illustrates the point I am making. The second often shows another translation that treats the conjunction differently.

20.6　It is especially important to highlight the conjunctions when phrasing.

- Coordinating conjunctions should be set off on their own line. Some teachers want them the same distance indented from the left to highlight the flow of thought.

- Subordinate conjunctions are indented under the word they modify, on the same line as their following phrase or clause.

- If the conjunction simply ties a series together, it is less important and the conjunction does not need to be highlighted.

Conjunctions are so important that you should memorize all the ones covered in this chapter.

Coordinating Conjunctions

20.7　Coordinate conjunctions connect grammatically equal units. They can connect two independent clauses (i.e., two sentences), two direct objects, two subjects, etc. They can even link paragraphs. Following are the main coordinate conjunctions in Greek.

καί

20.8　καί is the most common of all Greek conjunctions (occurring 9,161 times). It can mean "and" (*copulative*).

> Phil 4:9. The things you have learned *and* (καί) received *and* (καί) heard *and* (καί) seen in me, practice these things, *and* (καί) the God of peace will be with you (NASB).

> Whatever you have learned *or* (καί) received *or* (καί) heard from me, *or* (καί) seen in me—put it into practice. *And* (καί) the God of peace will be with you (NIV).

20.9 καί can also add emphasis to another word, as in the English "even" or "also" (*ascensive*). This use is sometimes left untranslated.

> Matt 5:46. For if you love those who love you, what reward have you? Do not *even* (καί) the tax collectors do the same? (RSV)

> Rom 8:29. For those God foreknew he *also* (καί) predestined to be conformed to the image of his Son, that he might be the firstborn among many brothers and sisters (NIV).

20.10 καί can also be used in a context in which the two clauses contrast each other, and καί is translated "but" by some translations while others use "and."

> Matt 12:43. When an evil spirit leaves a person, it goes into the desert, seeking rest *but* (καί) finding none (NLT).

> When an impure spirit comes out of a person, it goes through arid places seeking rest *and* (καί) does not find it (NIV).

20.11 When καί occurs at the beginning of a sentence, it is often marking the simple fact that the clause is a continuation of the previous discussion. Because we do not do this in English, this use of καί is often left untranslated.

> Heb 9:15 (καί) For this reason Christ is the mediator of a new covenant, that those who are called may receive the promised eternal inheritance (NIV).

> *And* (καί) for this cause he is the mediator of the new testament, that … they which are called might receive the promise of eternal inheritance (KJV).

δέ

20.12 δέ (2,792t) is a weaker connective, which means all it necessarily says is that there is a connection between the preceding and following. Often, when a sentence starts with δέ, it is not translated. The NET Bible has literally hundreds of footnotes that indicate every place they did not translate δέ.

> Matt 1:2. Abraham was the father of Isaac, (δέ) Isaac the father of Jacob, (δέ) Jacob the father of Judah and his brothers (NIV).

> Abraham was the father of Isaac, *and* (δέ) Isaac the father of Jacob, *and* (δέ) Jacob the father of Judah and his brothers (ESV).

> Rom 7:25 (δέ) I thank God—through Jesus Christ our Lord! So then, with the mind I myself serve the law of God, *but* (δέ) with the flesh the law of sin (NKJV).

20.13 Sometimes the force of the δέ is a little stronger and is translated as "and."

> John 3:19. *And* (δέ) this is the judgment, that the light has come into the world, and (καί) men loved darkness rather than light, because their deeds were evil (RSV).

> (δέ) This is the verdict: Light has come into the world, but (καί) people loved darkness instead of light because their deeds were evil (NIV).

20.14 Sometimes the δέ is helping the story to continue, and "now" or "then" among other words is used.

> Acts 2:5. *Now* (δέ) there were staying in Jerusalem God-fearing Jews from every nation under heaven (NIV).

> (δέ) Godly Jews from many nations were living in Jerusalem at that time (NLT).

> Luke 24:31. *Then* (δέ) their eyes were opened and (καί) they recognized him, and (καί) he disappeared from their sight (NIV).

> *And* (δέ) their eyes were opened, and (καί) they recognized him. And (καί) he vanished from their sight (ESV).

> *Suddenly* (δέ), their eyes were opened, and (καί) they recognized him. And (καί) at that moment he disappeared! (NLT).

20.15 δέ can also introduce a contrasting idea and is translated "but" (*adversative*). However, δέ is a weak adversative, which means it can only indicate a slight adversative relationship.

> Mark 15:23 (καί) They tried to give Him wine mixed with myrrh; *but* (δέ) He did not take it (NASB).

> Luke 16:17. *But* (δέ) it is easier for heaven and (καί) earth to pass away than for one dot of the Law to become void (ESV).

> (δέ) It is easier for heaven and (καί) earth to disappear than for the least stroke of a pen to drop out of the Law (NIV).

> *But* (δέ) that doesn't mean that the law has lost its force in even the smallest point. It is stronger and more permanent than heaven and (καί) earth (NLT).

> Acts 2:13. Some, *however*, (δέ) made fun of them and said, "They have had too much wine" (NIV).

> *But* (δέ) others in the crowd were mocking. "They're drunk, that's all!" they said (NLT).

John 1:12. *Yet* (δέ) to all who did receive him, to those who believed in his name, he gave the right to become children of God (NIV).

But (δέ) to all who did receive him, who believed in his name, he gave the right to become children of God (ESV).

20.16 If you want to get even more sophisticated, you can see that the English paragraph marker can perform the same function as the δέ, since it indicates a change of some sort. Luke 24:36-43 contains one of Jesus' post-resurrection appearances. V 44 starts a new paragraph introduced with δέ.

(δέ) He said to them, "This is what I told you while I was still with you: Everything must be fulfilled that is written about me in the Law of Moses, the Prophets and the Psalms" (NIV).

Now (δέ) He said to them, "These are My words which I spoke to you while I was still with you, that all things which are written about Me in the Law of Moses and the Prophets and the Psalms must be fulfilled" (NASB).

Then (δέ) he said to them, "These are my words that I spoke to you while I was still with you, that everything written about me in the Law of Moses and the Prophets and the Psalms must be fulfilled" (ESV).

In Matthew 28:11-15 we read about the Jewish leaders formulating the lie to explain away the empty tomb. V 16, in essence, starts a new paragraph by telling us what the disciples did.

But (δέ) the eleven disciples proceeded to Galilee, to the mountain which Jesus had designated (NASB).

Now (δέ) the eleven disciples went to Galilee, to the mountain to which Jesus had directed them (RSV).

Then (δέ) the eleven disciples went to Galilee, to the mountain where Jesus had told them to go (NIV).

How does the translator know when to translate δέ and when to drop it? Context! Are you seeing why translations can be so different? The translators' sense of English style and how they want to express these relationships can vary significantly.

γάρ

20.17 γάρ (1,041t) gives the reason or explanation for something (*explanatory*). It is usually translated "for."

John 4:7-8. There came a woman of Samaria to draw water. Jesus said to her, "Give Me a drink." *For* (γάρ) His disciples had gone away into the city to buy food (NASB).

Soon a Samaritan woman came to draw water, and Jesus said to her, "Please give me a drink." He was alone at the time *because* (γάρ) his disciples had gone into the village to buy some food" (NLT).

Rom 12:4. *For* (γάρ) as in one body we have many members, and the members do not all have the same function … (ESV).

(γάρ) *For* just as each of us has one body with many members, and these members do not all have the same function … (NIV).

20.18 But γάρ can also indicate that the author is simply continuing his discussion, and these occurrences are usually not translated, as illustrated by the second occurrence of γάρ in Romans 1:20.

Rom 1:19-20. For (διότι) what can be known about God is plain to them, *because* (γάρ) God has shown it to them. (γάρ) Ever since the creation of the world his invisible nature, namely, his eternal power and (καί) deity, has been clearly perceived in the things that have been made. So they are without excuse (RSV).

since (διότι) what may be known about God is plain to them, *because* (γάρ) God has made it plain to them. *For* (γάρ) since the creation of the world God's invisible qualities—his eternal power and (καί) divine nature—have been clearly seen, being understood from what has been made, so that men are without excuse (NIV).

ἀλλά, οὖν, ἤ

20.19 ἀλλά (638t) is a strong *adversative* conjunction, indicating that the following clause stands in contrast to the preceding. It is usually translated "but," but it can be translated many other ways that indicate a contrast.

Matt 5:17. Do not think that I have come to abolish the Law or the Prophets; I have not come to abolish them *but* (ἀλλά) to fulfill them (NIV).

Matt 5:15. Neither do people light a lamp and (καί) put it under a bowl. *Instead* (ἀλλά) they put it on its stand, and (καί) it gives light to everyone in the house (NIV).

Nor do people light a lamp and (καί) put it under a basket, *but* (ἀλλά) on a stand, and (καί) it gives light to all in the house (ESV).

Matt 9:17. Neither do people pour new wine into old wineskins. (δέ) If they do, the skins will burst; (καί) the wine will run out and (καί) the wineskins will be ruined. *No* (ἀλλά), they pour new wine into new wineskins, and (καί) both are preserved (NIV).

Nor do people put new wine into old wineskins; otherwise (δέ) the wineskins burst, and (καί) the wine pours out and (καί) the wineskins are ruined; *but* (ἀλλά) they put new wine into fresh wineskins, and (καί) both are preserved (NASB).

Matt 11:8. *If not* (ἀλλά), what did you go out to see? A man dressed in fine clothes? No, those who wear fine clothes are in kings' palaces (NIV).

What *then* (ἀλλά) did you go out to see? A man dressed in soft clothing? Behold, those who wear soft clothing are in kings' houses (ESV).

Mark 4:22. For (γάρ) there is nothing hid, except to be made manifest; nor is anything secret, *except* (ἀλλά) to come to light (RSV).

For (γάρ) whatever is hidden is meant to be disclosed, and whatever is concealed is meant (ἀλλά) to be brought out into the open (NIV).

Rom 6:5. For if we have been united like this in his death, we will *certainly* (ἀλλά) also (καί) be united with him in his resurrection (NIV).

Since we have been united with him in his death, we will (ἀλλά) also be raised as he was (NLT).

20.20 οὖν (499t) is the main *inferential* conjunction and is often translated "therefore."

Rom 12:1. *Therefore* (οὖν) I urge you, brethren, by the mercies of God, to present your bodies a living and (*no Greek conjunction*) holy sacrifice, acceptable to God, which is your spiritual service of worship (NASB).

And so (οὖν), dear brothers and sisters, I plead with you to give your bodies to God. Let them be a living and (*no Greek conjunction*) holy sacrifice—the kind he will accept. When you think of what he has done for you, is this too much to ask? (NLT).

20.21 οὖν can weaken to indicate a transition or continuation of the narrative.

John 9:18. The Jews *then* (οὖν) did not believe it of him, that he had been blind and (καί) had received sight (NASB).

The Jews (οὖν) did not believe that he had been blind and (καί) had received his sight (ESV).

[The Jews] *still (οὖν)* did not believe that he had been blind and *(καί)* had received his sight (NIV).

20.22 ἤ (343t) is the main conjunction for saying "or."

> Matt 5:18. For (γάρ) truly I say to you, until heaven and (καί) earth pass away, not the smallest letter *or (ἤ)* stroke shall pass from the Law until all is accomplished (NIV 1984).

> For (γάρ) truly, I say to you, until heaven and (καί) earth pass away, not an iota, (ἤ) not a dot, will pass from the Law until all is accomplished (ESV).

Did you notice how the comma performs the function of ἤ in the ESV example above?

Subordinate Conjunctions

20.23 Subordinate conjunctions introduce dependent clauses, which means these clauses will modify a main clause. This is significant for phrasing as you attempt to differentiate primary and secondary thoughts.

20.24 ὅτι (1,296t) can indicate the basis for an action and is usually translated "because."

> Rom 5:5. And (δέ) hope does not disappoint us, *because (ὅτι)* God's love has been poured into our hearts through the Holy Spirit which has been given to us (RSV).

20.25 ὅτι can also be the equivalent of "that" after certain types of verbs.

> John 15:18. If the world hates you, know *that (ὅτι)* it has hated me before it hated you (RSV).

20.26 ἵνα (663t) generally indicates *purpose* and can be translated "in order that," or "so that."

> John 3:16. For (γάρ) God so loved the world that he gave his only Son, *so that* (ἵνα) everyone who believes in him will not perish but (ἀλλ') have eternal life (NLT).

> Matt 7:1. Do not judge *so that* (ἵνα) you will not be judged (NASB).

> Judge not, *that* (ἵνα) you be not judged (ESV).

> Do not judge, *or* (ἵνα) you too will be judged (NIV).

> Stop judging others, *and* (ἵνα) you will not be judged (NLT).

20.27 ἵνα can also indicate the *result,* translated with "that."

> Matt 26:56. But (δέ) this has all taken place that (ἵνα) the writings of the prophets might be fulfilled (NIV).

The difference between purpose and result is subtle. If there was intention, it is purpose. If the action simply occurred, it is result. Some commentaries will try to split this hair.

20.28 ἵνα can also lose all of its purpose/result nuance and simply introduce the content of what is expressed by the verb.

> Mark 9:30. He did not want (ἵνα) anyone to know it (NRSV).

20.29 εἰ (502t) is the main *conditional* conjunction meaning "if."

> Luke 22:67. *If* (εἰ) you are the Christ, tell us (RSV).

20.30 ἐάν (334t) is another form of ἐι, also meaning "if."

> Matt 5:13. You are the salt of the earth; but (δέ) *if* (ἐάν) the salt has become tasteless, how can it be made salty again? It is no longer good for anything, except (εἰ μή) to be thrown out and (*no Greek conjunction*) trampled under foot by men (NASB).

20.31 ὅτε (103) is the main temporal conjunction meaning "when."

> Gal 4:4. But (δέ) *when* (ὅτε) the right time came, God sent his Son, born of a woman, subject to the law (NLT).

Correlative Conjunctions

20.32 Correlative conjunctions are pairs of conjunctions that work together. The most common are:

μέν ... δέ	on the one hand ... but on the other
καί ... καί	both ... and
ἤ ...ἤ	either ... or
μήτε ... μήτε	neither ... nor
οὔτε ... οὔτε	neither ... nor
οὐκ ... ἀλλά (or δέ)	not ... but
τε ... καί	both ... and

Rev 3:15. I know your works: you are *neither* (οὔτε) cold *nor* (οὔτε) hot. Would that you were cold or (ἤ) hot! (RSV)

20.33 Sometimes the first of the pair is not translated because of English style.

Matt 9:37. Then he said to his disciples, "(μέν) The harvest is plentiful, *but* (δέ) the laborers are few" (RSV).

20.34 The translation of conjunctions can become quite nuanced. For example, in the NASB of 1 Corinthians 7:7 the μέν … δέ is represented by the change from "one" to "another."

1 Cor 7:7. *one* (μέν) in this manner, and *another* (δέ) in that.

20.35 The correlatives can often be tricky to spot because of intervening words.

1 Peter 2:4	ὑπο	ἀνθρώπων	μὲν	ἀποδεδοκιμασμένον	παρὰ	δὲ	θεῷ	ἐκλεκτόν
	by	men		rejected	before	but	God	chosen

rejected by men but chosen by God

Notice how μέν comes after ὑπὸ ἀνθρώπων and δέ after παρά. In *IRU* I listed μέν and δέ as the first word in each phrase.

	rejected	by	men	but	chosen	by	God
μὲν	ἀποδεδοκιμασμένον	ὑπὸ	ἀνθρώπων	δὲ	ἐκλεκτὸν	παρὰ	θεῷ
pl	pt.rp.asm	p.g	n.gpm	cj	a.asm	p.d	n.dsm
3525	627	5679	476	1254	1723	4123	2536

Vocabulary

20.36 There is vocabulary for this chapter in the online class.

This photo is of a cursive (see pg. 258) New Testament manuscript, copied in the twelfth century. It contains Matthew 15:13–27a. Photo provided by the Center for the Study of the New Testament Manuscripts (Daniel Wallace, director) and used by permission of Institut für neutestamentliche Textforschung.

Chapter 21

Phrasing 102

In Chapter 14 we learned the basics of phrasing. Let's review! The purpose of phrasing is to identify the beginning and end of the passage, divide it into manageable sections if necessary, find the main point(s) of each section, and then see how the remaining phrases relate to those main points.

We are going to do some more phrasing, this time with the letter of Jude. This is a harder book to phrase, but if you can get through Jude, you can deal with most of the New Testament.

Jude

I have listed the NIV (1984) text of Jude on the next two pages without paragraphs and headings. Make a copy of the pages and work from it, not your Bible, or copy the text from your Bible software and paste it into your word processor.

Step 1: Find the Beginning and the End

Because we want to phrase all of Jude, this step is done for us. We are going to work with all 25 verses.

Step 2: Identify the Sections

Work through Jude and discover how many basics sections it has. Place headings with each. My work is on page 161, so don't look ahead until you are done.

Titus 2:11-14   21:24

It would seem obvious what these signs are giving directions to.

Jude

1:1   Jude, a servant of Jesus Christ and a brother of James,

To those who have been called, who are loved by God the Father and kept by Jesus Christ:

1:2   Mercy, peace and love be yours in abundance.

1:3   Dear friends, although I was very eager to write to you about the salvation we share, I felt I had to write and urge you to contend for the faith that was once for all entrusted to the saints.

1:4   For certain men whose condemnation was written about long ago have secretly slipped in among you. They are godless men, who change the grace of our God into a license for immorality and deny Jesus Christ our only Sovereign and Lord.

1:5   Though you already know all this, I want to remind you that the Lord delivered his people out of Egypt, but later destroyed those who did not believe.

1:6   And the angels who did not keep their positions of authority but abandoned their own home—these he has kept in darkness, bound with everlasting chains for judgment on the great Day.

1:7   In a similar way, Sodom and Gomorrah and the surrounding towns gave themselves up to sexual immorality and perversion. They serve as an example of those who suffer the punishment of eternal fire.

1:8   In the very same way, these dreamers pollute their own bodies, reject authority and slander celestial beings.

1:9   But even the archangel Michael, when he was disputing with the devil about the body of Moses, did not dare to bring a slanderous accusation against him, but said, "The Lord rebuke you!"

1:10   Yet these men speak abusively against whatever they do not understand; and what things they do understand by instinct, like unreasoning animals—these are the very things that destroy them.

1:11   Woe to them! They have taken the way of Cain; they have rushed for profit into Balaam's error; they have been destroyed in Korah's rebellion.

1:12   These men are blemishes at your love feasts, eating with you without the slightest qualm—shepherds who feed only themselves. They are clouds without rain, blown along by the wind; autumn trees, without fruit and uprooted—twice dead.

1:13   They are wild waves of the sea, foaming up their shame; wandering stars, for whom blackest darkness has been reserved forever.

1:14   Enoch, the seventh from Adam, prophesied about these men: "See, the Lord is coming with thousands upon thousands of his holy ones

1:15   to judge everyone, and to convict all the ungodly of all the ungodly acts they have done in the ungodly way, and of all the harsh words ungodly sinners have spoken against him."

1:16   These men are grumblers and faultfinders; they follow their own evil desires; they boast about themselves and flatter others for their own advantage.

1:17   But, dear friends, remember what the apostles of our Lord Jesus Christ foretold.

1:18   They said to you, "In the last times there will be scoffers who will follow their own ungodly desires."

1:19   These are the men who divide you, who follow mere natural instincts and do not have the Spirit.

1:20   But you, dear friends, build yourselves up in your most holy faith and pray in the Holy Spirit.

1:21   Keep yourselves in God's love as you wait for the mercy of our Lord Jesus Christ to bring you to eternal life.

1:22   Be merciful to those who doubt;

1:23   snatch others from the fire and save them; to others show mercy, mixed with fear—hating even the clothing stained by corrupted flesh.

1:24   To him who is able to keep you from falling and to present you before his glorious presence without fault and with great joy—

1:25   to the only God our Savior be glory, majesty, power and authority, through Jesus Christ our Lord, before all ages, now and forevermore! Amen.

(NIV 1984)

Salutation

1:1   Jude, a servant of Jesus Christ and a brother of James,

         To those who have been called, who are loved by God the Father and kept by Jesus Christ:

1:2   Mercy, peace and love be yours in abundance.

Occasion for Writing

1:3   Dear friends, although I was very eager to write to you about the salvation we share, I felt I had to write and urge you to contend for the faith that was once for all entrusted to the saints.

1:4   For certain men whose condemnation was written about long ago have secretly slipped in among you. They are godless men, who change the grace of our God into a license for immorality and deny Jesus Christ our only Sovereign and Lord.

Description and Condemnation of the Troublemakers

1:5   Though you already know all this, I want to remind you that the Lord delivered his people out of Egypt, but later destroyed those who did not believe.

. . . . .

Call to Perseverance

1:20   But you, dear friends, build yourselves up in your most holy faith and pray in the Holy Spirit.

1:21   Keep yourselves in God's love as you wait for the mercy of our Lord Jesus Christ to bring you to eternal life.

1:22   Be merciful to those who doubt;

1:23   snatch others from the fire and save them; to others show mercy, mixed with fear—hating even the clothing stained by corrupted flesh.

Doxology

1:24   To him who is able to keep you from falling and to present you before his glorious presence without fault and with great joy—

1:25   to the only God our Savior be glory, majesty, power and authority, through Jesus Christ our Lord, before all ages, now and forevermore! Amen.

So how did you do? I see five basic sections. The salutation and doxology are pretty evident. Vv 3-4 tell us why Jude wrote and introduces us to the troublemakers.

The heart of the letter is vv 5-23, but there is a shift between v 19 and v 20 as Jude moves from describing the troublemakers to encouraging the church to persevere. In other words, there is a shift of audience and a shift in his basic message.

Some people don't split it this way. Some see a shift at 1:17, especially because of the beginning "Dear friends." That's okay. I may not be right. But when I break a passage into its sections, what I am looking for is a unifying theme, something that holds the verses together. In vv 5-23 I see Jude doing the same thing: whether he is describing people or explicitly judging them, all of it functions as a condemnation of sin, asserting that God always punishes evil.

Steps 3-4

Go ahead and phrase the salutation. It has similarities to 1 Peter 1:1-2 and shouldn't give you a problem. Also phrase vv 3-4. Pay special attention to why Jude says they are godless.

When you are done, check my work on the next page.

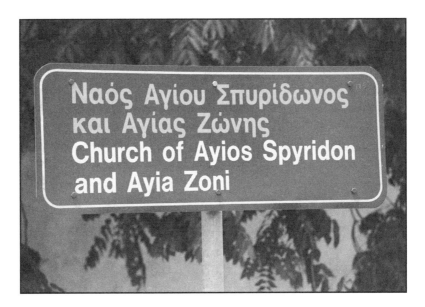

A sign of a church. Can you spot any variances from the transliteration scheme you were instructed in this book?

Salutation

1:1   Jude,

          a servant of Jesus Christ and

          a brother of James,

     To those

          who have been called,

          who are   loved by God the Father and

                   kept by Jesus Christ:

1:2   Mercy, peace and love be yours in abundance.

Occasion for Writing

1:3   Dear friends,

          although I was very eager to write to you about the salvation we share,

     I felt I had to write and urge you to contend for the faith

               that was once for all entrusted to the saints.

1:4   For

    certain men ... have secretly slipped in among you.

          whose condemnation was written about long ago

          They are godless men,

                   who change the grace of our God into a license for immorality and

                   deny Jesus Christ our only Sovereign and Lord.

We have the usual three-part salutation, with Jude emphasizing that those who have been called are loved and kept both by God the Father and Jesus Christ.

Jude then moves into the occasion for writing. He had wanted to write a different type of letter, one about the salvation he shares with the church; but instead, because of the troublemakers, he felt the need to write them to contend, to fight, for the faith. Why? Because certain godless men had snuck into the church, and their heresy was twofold. They taught that holiness didn't matter, that God's grace gave them license to live immoral lives. Second, they denied that Jesus was the believer's only Sovereign and Lord.

I connected the "For" in v 4 back to "felt," precisely identifying v 4 as the *reason* for why Jude felt this way. Without the line, it may not have been visually clear that "For" is indented under "felt."

Notice the use of ellipsis in v 4: "certain men … have secretly slipped in." While I prefer to keep the word order of the translation, sometimes it is not possible. In biblical order, the phrase, "whose condemnation was written about long ago," separates the subject "men" from its verb "slipped in" and is parallel with the following phrase, "they are godless men." So I pulled the phrase out, marked its place with an ellipsis, and placed it under "men."

Notice also what I did with the last two statements. They were too long to fit on one line, so I put extra space between the two. Without that space, you might think there were three phrases modifying "men."

A picture of the ruins of Acropolis, towering over the city of Athens.

Description and Condemnation of the Troublemakers

1:5   Though you already know all this, I want to remind you that the Lord delivered his people out of Egypt, but later destroyed those who did not believe.

1:6   And the angels who did not keep their positions of authority but abandoned their own home—these he has kept in darkness, bound with everlasting chains for judgment on the great Day.

1:7   In a similar way, Sodom and Gomorrah and the surrounding towns gave themselves up to sexual immorality and perversion. They serve as an example of those who suffer the punishment of eternal fire.

1:8   In the very same way, these dreamers pollute their own bodies, reject authority and slander celestial beings.

1:9   But even the archangel Michael, when he was disputing with the devil about the body of Moses, did not dare to bring a slanderous accusation against him, but said, "The Lord rebuke you!"

1:10   Yet these men speak abusively against whatever they do not understand; and what things they do understand by instinct, like unreasoning animals—these are the very things that destroy them.

1:11   Woe to them! They have taken the way of Cain; they have rushed for profit into Balaam's error; they have been destroyed in Korah's rebellion.

1:12   These men are blemishes at your love feasts, eating with you without the slightest qualm—shepherds who feed only themselves. They are clouds without rain, blown along by the wind; autumn trees, without fruit and uprooted—twice dead.

1:13   They are wild waves of the sea, foaming up their shame; wandering stars, for whom blackest darkness has been reserved forever.

1:14   Enoch, the seventh from Adam, prophesied about these men: "See, the Lord is coming with thousands upon thousands of his holy ones

1:15   to judge everyone, and to convict all the ungodly of all the ungodly acts they have done in the ungodly way, and of all the harsh words ungodly sinners have spoken against him."

1:16   These men are grumblers and faultfinders; they follow their own evil desires; they boast about themselves and flatter others for their own advantage.

1:17   But, dear friends, remember what the apostles of our Lord Jesus Christ foretold.

1:18   They said to you, "In the last times there will be scoffers who will follow their own ungodly desires."

1:19   These are the men who divide you, who follow mere natural instincts and do not have the Spirit.

Repeat of Steps 1 and 2

What are we going to go with vv 5-19? Jude is describing the troublemakers and condemning them, and he is talking about other people who got in trouble. But vv 5-19 are probably too many verses to handle at one time, so what is a "phraser" to do?

Basically, we treat the section (vv 5-19) as a new passage, and repeat Step 2 by dividing the section into its subsections. Read and reread vv 5-19 until the Bible tells you where the natural breaks are. Go ahead and do it now, and be sure to write a heading for each subsection. (Write the subsection headings in some form that differentiates them from the main section headings.) Then do Steps 3 and 4 for each subsection. My work is on the next few pages.

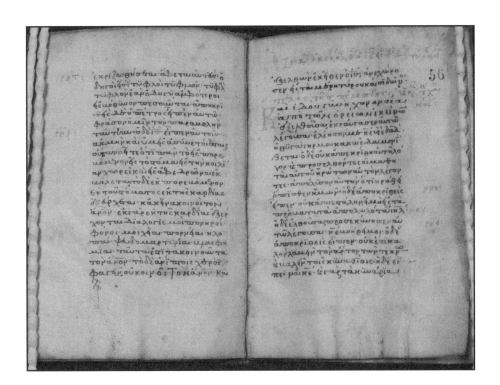

This is a lectionary from the thirteenth to fourteenth century, containing parts of Matthew and John. Photo provided by the Center for the Study of New Testament manuscripts (Daniel Wallace, director) and used by permission of Institut für neutestamentliche Textforschung.

Three Parallels

1:5   Though you already know all this, I want to remind you that

{1} the Lord delivered <u>his people</u> out of Egypt,
>   but later destroyed those who did not believe.

1:6   And
{2} the <u>angels</u> who did not keep their positions of authority but abandoned their own home
>   —these he has kept in darkness, bound with everlasting chains for judgment on the great Day.

1:7   In a similar way,
{3} <u>Sodom and Gomorrah</u> and the surrounding towns gave themselves up to sexual immorality and perversion.
>   They serve as an example of those who suffer the punishment of eternal fire.

Description of the Troublemakers

1:8   In the very same way,
<u>these dreamers</u>
>   {1} pollute their own bodies,
>   {2} reject authority and
>   {3} slander celestial beings.

1:9   But even the archangel <u>Michael,</u> →
when he was disputing with the devil about the body of Moses,
>   →   did not dare to bring a slanderous accusation against him,
>   but said, "The Lord rebuke you!"

1:10   Yet <u>these men</u>
>   {4} speak abusively against whatever they do not understand; and
>   {5} what things they do understand by instinct, like unreasoning animals—these are the very things that destroy them.

I see six subsections. I could be wrong, but that is how the passage divides to my way of thinking.

(1) Vv 5-7 spell out *three situations* that parallel the situation Jude is addressing: people delivered from Egypt; angels; Sodom and Gomorrah. The parallelism is that these three groups represent that fact that God always punishes sin. The first two groups are especially privileged people, and even they were punished. The implication is that these "certain men" in Jude's time will likewise be punished for their sins.

Notice that I numbered the three points. As I said in chapter 14, whenever I want to add something in my phrasing to the biblical text, I use curly brackets so I never confuse my scribblings with God's Word.

I could have broken v 6b into two parts, showing that the angels {1} have been kept in darkness and {2} are bound with everlasting chains. But I divided it up the way I did because I like to see the symmetry of three groups of beings who each experienced punishment: the Israelites were destroyed; the angels are bound in darkness; the people of Sodom and Gomorrah were punished with fire.

(2) In vv 8-10 we see Jude doing two things. First, he is describing the troublemakers, the "dreamers," and emphasizing how bad they are. In v 8 he gives three characteristics, and two more in v 10. But what is v 9 about?

As you worked on your phrasing, hopefully you saw that v 9 goes with the third description of the dreamers. They "slander celestial beings" (v 8), but even the archangel Michael wouldn't slander Satan but simply said, "The Lord rebuke you!" (Don't go looking for this story in your Bible.)

Notice my use of space (e.g., between v 8 and v 9) to group different ideas. Notice also how underlining the most essential elements of the discussion help you focus on the basics of the passage and not become lost in the details.

In v 9 the subject ("Michael") and the main verb ("did not dare") are separated by the temporal clause ("when …"). The arrows ("→") are my way of hooking "Michael did not dare" together.

Statement of Judgment

1:11   Woe to them!

        {1} They have taken the way of Cain;

        {2} they have rushed for profit into Balaam's error;

        {3} they have been destroyed in Korah's rebellion.

1:12   {4} These men are blemishes at your love feasts,

                eating with you without the slightest qualm

                —shepherds who feed only themselves.

        {5} They are clouds without rain, blown along by the wind;

        {6} autumn trees, without fruit and uprooted—twice dead.

1:13   {7} They are wild waves of the sea, foaming up their shame;

        {8} wandering stars, for whom blackest darkness has been reserved forever.

Prophecies

1:14   Enoch, the seventh from Adam, prophesied about these men:

       "See, the Lord is coming with thousands upon thousands of his holy ones

1:15   to judge everyone, and

          to convict all the ungodly

             of all the ungodly acts they have done in the ungodly way, and

             of all the harsh words ungodly sinners have spoken against him."

Continued Descriptions

1:16   {1} These men are grumblers and faultfinders;

        {2} they follow their own evil desires;

        {3} they boast about themselves and flatter others for their own advantage.

(3) The third subsection moves into Jude's statements of woe, his statement of judgment on these dreamers. Again, notice the numbering of the series.

(4) Jude continues by pointing out that Enoch prophesied about these men. Enoch didn't prophesy that these specific men would come, but that the Lord would judge all the ungodly for what they said and did.

(5) In v 16 Jude resumes his description of the dreamers. If you wanted to connect them back to vv 11-13, you could continue the numbering with {9}, {10}, and {11}. However, you may have noticed that Jude likes series of three, so I left them {1}, {2}, and {3}.

The entrance to an archaeological site of ancient Corinth.

1:17   But, dear friends,

remember what the apostles of our Lord Jesus Christ foretold.

1:18   They said to you,

"In the last times there will be scoffers

who will follow their own ungodly
desires."

1:19   These are the men   who divide you,

who follow mere natural instincts and

do not have the Spirit.

Call to Perseverance

1:20   But you, dear friends, build yourselves up in your most holy faith and pray in the Holy Spirit.

1:21   Keep yourselves in God's love as you wait for the mercy of our Lord Jesus Christ to bring you to eternal life.

1:22   Be merciful to those who doubt;

1:23   snatch others from the fire and save them; to others show mercy, mixed with fear—hating even the clothing stained by corrupted flesh.

Doxology

1:24   To him who is able to keep you from falling and to present you before his glorious presence without fault and with great joy—

1:25   to the only God our Savior be glory, majesty, power and authority, through Jesus Christ our Lord, before all ages, now and forevermore!

(6) In the sixth subsection, Jude refers to the prophecies of the apostles, that evil people will come in the last days; the dreamers are the fulfillment of those prophecies. What is important to note, in all these descriptions, is that Jude is also condemning them, and that note of judgment is what ties vv 5-19 together.

Some people see a major break at v 17, which starts with what appears to be a transitional phrase ("But, dear friends") and which addresses the church directly. It is good to have a sensitivity to this type of change. However, because the overall thrust of this subsection is once again to describe the dreamers as evil people and so continue the judgment theme, I prefer to keep vv 17-19 with the preceeding and not start a new subsection.

How do my subsections compare to yours? How about our headings? If you found a different structure, you may want to go back and reread the passage. But again let me stress that the point here is for *you* to study *your* own Bible and to let the Bible and the Holy Spirit talk to you about what it is saying.

Okay, we are almost done. Phrase vv 20-25 (page 170) and then turn the page.

It is probably a good thing both Greek and English are written here. The Greek phrase literally reads, "Do not come near."

Call to Perseverance

1:20   But you, dear friends,

           {1} build yourselves up in your most holy faith and

           {2} pray in the Holy Spirit.

1:21   {3} Keep yourselves in God's love

        as you wait for the mercy of our Lord Jesus Christ to bring you to eternal life.

1:22   {4} Be merciful to those who doubt;

1:23   {5} snatch others from the fire and save them;

        {6} to others show mercy, mixed with fear

        {7}—hating even the clothing stained by corrupted flesh.

Doxology

1:24   To him

          who is able   to keep you from falling and

                    to present you before his glorious presence

                          without fault and with great joy—

1:25   to the only God our Savior

      be glory, majesty, power and authority,

       through Jesus Christ our Lord,

       before all ages, now and forevermore!

      Amen.

Vv 20-23 are a call to perseverance in face of the opposition from the dreamers. This is the point to which Jude has been heading. He is not describing them just to condemn them; he wants his "dear friends" to see that the dreamers are evil people and to stand firm in the face of their opposition.

Vv 24-25 end with a glorious doxology. Did you notice the themes in the doxology that were introduced in vv 1–2? These themes of God's protection and the person of Jesus Christ serve as theological bookends to Jude's call for perseverance.

Let me again stress that while phrasing is not grammatical diagramming, recognizing conjunctions and dependent clauses goes a long way in helping us see the author's flow of thought.

Do you see what just happened? You took twenty-five verses that perhaps were not the easiest to understand, you discovered their main points, you identified several modifying assertions, and you can see how they all relate to the main points. Welcome to the heart of Bible study!

You figure out what works for you. That's the point. There isn't always a right and wrong way to phrase. You can take this basic process and mold and shape it until it works for you, until you find a way that helps you see most clearly what the Bible is saying. And what works for me may not work for you. But take the time, experiment, and let the Bible teach you what it says and means.

One last point. One of the purposes of this text is to help you to be able to read the better commentaries. The kind of work we have been doing here is what you will find in them. Perhaps the authors will not be as deliberate and obvious as I have been, but this is precisely the type of work that underlies a good commentary. You will see an example of this in Phrasing 104 (chapter 30).

For large Greek cities, roadsigns have Greek and English. If you want to go to smaller localities, you will need to know how to read Greek.

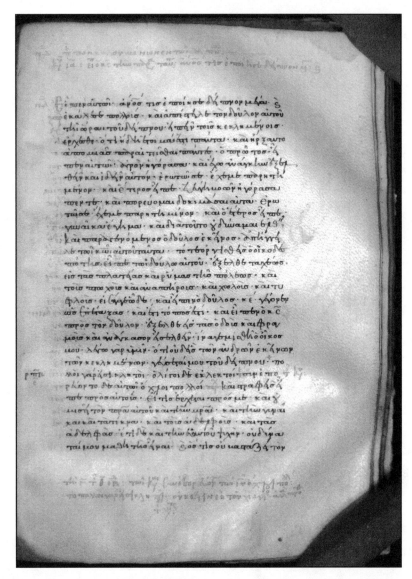

Codex 2882 is a 10th-11th century Greek manuscript of Luke's Gospel. The manuscript, which contains 46 leaves (92 pages), was previously owned by a man who came from Greece to America in the early decades of the twentieth century. After he died, the manuscript was purchased by a rare book and manuscript store in Pennsylvania. It was then purchased in 2005 by the Center for the Study of New Testament Manuscripts. The manuscript was registered with the Institut für neutestamentliche Textforschung (the Institute for New Testament Textual Research) in Münster, Germany in January 2008 and given the Gregory-Aland number 2882.

The manuscript contains all of Luke except for 22.5b–35, a single leaf which was the first leaf of an original 8-leaf quire. It would have been a double-leaf, constituting the outer double-leaf of the quire, with Luke 22.5b–35 on the front leaf and John 1.1ff most likely on the back leaf. The MS currently ends with the kephalaia for John and a hymn about the evangelist on 46b.

Part III

Functional Greek

In this third and final section of *Greek for the Rest of Us*, we will become functional in the use of traditional Greek-English interlinears. In order to do so, we must learn a lot more technical information about Greek. It is critrical that you do as much of the homework as you possibly can. Practice is what will cement the knowledge in your head, and you should go to the online class for many examples and assignments. Our specific goals are:

- Finish intermediate Greek grammar (nouns and verbs)

- Learn to phrase in Greek

- Tie everything together by looking at translational differences

Chapter 22

Pronouns

Now that we are into Greek-English interlinears, it is time to make sure your knowledge of the pronouns is well established. These words occurs with a high frequency and with some flexibility of meaning.

First and Second Person Personal Pronouns

22.1 If you did not memorize the Greek personal pronouns in Church Greek, you need to do so now.

	first person			*second person*		
nom sg	ἐγώ		I	σύ		you
gen sg	μου	(ἐμοῦ)	my	σου	(σοῦ)	your
dat sg	μοι	(ἐμοί)	to me	σοι	(σοί)	to you
acc sg	με	(ἐμέ)	me	σε	(σέ)	you
nom pl	ἡμεῖς		we	ὑμεῖς		you
gen pl	ἡμῶν		our	ὑμῶν		your
dat pl	ἡμῖν		to us	ὑμῖν		to you
acc pl	ἡμᾶς		us	ὑμᾶς		you

22.2 When the genitive of these pronouns is used to show possession, they generally follow the noun they modify.

John 20:28 ὁ κύριός μου καὶ ὁ θεός μου
Lord *my* and God *my*
My Lord and *my* God.

22.3 **Accents.** In the first person singular, the genitive, dative, and accusative cases will sometimes include an epsilon and an accent (ἐμοῦ, ἐμοί, ἐμέ). The second person pronoun will not add an epsilon but it can add an accent (σοῦ, σοί, σέ). These accented forms are called the **emphatic** forms.

The emphatic and unemphatic forms have the same basic meaning. The emphatic form is used when the author wants to be especially emphatic, often in contrasting one person with another.

John 13:35 ἐμοὶ μαθηταί ἐστε, ἐὰν ἀγάπην ἔχητε ἐν ἀλλήλοις.
to me disciples you are if love you have to one another
You are my disciples, if you have love for one another."

Emphatic forms also tend to be used after prepositions.

Mt 26:10 ἔργον γὰρ καλὸν ἠργάσατο εἰς ἐμέ.
Thing for good she has done to me
For she has done a beautiful thing *to me.*

Enclitics, Proclitics, and Double Accents

22.4 Generally, there is one accent per word. However, there are times you may have seen where a word has two accents and another has no accent. What are these?

22.5 An **enclitic** is a word that was pronounced so closely with the *preceeding* word that it moved its accent back to that word, which can produce one word with two accents and the enclitic with none. Common enclitics you know are μοῦ, μοί, μέ, σοῦ, σοί, σέ, τις, and most forms of εἰμί.

Matt 1:20 τὸ γὰρ ἐν αὐτῇ γεννηθὲν ἐκ πνεύματός ἐστιν ἁγίου.
the for in her conceived by spirit *is* holy
For that which has been conceived in her *is* by the Holy Spirit

ἐστιν loses its accent to πνεύματός.

22.6 A **proclitic** connects itself to the *following* word, and is only accented when that word pushes its own accent back to the proclitic. Common proclitics you know are are ὁ, ἡ, οἱ, αἱ, εἰς, ἐκ, ἐν, εἰ, ὡς, and οὐ. Technically, all prepositions are proclitics.

Matt 12:35 ὁ ἀγαθὸς ἄνθρωπος ἐκ τοῦ ἀγαθοῦ θησαυροῦ ἐκβάλλει ἀγαθά.
the good man *out of* the good treasure brings good things
NRSV: *The* good person brings good things *out of* a good treasure.

αὐτός

22.7 If you did not memorize αὐτός in Church Greek, you need to do so now.

	masc	*fem*	*neut*	*translation as the personal pronoun*		
nom sg	αὐτός	αὐτή	αὐτό	he	she	it
gen sg	αὐτοῦ	αὐτῆς	αὐτοῦ	his	her	its
dat sg	αὐτῷ	αὐτῇ	αὐτῷ	to him	to her	to it
acc sg	αὐτόν	αὐτήν	αὐτό	him	her	it
nom pl	αὐτοί	αὐταί	αὐτά	they		
gen pl	αὐτῶν	αὐτῶν	αὐτῶν	their		
dat pl	αὐτοῖς	αὐταῖς	αὐτοῖς	to them		
acc pl	αὐτούς	αὐτάς	αὐτά	them		

22.8 There are three uses of αὐτός. The most common is as the **third person personal pronoun** (meaning shown above).

22.9 When αὐτοῦ and other genitive forms such as αὐτῶν are indicating possession (e.g., "his"), like μου and σου they tend to follow the word they are modifying.

> *Matt 2:14* παρέλαβεν τὸ παιδίον καὶ τὴν μητέρα αὐτοῦ νυκτὸς
> he took   the   child   and   *mother*   his   by night
> He took the child and *his mother* by night.

22.10 In translation, αὐτός is sometimes replaced by its antecedent, usually for one of two reasons.

- There might be confusion in reading the text if the translator simply writes "he." For example, in Matt 8:24, who was the "he" who was sleeping?

   Suddenly a furious storm came up on the lake, so that the waves swept over the boat. But *Jesus* was sleeping (αὐτὸς δὲ ἐκάθευδεν) (NIV).

   The Greek only has "he (αὐτὸς) was sleeping," and the NIV inserts "Jesus."

- Sometimes at the beginning of a paragraph, the simple translation of αὐτός as "he" might also be confusing. This is especially true if the translators think the reader will be working with this one paragraph and not in the context of the preceding paragraphs. On Matthew 9:10 the ESV writes,

   And as Jesus (αὐτοῦ) reclined at table in the house, behold, many tax collectors and sinners came and were reclining with Jesus and his disciples.

   The footnote on the first "Jesus" reads, "Greek *he*."

22.11 Adjectival intensive. αὐτός can function intensively when it is used adjectivally.[1] The closest construction we have in English is the reflexive pronoun (himself, herself, itself, themselves, etc.).

In this usage, αὐτός modifies another word and is usually in the predicate position. αὐτὸς ὁ ἀπόστολος → the apostle himself. αὐτὸ τὸ δῶρον → the gift itself.

Mark 6:17	Αὐτὸς γὰρ ὁ Ἡρῴδης	ἀποστείλας	ἐκράτησεν	τὸν Ἰωάννην.	
	himself For Herod	sending	seized	John.	

For Herod *himself* had sent for and arrested John.

αὐτός agrees with the noun it modifies in case, number, and gender. In English, choose the gender of the reflexive pronoun based on the natural gender of the word αὐτός modifies. ἐγὼ αὐτός → I myself. ἡ ἐκκλησία αὐτή → the church itself/herself.

Do not confuse this with the predicate position of an adjective. When an adjective is in the predicate position, you must insert the verb "to be." When αὐτός is functioning as an adjectival intensive, it is modifying the noun.

ὁ Ἰησοῦς ἀγαθός	Jesus is good (predicate position)
αὐτὸς ὁ Ἰησοῦς	Jesus himself (adjectival intensive)

22.12 When functioning as an intensive, αὐτός is usually in the nominative case and modifies the subject.

Mark 12.36	αὐτὸς	Δαυὶδ	εἶπεν	ἐν	τῷ πνεύματι τῷ	ἁγίῳ	
	himself	David	spoke	by	the Holy	the Spirit.	

David *himself* spoke by the Holy Spirit

John 4:2	Ἰησοῦς	αὐτὸς	οὐκ	ἐβάπτιζεν	ἀλλ'	οἱ	μαθηταὶ αὐτοῦ.	
	Jesus	*himself*	not	was baptizing	but	the	disciples his	

Jesus *himself* was not baptizing, but his disciples.

22.13 The subject of the verb does not have to be third person. When used with the first or second person, αὐτός still adds emphasis.

σὺ	αὐτὸς	λέγεις	τοῖς	ἀνθρώποις.
You	*yourself*	speak	to	the men.

You *yourself* say to the men.

Different suggestions are made on how to translate this use of αὐτός. Some suggest using a reflexive pronoun as in the illustrations above. It is David himself and not

---

[1] *Accordance* lists 143 occurrences in the New Testament of αὐτός as the adjectival intensive pronoun, but it includes the uses of αὐτός as the identical adjective (below). It lists 14t as a reflexive pronoun.

someone else who spoke by the Holy Spirit. The argument is that this use of αὐτός is unnecessary and therefore its presence is emphatic. Others suggest ignoring the intensive use of αὐτός because this translation does not sound proper to English ears and feels a bit over-translated.

22.14 **Identical adjective**. αὐτός is sometimes used as the identical adjective meaning "same." This is its least frequent usage. It is normally in the attributive position when used this way, but not always.[2] Its case, number, and gender are determined by the word it modifies, as with any adjective.

> *Mark 14:39*   καὶ πάλιν ἀπελθὼν   προσηύξατο τὸν αὐτὸν λόγον
> And   again   after going away he prayed   *the*   *same*   *word*.
> And again, after going away, He prayed the *same* prayer.

Demonstratives

22.15 The demonstrative pronouns in Greek are οὗτος ("this/these"; occurs 1,387 times) and ἐκεῖνος ("that/those"; occurs 265 times). They function the same way as the demonstratives do in English, both as pronouns and as adjectives.

22.16 If a demonstrative is functioning as an adjective, it will be anarthrous. In other words, it will be in the predicate position.

οὗτος ὁ ἄνθρωπος	αὕτη ἡ γυνή
This man	This woman
ὁ ἄνθρωπος οὗτος	ἡ γυνή αὕτη
This man	This woman
ἐκεῖνοι οἱ ἄνθρωποι	ἐκεῖναι αἱ γυναικός
Those men	Those women

This is the opposite of regular adjectives, so do not get them confused. The noun that the demonstrative adjective modifies will always have the article.

> *Matt 4:3*   εἰπὲ ἵνα οἱ λίθοι οὗτοι   ἄρτοι γένωνται.
> say   that stones *these*   bread become
> Tell *these* stones to become bread.

> *Matt 3:1*   Ἐν δὲ ταῖς ἡμέραις ἐκείναις   παραγίνεται Ἰωάννης ὁ βαπτιστὴς
> in   but days   *those*   appeared   John   the Baptist
> Now in *those* days, John the Baptist appeared.

---

2   αὐτός is found in the attributive position 60 times in the New Testament.

22.17 If a demonstrative is functioning as a pronoun, translators will sometimes add in words to make proper English, but not always (as is true of any adjective).

Matt 9:3   τινες τῶν γραμματέων εἶπαν ἐν   ἑαυτοῖς· οὗτος βλασφημεῖ.
some   of the scribes   said   to   themselves *this*   blasphemes

NRSV: Some of the scribes said to themselves, "*This man* is blaspheming."
NIV: Some of the teachers of the law said to themselves, "*This fellow* is blaspheming!"

Matt 3:17   οὗτός ἐστιν ὁ υἱός μου ὁ   ἀγαπητός
this   is   son   my   the   beloved

This is my beloved son.

22.18 Sometimes the demonstrative pronoun weakens in its force and functions as a personal pronoun.

Luke 1:32   οὗτος ἔσται   μέγας καὶ   υἱὸς ὑψίστου   κληθήσεται
this   will be   great   and   son   of Most High   he will be called

He will be great and will be called "Son of the Most High."

Matt 13:11   ἐκείνοις δὲ οὐ δέδοται.
to those   but not   is given

But *to them* it is not given.

22.19 There are two other common adjectives that function attributively in the predicate position: πᾶς and ὅλος.

1 Tim 2:4   ὃς   πάντας ἀνθρώπους θέλει   σωθῆναι
who   *all*   people   wishes   to be saved

Who wishes *all* people to be saved

Titus 1:11   οὓς   δεῖ   ἐπιστομίζειν, οἵτινες ὅλους οἴκους   ἀνατρέπουσιν
whom   it is necessary   to muzzle   who   *entire*   households   are upsetting

It is therefore necessary to muzzle those who are upsetting *entire* households.

Vocabulary and Exercises

22.20 There is vocabulary for this chapter in the online class, and all the exercises are available on the class' website, at:

www.teknia.com/functionalgreek

Chapter 23

Definite Article, and Odds 'n Ends

23.1 ὁ, which we usually call the Greek "definite article" or just the "article," is much more than the word "the." It actually has one of the widest ranges of meaning of all Greek words.

23.2 The function of ὁ is *not* to make something definite that would otherwise be indefinite. This is a common mistake in exegesis. We have already seen ὁ used in the first three situations below.

23.3 ὁ can function as the definite article.

Luke 5:33 οἱ μαθηταὶ   Ἰωάννου   νηστεύουσιν   πυκνά
             the disciples   of John   fast   often
             The disciples of John often fast.

23.4 Greek uses ὁ when English does not use the definite article, such as with proper names.

Matt 3:15 ἀποκριθεὶς   δὲ   ὁ   Ἰησοῦς   εἶπεν   πρὸς   αὐτόν
             answering   but   *the*   Jesus   said   to   him
             NASB: But Jesus answering said to him

23.5 Greek doesn't use ὁ when English requires the definite article, in which case the translator can add it back in. This is especially true in prepositional phrases.

John 1:1 Ἐν   ἀρχῇ   ἦν   ὁ   λόγος
            in   beginning   was   the   Word
            NIV: In *the* beginning was the Word.

23.6 ὁ can also function as a grammatical marker, for example showing that the following word modifies the previous word. I will discuss this in the next chapter.

Mark 8:38 μετὰ   τῶν   ἀγγέλων   τῶν   ἁγίων.
             with   the   angels   *the*   holy
             with the holy angels

23.7 ὁ can function as a personal pronoun.

Matt 12:3   ὁ   δὲ   εἶπεν   αὐτοῖς·   οὐκ   ἀνέγνωτε   τί   ἐποίησεν   Δαυὶδ
the   but   said   to them   not   you read   what   did   David
But *he* said to them, "Have you not read what David did?"

Luke 5:33   Οἱ   δὲ   εἶπαν   πρὸς   αὐτόν
the   and   said   to   him
NASB: And *they* said to Him

23.8 ὁ can function as a possessive pronoun.

Eph 5:25   Οἱ   ἄνδρες,   ἀγαπᾶτε   τὰς   γυναῖκας
the   men   love!   *the*   wives
NASB: Husbands, love *your* wives.

23.9 Sometimes ὁ functions with a word or phrase, in essence turning the construction into a substantive or a modifier.

Matt 5::3   Μακάριοι   οἱ   πτωχοὶ   τῷ πνεύματι
blessed   *the*   poor   *in spirit*
Blessed are *the poor in spirit*.

πτωχοί is an adjective functioning with οἱ as a noun.

Matt 2:2   ποῦ   ἐστιν   ὁ   τεχθεὶς   βασιλεὺς   τῶν Ἰουδαίων;
where   is   *the*   *being born*   king   *of the Jews*
Where is *the one who is born King of the Jews*?

τεχθείς is a participle functioning with ὁ as a noun.

Luke 7:32   ὅμοιοί   εἰσιν   παιδίοις   τοῖς   ἐν   ἀγορᾷ   καθημένοις
like   they are   children   *who*   *in*   *marketplace*   *sitting*
NASB: They are like children *who sit in the market place*.
NIV: They are like children *sitting in the marketplace*.

τοῖς … καθημένοις is functioning as a noun, and is modified by the prepositional phrase ἐν ἀγορᾷ.

As I have said before, don't be surprised to find a lot of flexibility in translating ὁ.

Diacriticals

23.10 Because this has been a short chapter, this is a good place to cover a few other points. In some words we find two vowels that normally form a diphthong, but in a few cases both vowels are pronounced. To show that these two vowels are pronounced as two separate sounds, a **diaeresis** (¨) is placed over the second vowel. This is like the French word *naïve* that was brought over into English.

Ἡσαΐας (Ἡ-σα-ΐ-ας) means Isaiah.

23.11 Sometimes the final vowel of a word drops off, and the word is marked for **elison** with an apostrophe (ἀλλα → ἀλλ'). English does something similar (e.g., "was not" → "wasn't").

Punctuation

23.12 If the last syllable of a word has an acute accent and that word is not followed by a punctuation mark, the acute becomes a grave.

καί εἰρήνη → καὶ εἰρήνη

When a commentator cites a single word that has a grave (e.g., καὶ), the grave is returned to the acute (καί).

Lexical forms

23.13 We have seen that most people list the lexical form of verbs in the first person singular, present indicative (λέγω, "I say"). However, some of the older grammars and some modern commentaries list the infinitive form as the lexical form (λέγειν, "to say").

Postpositives

23.14 A postpositive is a word that cannot occur as the first word in the Greek clause. They usually are the second word, sometimes third, and rarely fourth (or more). We usually translate these words as the first word in the English clause.

23.15 The postpositives you know are γάρ, δέ, and οὖν.

Gal 6:5	ἕκαστος	γὰρ	τὸ ἴδιον	φορτίον	βαστάσει.
	each	for	his own	load	will carry

For each one will bear his own load.

Matt. 27:39   Οἱ   δὲ   παραπορευόμενοι   ἐβλασφήμουν   αὐτὸν   κινοῦντες   τὰς   κεφαλὰς   αὐτῶν.
those *and* passing by   derided   him   wagging   heads   their
And those who passed by derided him, wagging their heads.

1 Tim 3:2   δεῖ   οὖν   τὸν ἐπίσκοπον   ἀνεπίλημπτον   εἶναι
it is necessary   *therefore*   the elder   above reproach   to be
Therefore, it is necessary for the elder to be above reproach.

Subject and Predicate

23.16 A sentence can be broken into two basic parts, the subject and the predicate. (I am sorry we don't have a different word than "subject" since it gets confused with the "subject" of the verb, but nobody checked with me when these grammatical terms were created!)

23.17 The **subject** is the subject of the main verb and anything that modifies it. Consider this sentence.

> The great big dog lying under the table is licking my toes.

"Dog" is the subject of the verb "is licking," and "The great big dog lying under the table" is considered the subject of the entire sentence.

23.18 The **predicate** is everything else, including the main verb. In the sentence above, "is licking my toes" is the predicate. It contains the verb "is licking," the direct object "toes," and an adjectival modifier "my."

Types of Sentences

23.19 There are different types of sentences, grammatically. A **simple** sentence has one subject and one verb.

> I love Greek!

The subject and/or the verb can be compound.

> Kiersten and I love Greek and Hebrew.

23.20 A **compound** sentence has two or more independent clauses connected with a coordinating conjunction or punctuation.

> Kiersten loves Greek and Tyler loves Hebrew.
>
> Kiersten loves Greek; Tyler loves Hebrew.

23.21 A **complex** sentence has one independent clauses and one (or more) dependent clauses.

> Whenever I think back to Hebrew class, I start to sweat.

23.22 A **compound-complex** sentence has two (or more) independent clauses and one (or more) dependent clauses.

> I went to class and Hayden went home because he was tired.

23.23 Greek is a **hypotactic** language. This means that it tends toward having a main clause with a series of dependent clauses or participial phrases modifying it. This is opposed to a language like English and to a greater degree Hebrew, which are **paratactic**. These languages are more linear, tending to link one independent clause to the next with coordinating conjunctions such as "and" and "but." Greek narrative tends to be more paratactic, especially John, but not Paul.

This is why understanding clauses and phrases and how they relate to each other is so important; it is a reflection of the way the language is written.

Word order

23.24 It is difficult to speak of "normal" Greek word order, since most Greek sentences do not follow it. But in a general sense, the normal word order is conjunction, verb, subject, object.

23.25 Why would a Greek speaker alter the order? Mostly for emphasis. If they wanted to emphasize a word, they would tend to move it to an "unusual" location, normally forward in the sentence. Sometimes English can translate the nuance of the word order, but normally not. What is the point of the word order here?

1 Tim 2:4	πάντας	ἀνθρώπους	θέλει	σωθῆναι
	all	people	he wishes	to be saved

ESV: [God] desires *all* people to be saved.

Eph 2:8   Τῇ   γὰρ χάριτί   ἐστε   σεσωσμένοι
by   for *grace*   you are   having been saved
NASB: For *by grace* you have been saved.
NIV: For *it is by grace* you have been saved.

Idioms

23.26   Idioms are collections of words, usually two, that have a special meaning when the words occur together, a meaning that the words don't have when they are isolated.

- εἰ μή means "except" or "unless," even though the two words separately mean "if" "not."

- διὰ τοῦτο, "through this," means "on account of this" or "therefore."

Noun phrases

23.27   I haven't used this term before, but I am thinking of phrases that are not prepositional or participial, but nonetheless have an internally consistent meaning. It is important to view them as units of thought when phrasing.

23.28   Dative noun phrases can stand somewhat on their own, like τῷ κόσμῳ, "to the world."

Matt 18:7   Οὐαὶ   τῷ   κόσμῳ   ἀπὸ   τῶν   σκανδάλων.
woe   *to the*   *world*   from   the   enticements
Woe *to the world* because of the things that cause people to sin!

23.29   Genitive noun phrases are generally modifying something.

Matt 4:8   δείκνυσιν   αὐτῷ   πάσας   τὰς βασιλείας   τοῦ κόσμου   καὶ   τὴν δόξαν   αὐτῶν
he showed   him   all   the kingdoms   *of the world*   and   glory   their
He showed him all the kingdoms *of the world* and their splendor.

23.30   Related are phrases that stand in apposition to a noun. Be sure to identify the beginning and end of these phrases.

John 3:1   Ἦν   δὲ ἄνθρωπος … Νικόδημος   ὄνομα   αὐτῷ,   ἄρχων   τῶν Ἰουδαίων.
there was   and man …   *Nicodemus*   *name*   *to him ruler*   *of the Jews*
And there was a man …, *his name was Nicodemus, a ruler of the Jews.*

Νικόδημος ὄνομα αὐτῷ is in apposition to ἄνθρωπος, and ἄρχων τῶν Ἰουδαίων is in apposition to Νικόδημος.

Chapter 24

Adjectives

English

24.1 As we have seen, adjectives can function *adjectivally* —like a regular adjective, also called an *attributive* adjective.

> He is a *good* student.

24.2 An adjective can also function *substantivally* —as if it were a noun. In this case the adjective does not modify anything but performs a function in the sentence, such as the subject, direct object, etc.

> The *Good,* the *Bad,* and the *Ugly* are all welcome here.
>
> Out with the *old* and in with the *new.*

Substantival adjectives get their number and gender from the word they stand for. Their case is determined by usage. If they are the subject, they will be in the subjective case; if they are the direct object, they will be in the objective case.

24.3 Adjectives can appear in the predicate, which means they occur after the verb.

> The Bible is *black.*

Greek Adjective

24.4 Greek adjectives are not always right before the noun as in English. Because reverse interlinears follow English order, this has not been an issue for you. But because Functional Greek uses Greek-English interlinears, you need to understand the basics of what is happening with Greek adjectives.

24.5 There are two grammatical terms you need to know.

- If a word is preceded by ὁ, we say the word is *articular.*
- If a word is not preceded by ὁ, we say the word is *anarthrous.*

Attributive adjectives tend to be articular; predicate adjectives are anarthrous.

24.6 **First Attributive Postion**. Greek can use adjectives in the order article–modifier–substantive.

Phil 1:15 ἀπὸ τῆς πρώτης ἡμέρας ἄχρι τοῦ νῦν
from the *first* day until the now
from the *first* day until now

It is easy to see that τῆς πρώτης ἡμέρας means "the first day," with τῆς meaning "the," πρώτης being the adjective, and ἡμέρας the noun. It is easy because this is how English does it.

24.7 **Second Attributive Postion**. Greek often lists the adjective in the order article–noun–article–adjective.

Eph 4:30 τὸ πνεῦμα τὸ ἅγιον
the spirit the *holy*
The *Holy* Spirit

Greek could write "the Holy Spirit" or "the Spirit the Holy" with no significant difference in meaning. In *IRU* these two phrases have been listed like this.

the	Holy	Spirit
τὸ	⌞τὸ ἅγιον⌟	πνεῦμα
	a.asn	n.asn
	41	4460

As you can see, I kept the second article with its adjective. But from now on you will see the Greek word order.

What these two attributive positions have in common is that the attributive adjective is articular in both.

24.8 **Predicate Position**. As in English, the Greek anarthrous adjective can be in the predicate, and there does not have to be an explicit verb in the Greek sentence (although there may be). The translator will have added the verb, normally a form of the verb "to be."

Matt 7:13 πλατεῖα ἡ πύλη καὶ εὐρύχωρος ἡ ὁδὸς
wide the gate and easy the way
The gate *is* wide and the way *is* easy.

The **first predicate position** is adjective–article–noun.

Matt 5:9 μακάριοι οἱ εἰρηνοποιοί
blessed the peacemakers
Blessed *are* the peacemakers.

The **second predicate position** is article–noun–adjective.

Matt 5:12   χαίρετε καὶ ἀγαλλιᾶσθε, ὅτι ὁ μισθὸς ὑμῶν πολὺς
           rejoice and be glad   for the reward your *great*
           Rejoice and be glad, for your reward *is great.*

John 3:33   ὁ θεὸς ἀληθής ἐστιν.
           God   is   *true*
           God is *true.*

Substantival

24.9   Greek adjectives can function substantivally. Their gender and number are determined by the word they stand for; their case is determined by their function in the sentence.

It is often necessary to add a word to the translation to make sense of this usage, and it is usually clear from context what word needs to be added. In Matthew 1:19, δίκαιος is an adjective meaning "righteous." If the translator's sense of English wants to treat the adjective substantivally, you need to add a word like "man."

Matt 1:19   Ἰωσὴφ δὲ ὁ ἀνὴρ αὐτῆς, δίκαιος ὢν
           Joseph but the husband of her   righteous   being
           NIV 1984: Because Joseph her husband was a righteous *man*
           NLT: Joseph, her fiancé, was a good *man.*

24.10   The most famous example of a possible substantival adjective is from the Lord's Prayer. The question is, are we to pray that we be delivered from evil, or from the evil one, i.e., Satan? πονηροῦ is an adjective meaning "evil."

Matt 6:13   ῥῦσαι ἡμᾶς ἀπὸ τοῦ πονηροῦ
           deliver us   from the   *evil*
           NASB: Deliver us from evil.
           NIV: Deliver us from the evil *one.*

In adding "one," the NIV is not adding to Scripture. This is simply how language functions, and these words are often necessary if you are going to say in one language what was said in another.

Anarthrous

24.11 Sometimes both the noun and the adjective will be anarthrous; there will be no article helping you see if the adjective is functioning as an attributive, substantive, or predicate. In this situation, let context be your guide. What fits the context?

Matt 3:15   πρέπον ἐστὶν ἡμῖν πληρῶσαι πᾶσαν δικαιοσύνην.
             fitting   it is for us to fulfill *all*   *righteousness*
             It is fitting for us to fulfill *all righteousness.*

πᾶσαν is giving an attribute of δικαιοσύνην.

Luke 11:34   ἐπὰν δὲ πονηρὸς ᾖ, καὶ τὸ σῶμά σου σκοτεινόν
              when but bad   is and the body your *darkness*
              ESV: But when it is bad, your body *is full of darkness.*

Context shows that σκοτεινόν is in the predicate, with σῶμά as the subject.

Degrees of an adjective

24.12 An adjective can have three "degrees."

- The *positive* degree is the uncompared form of the adjective: "large" (μέγας).

- The *comparative* degree denotes the greater of two items: "larger" (μείζων).

- The *superlative* degree describes the greatest, or a comparison of three or more: "largest" (μέγιστος).

24.13 In Koine Greek the superlative was dying out and its function was being assumed by the comparative. For example, someone might use μείζων when context technically requires μέγιστος. As usual, context is the key in translation (*BNTS*, 131-35).

Chapter 25

Phrases and Clauses

Prepositional Phrases

25.1 We have seen that Greek regularly drops ὁ in a prepositional phrase. "In the world" could be written in Greek as ἐν τῷ κόσμῳ, or without ὁ, as ἐν κόσμῳ. In this situation, and if it fits the context, the translator may put the article back in.

> *Rom 5:13*   ἁμαρτία ἦν ἐν κόσμῳ
>   sin   was in world
>   NIV: Sin was in *the* world.

25.2 Earlier I showed you that adjectives can occur in the "article–noun–article–adjective" position. Actually, that last word should be "modifier": article–noun–article–modifier. Even a prepositional phrase can act as a modifier.

> *Phil 2:9*   τὸ ὄνομα τὸ ὑπὲρ πᾶν ὄνομα
>   the name   *the* *above* *every* *name*
>   RSV: the name *which is above every name*

The second τό shows that the following prepositional phrase (ὑπὲρ πᾶν ὄνομα) modifies the preceding noun (ὄνομα).

When a prepositional phrase functions attributively, it is normally in the second attributive position.

Other times the article will not be translated, which is fine since all it is doing is showing that the following phrase is modifying the previous word.

> *Phil 3:11*   τὴν ἐξανάστασιν τὴν ἐκ νεκρῶν
>   the resurrection   *the* *from* *dead*
>   RSV: the resurrection *from the dead*

The second τὴν shows that ἐκ νεκρῶν modifies ἐξανάστασιν.

Because we do not have the same construction in English, translations handle this situation in different ways. Usually the "article + prepositional phrase" is turned into a relative clause, which means a verb must be added.

Matt 5:12 οὕτως γὰρ ἐδίωξαν τοὺς προφήτας τοὺς πρὸ ὑμῶν.
in this way for they persecuted the prophets *the* before you

For that is how they persecuted the prophets *who were before you.*

The articular (τοὺς) prepositional phrase πρὸ ὑμῶν is in an attributive position to προφήτας.

25.3 Like adjectives, an articular prepositional phrase can function substantivally.

Mark 3:34 περιβλεψάμενος τοὺς περὶ αὐτὸν κύκλῳ καθημένους
looking around at *the* around him in a circle sitting

Looking around at *those who were sitting around him in a circle*

Participial phrases

25.4 A participial phrase can also function attributively.

Matt 2:18 Ῥαχὴλ κλαίουσα τὰ τέκνα αὐτῆς
Rachel *weeping* the children her

Rachel, *weeping for her children*

The anarthrous participle κλαίουσα is modifying Ῥαχὴλ.

25.5 When used with ὁ, the participial phrase will normally be in the second attributive position.

Matt 4:16 ὁ λαὸς ὁ καθήμενος ἐν σκότει φῶς εἶδεν μέγα.
the people *the* sitting in darkness light saw great

The people *living in darkness* have seen a great light.

25.6 Like adjectives, a participial phrase can function substantivally.

Matt 5:4 μακάριοι οἱ πενθοῦντες, ὅτι αὐτοὶ παρακληθήσονται.
blessed *the* mourning for they will be comforted

Blessed are *those who mourn*, for they will be comforted.

In this verse, the participial phrase is functioning as the predicate nominative.

Clauses

25.7 If a translator wants to break a long Greek sentence into multiple sentences, the break will almost always come between clauses, and this will often necessitate adding some words to the clause to make it into a sentence. For example, the NIV adds "I pray" to the beginning of Ephesians 3:16 since in Greek it is a content clause (ἵνα) and not a complete sentence.

> *I pray* that (ἵνα) out of his glorious riches he may strengthen you with power through his Spirit in your inner being.

Relative Clause

25.8 Relative pronouns can be changed to indefinite relative pronouns (e.g., to "whoever, whichever, whatever") when they are followed by ἄν (or an alternate form such as ἐάν).

> Matt 5:19. "*Anyone* (ὃς ἐὰν) who sets aside one of the least of these commands and teaches others accordingly will be called least in the kingdom of heaven, but *whoever* (ὃς ἐὰν) practices and teaches these commands will be called great in the kingdom of heaven" (NIV).

25.9 In your phrasing, always connect a relative pronoun to its antecedent. Remember, the relative pronoun must agree with its antecedent in number and gender. So, for example, if the pronoun is masculine plural, look for an antecedent that is masculine plural.

25.10 When Greek relative clauses perform a function, it is often necessary for the translator to add a word to the clause to make better sounding English. For example, in the sentence "Who will be first will be last," the relative clause "Who will be first" is the subject of the verb "will be." To make the translation smoother you could add a word such as a personal pronoun, "*He* who will be first will be last."

> *John 1:26*   μέσος ὑμῶν ἕστηκεν   ὃν   ὑμεῖς οὐκ   οἴδατε
> midst of you stands   whom you   not   know
> NRSV: Among you stands *one* whom you do not know.
>
> The antecedent of ὃν is not expressed but only implied. This is not that unusual.

25.11 Because Greek is an inflected language, Greek writers are comfortable separating pronouns from their antecedents by quite some distance. The grammar would allow the Greek reader to see the pronoun's antecedent. However, English requires pronouns to be much closer to their antecedent. Because of this difference, translators sometimes substitute the antecedent for the pronoun if they think that the English reader might not be able to identify the pronoun's antecedent. Consider Romans 6:10.

Rom 6:10   ὃ   γὰρ ἀπέθανεν, τῇ   ἁμαρτίᾳ ἀπέθανεν ἐφάπαξ
             which *for* *he died,* *to the* *sin*   *he died*   *once for all*

KJV: For in *that* he died, he died unto sin once.
ESV: The *death* he died, he died to sin once for all.

For the pronoun ὅ, the ESV substitutes "death."

25.12 Sometimes a Greek sentence is too long and must be broken into smaller units for the sake of English style (cf. 25.7). When this is done, relative clauses are often used to start a new sentence, and in this case the antecedent is often supplied for the pronoun. A word-for-word translation of Romans 2:5b-6 reads like this:

ἀποκαλύψεως δικαιοκρισίας   τοῦ θεοῦ ὃς ἀποδώσει
revelation   *of righteous verdict* *of God* *who* *he will give judgment*

ἑκάστῳ   κατὰ   τὰ ἔργα   αὐτοῦ
to each *according to* *the works* *of him*

There is no question as to the identity of the "who" (ὅς), especially since it immediately follows "God" (θεοῦ). However, if the translators feel that the sentence is too long and they decide to start a new sentence at ὅς, the "who" becomes separated from its antecedent.

- The NASB does not start a new sentence,

  who will render to each person according to his deeds.

- The ESV starts a new paragraph at v 6 and so can't write "who." It says,

  He will render to each one according to his works.

- The NIV supplies the antecedent of the relative pronoun, without a footnote.

  God "will repay each person according to what they have done."

Sometimes the pronoun refers back to an idea in general, or to a group of words. In Colossians 2:23, the antecedents of the pronoun ἅ translated "such regulations" are those specifically mentioned in v 21. "Do not handle! Do not taste! Do not touch!" The NIV translates,

Such regulations indeed have an appearance of wisdom, with their self-imposed worship, their false humility and their harsh treatment of the body, but they lack any value in restraining sensual indulgence.

The translators are not "adding to" Scripture. The Greek makes the connection between pronoun and its antecedent(s) clear, and the translators don't want you to misunderstand.

25.13 **Attraction**. Greek, as is the case with any language, does not always follow its own rules. All spoken languages are in a constant state of flux, so nice, neat grammatical rules often break down.

This is the case with the relative pronoun. Its case is supposed to be determined by its function inside the relative clause, but in certain situations you will see that the relative pronoun is altered to be the same case as its antecedent, as if it were modifying it. This is called "attraction," and in this situation the relative pronoun is modifying the antecedent in gender, number, *and* case.

Attraction usually happens when the relative pronoun occurs in the immediate proximity to the antecedent, when the antecedent is dative or genitive, and when the relative pronoun normally would be accusative.

Acts 7:17	ἤγγιζεν	ὁ χρόνος	τῆς ἐπαγγελίας	ἧς	ὡμολόγησεν	ὁ θεὸς	τῷ Ἀβραάμ
	drew near	the time	of the promise	which	assured	God	to Abraham

The time of the promise *that* God assured to Abraham was drawing near.

The relative pronoun ἧς *should* have been the accusative ἥν because it is the direct object of ὡμολόγησεν, but it was attracted to the genitive case of its antecedent ἐπαγγελίας.

Conditional Sentences

25.14 We have seen that a "conditional sentence" is an "if… then… " type sentence. The "if" clause is called the **protasis**; the "then" clause is the **apodosis**. There are four basic types of conditional sentences in Greek based on their form, and each one has its own nuance of meaning.

Type	*Protasis*	*Apodosis*
First class	εἰ + indicative any tense	any mood or tense
Second class	εἰ + indicative past tense	(ἄν) + indicative past tense
Third class	ἐάν + subjunctive any tense	any mood or tense
Fourth class	εἰ + optative present or aorist	ἄν + optative present or aorist

25.15 **First class**. Also called a "condition of fact." The protasis begins with εἰ ("if") and the verb is in the indicative. These sentences are saying that if something is true, and let's assume for the sake of the argument that it is true, then such and such will occur.

Matt 5:29 εἰ   δὲ   ὁ ὀφθαλμός σου   ὁ δεξιὸς   σκανδαλίζει   σε,   ἔξελε   αὐτὸν
         if   but   the eye   your   right   causes to sin   you   tear out   it

If your right eye causes you to sin, tear it out.

Sometimes the apodosis is clearly true, and translators might use "since" instead of "if."[3] But it seems to me that there is often something to be gained by saying "if ..." even when you know it is true. It causes you to affirm the truthfulness of the apodosis.

Luke 4:3 εἰ υἱὸς εἶ   τοῦ θεοῦ, εἰπὲ τῷ λίθῳ   τούτῳ   ἵνα   γένηται   ἄρτος.
        if son you are of God   say   to the stone this   that it become   bread

NRSV: If you are the Son of God, command this stone to become a loaf of bread.

Satan certainly knew who Jesus was. However, there are times in which saying "if" makes something sound conditional when it is not.

Matt 12:28 εἰ   δὲ   ἐν   πνεύματι   θεοῦ   ἐγὼ   ἐκβάλλω   τὰ   δαιμόνια
          if   but   by   Spirit   of God   I   cast out   the demons

But if I, by the Spirit of God, cast out demons

Jesus knew he was casting out demons by God's Spirit.

25.16 **Second class**. Also called "contrary to fact." The protasis begins with εἰ ("if") and the verb is a past tense in the indicative. These sentences are saying that if something is true, even though it is not, then such and such would occur. The falseness of the protasis is assumed in the argument.

John 5:46 εἰ   γὰρ   ἐπιστεύετε   Μωϋσεῖ,   ἐπιστεύετε   ἂν   ἐμοί
         if   for   you believed   Moses   you believe   would   me

If you believed Moses, you would believe me.

---

[3] Wallace says that 37% of first class conditions could be translated this way, but argues that this is over-translating (*BNTS*, 310).

25.17 **Third class**. The protasis begins with ἐάν ("if") and the verb is in the subjunctive mood. There are two subcategories of the third class condition, although they are identical in form.

1. More Probable Future. Sometimes a third class condition is used to say that if some specific event in the future happens, and it is probable that it will, then something else will happen.

Mark 5:28   ἐὰν ἅψωμαι κἂν τῶν ἱματίων αὐτοῦ σωθήσομαι
            if   I touch   might   clothes   his   I will be healed
            If I can only touch his clothes, I will be healed.

She thought that if she could only touch Jesus' clothing—and it was likely that she could—then she would be healed.

Matt 4:9   ταῦτά σοι πάντα δώσω, ἐὰν πεσὼν προσκυνήσῃς μοι.
          these   to you   all   I will give   if   falling down   you worship   me
          All these I will give you, if you will fall down and worship me.

Did Satan really believe it was likely Jesus would do this? Seems unlikely, although we do not know what Satan did know and did not know about Jesus. Perhaps the use of this particular grammatical form was meant to suggest to Jesus that he might do this. Satan was wrong! This points to the problem of this label, "more probable." There are many examples in the Greek Testament where the "if" clause is not likely to happen.

2. Present General. This same form is also used to state a general truth, an axiomatic truth. The subjunctive mood is appropriate because the truth of the statement is timeless.

John 11:9   ἐάν τις περιπατῇ ἐν τῇ ἡμέρα, οὐ προσκόπτει
          if   anyone   walks   in   the day   not   he stumbles
          If anyone walks in the day, he does not stumble.

Jesus is not thinking of any particular event in the future; he is stating a general truth.

25.18 **Fourth class**. Also called a "less probable future" condition. The writer is saying that if something happens, and it is *not* likely to happen, then something else would happen. There is no complete illustration of this form in the New Testament. Moreover, it uses a mood you are not learning here—the optative mood.

You should also know that the forms of conditional sentences can be mixed, a protasis from one and an apodosis from another.

Chapter 26

Phrasing 103

By now you are experienced in phrasing, and in doing so you are learning how to understand the better commentaries. But Greek answers many mysteries of the phrasing world, and it is time to jump in to Greek phrasing. We are going to start with John 3, and in Phrasing 104 we will graduate to Ephesians 1.

26.1   Be sure to work through the exercises for this chapter in the online class. It is crucial to develop the right habits for using Greek-English interlinears, and so I have made a large number of screen casts where you can watch me walk through the verses.

26.2   Also, please be patient with yourself. Now that we are moving into the Greek text, you are going to see many things that will not make sense to you. Some of them will still be explained in the remaining chapters of this book. But others will just have to be skipped since no approach to first and second year Greek is able to teach you everything.

Preparing the Greek text

26.3   Start by preparing the text. Here are the steps I take.

- Copy the Greek text into your word processor.

- I remove all of the verse references except the book and chapter.

- Put a tab between the reference and the text

- Set your hanging indent to half an inch

- Set each paragraph to have a little space above each paragraph; I use 6 points.

- I place a tab at an inch so I don't have to click on every phrase and set a tab. Be sure you do not use spaces to align the phrases; use tabs.

This is just how I do it; you can formulate your own procedure. You can see a sample of my formatting on the next page.

3:1   Ἦν δὲ ἄνθρωπος ἐκ τῶν Φαρισαίων, Νικόδημος ὄνομα αὐτῷ, ἄρχων τῶν Ἰουδαίων·

3:2   οὗτος ἦλθεν πρὸς αὐτὸν νυκτὸς καὶ εἶπεν αὐτῷ· ῥαββί, οἴδαμεν ὅτι ἀπὸ θεοῦ ἐλήλυθας διδάσκαλος· οὐδεὶς γὰρ δύναται ταῦτα τὰ σημεῖα ποιεῖν ἃ σὺ ποιεῖς, ἐὰν μὴ ᾖ ὁ θεὸς μετ' αὐτοῦ.

3:3   ἀπεκρίθη Ἰησοῦς καὶ εἶπεν αὐτῷ· ἀμὴν ἀμὴν λέγω σοι, ἐὰν μή τις γεννηθῇ ἄνωθεν, οὐ δύναται ἰδεῖν τὴν βασιλείαν τοῦ θεοῦ.

3:4   λέγει πρὸς αὐτὸν [ὁ] Νικόδημος· πῶς δύναται ἄνθρωπος γεννηθῆναι γέρων ὤν; μὴ δύναται εἰς τὴν κοιλίαν τῆς μητρὸς αὐτοῦ δεύτερον εἰσελθεῖν καὶ γεννηθῆναι;

3:5   ἀπεκρίθη Ἰησοῦς· ἀμὴν ἀμὴν λέγω σοι, ἐὰν μή τις γεννηθῇ ἐξ ὕδατος καὶ πνεύματος, οὐ δύναται εἰσελθεῖν εἰς τὴν βασιλείαν τοῦ θεοῦ.

3:6   τὸ γεγεννημένον ἐκ τῆς σαρκὸς σάρξ ἐστιν, καὶ τὸ γεγεννημένον ἐκ τοῦ πνεύματος πνεῦμά ἐστιν.

3:7   μὴ θαυμάσῃς ὅτι εἶπόν σοι· δεῖ ὑμᾶς γεννηθῆναι ἄνωθεν.

3:8   τὸ πνεῦμα ὅπου θέλει πνεῖ καὶ τὴν φωνὴν αὐτοῦ ἀκούεις, ἀλλ' οὐκ οἶδας πόθεν ἔρχεται καὶ ποῦ ὑπάγει· οὕτως ἐστὶν πᾶς ὁ γεγεννημένος ἐκ τοῦ πνεύματος.

3:9   ἀπεκρίθη Νικόδημος καὶ εἶπεν αὐτῷ· πῶς δύναται ταῦτα γενέσθαι;

3:10   ἀπεκρίθη Ἰησοῦς καὶ εἶπεν αὐτῷ· σὺ εἶ ὁ διδάσκαλος τοῦ Ἰσραὴλ καὶ ταῦτα οὐ γινώσκεις;

Configuring your interlinear

26.4   The starting point is to get your interlinear set up the way you want to use it. How you do this depends greatly on what software package you are using. I will be illustrating using Accordance, but you are able to do the same types of things in Logos, The Bible Study App (OliveTree), WORDsearch, and some online sites.

26.5   Start by cleaning up your window, removing all but one zone and one text. Then select the Greek text, find John 1:1, and choose Show Interlinear.

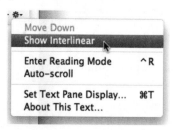

26.6 Click on the interlinear button and select what you want displayed in the interlinear. My encouragement is to display the Greek text, key number, lemma, part of speech, tag, and a couple English translations (which must be Key number texts).

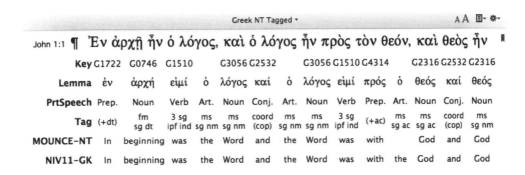

26.7 Finally, you should save this format so you can choose it quickly for further study. Click the interlinear button, go to the bottom, and select Save as New Interlinear.

Give it a name. When you want to use it, select it from the menu.

Time to play

26.8 You need to give yourself some time to get used to the interlinear. Be sure the Instant Details window is open so you can see the parsings as you mouse over words (see next page).

As you get used to the interlinear, you may find that you want to display different items. For example, if you are comfortable seeing the parsings in the Instant Details window, you can remove them from the interlinear display.

On the next two pages you can see a few other software programs and their interlinears.

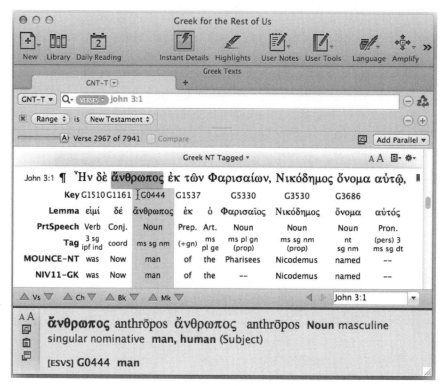

Accordance

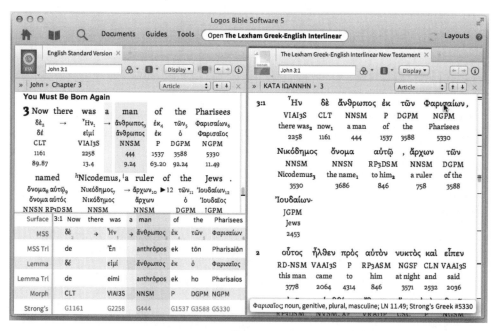

Logos

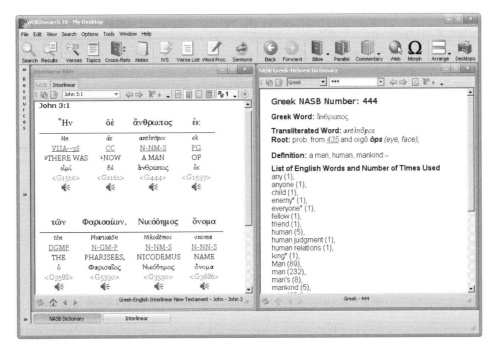

WORDsearch

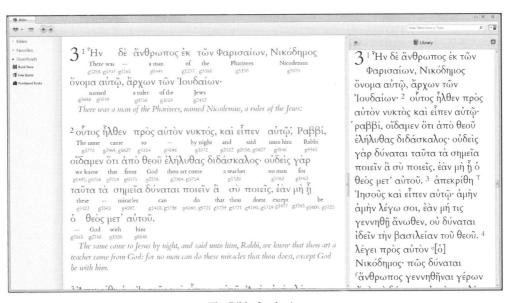

The Bible Study App

John 3:1 (Mounce Reverse-Interlinear New Testament)

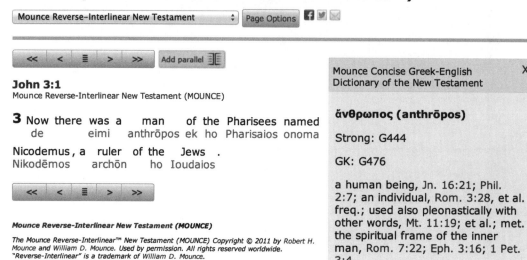

Mounce Reverse-Interlinear New Testament ⇕   Page Options f y ✉

‹‹ ‹ ≡ › ››   Add parallel ▤

John 3:1
Mounce Reverse-Interlinear New Testament (MOUNCE)

3 Now there was a   man   of the Pharisees named
de   eimi anthrōpos ek ho Pharisaios onoma

Nicodemus, a ruler of the   Jews .
Nikodēmos   archōn   ho Ioudaios

‹‹ ‹ ≡ › ››

Mounce Reverse-Interlinear New Testament (MOUNCE)

The Mounce Reverse-Interlinear™ New Testament (MOUNCE) Copyright © 2011 by Robert H. Mounce and William D. Mounce. Used by permission. All rights reserved worldwide. "Reverse-Interlinear" is a trademark of William D. Mounce.

Mounce Concise Greek-English Dictionary of the New Testament   X

ἄνθρωπος (anthrōpos)

Strong: G444

GK: G476

a human being, Jn. 16:21; Phil. 2:7; an individual, Rom. 3:28, et al. freq.; used also pleonastically with other words, Mt. 11:19; et al.; met. the spiritual frame of the inner man, Rom. 7:22; Eph. 3:16; 1 Pet. 3:4

BibleGateway.com

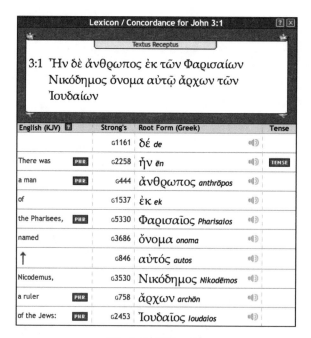

BlueLetterBible.com

John 3

26.9 Let's start to work through John 3, and you start by asking yourself what you are looking for. What are the Greek clues to help phrase this passage even better than we could in English. You are looking for at least the following:

- Beginning and ending of the sentence (which could be much longer in Greek than in English)

- Punctuation. Even though the punctuation is an editorial edition, not part of the text itself, they are good helpers in exegesis.

- Prepositional phrases

- Participial phrases (especially anarthrous)

- Relative clauses

- Dative and genitive noun phrases

- The use of the article to indicate a modifier or substantival idea

- Sentence structure (compound and complex)

Remember too why we learned a little vocabulary. When it comes to prepositions, ὁ, and ὅς, you shouldn't have to check the Instant Details windows; you should recognize them in the text itself.

I am going to move slowly through the first several verses and then speed up. When I ask a question, the answer will be given on the online class, unless for some reason I decide to include it here in the parentheses.

3:1 John 3 is a simple passage, which is why I started with it, but that also means the Greek phrasing will not be as helpful as it will in Ephesians 1. But it is a good start.

Ἦν δὲ ἄνθρωπος ἐκ τῶν Φαρισαίων, Νικόδημος ὄνομα αὐτῷ, ἄρχων τῶν Ἰουδαίων.

As you mouse over the verse, what do you notice?

- There is no expressed subject to Ἦν, so it must come from the personal endings. It is quite common to have to add a "there" to this verb: "There was."

- Why is ἄνθρωπος in the nominative?

- ἐκ τῶν Φαρισαίων is a prepositional phrase, so you will start a new line in phrasing with this construction.

- Why is Νικόδημος nominative?

- ὄνομα αὐτῷ is a little strange. This is the way Greeks would say, "his name is." "Name to him."

- ἄρχων τῶν Ἰουδαίων begins with a noun, telling something about "Nicodemus," and therefore is in apposition to Νικόδημος. But following ἄρχων you see a genitive modifier, so all three words belong together.

Let's phrase John 3:1. The trick here is not to have a lot of Greek on the screen that is meaningless to you. So what do you do? I can't take credit for this. I taught the Pastoral Epistles in Hong Kong a while back, and I used phrasing as my basic lecture notes. But only half the students could speak English, so they came up with this idea of doing a literal word-for-word translation below the Greek (of course, using Mandarin). In the translation:

- When there is a genitive, use "of" before the noun.

- When there is a dative, use "to," "in," "by," or "with," whatever fits the context.

- Translate plurals as plurals.

Based on what we saw in the interlinear, there is a prepositional phrase and a noun clause that need their own line. Break v 1 down into its Greek phrases.

Ἦν δὲ ἄνθρωπος

ἐκ τῶν Φαρισαίων,

Νικόδημος ὄνομα αὐτῷ,

ἄρχων τῶν Ἰουδαίων·

Now, do a word-for-word translation under each phrase. Different word processors may do this differently, but on most a SHIFT-RETURN creates a new line and keeps the two lines in the same paragraph. This way the two lines will move together. (If you use just RETURN, then you will have two paragraphs and they will not move together as easily.)

Ἦν δὲ ἄνθρωπος
There was but man

ἐκ τῶν Φαρισαίων,
of the Pharisees

Νικόδημος ὄνομα αὐτῷ,
Nicodemus name to him

ἄρχων τῶν Ἰουδαίων·
ruler of the Jews

Identify the main thought, and the supporting thoughts. Use what you know of Greek grammar to put the right phrase under the right word.

Ἦν δὲ ἄνθρωπος
There was but man

> ἐκ τῶν Φαρισαίων,
> of the Pharisees
>
> Νικόδημος ὄνομα αὐτῷ,
> Nicodemus name to him
>
> ἄρχων τῶν Ἰουδαίων·
> ruler of the Jews

So there you have it. The main thought is to introduce a man, and then John gives us three qualities: he is a Pharisee; his name is Nicodemus; he is a Jewish authority.

If you were doing a fuller study, you might wonder about this introduction, "but there was a man." Why start with "man"? If you look at the last two verses of chapter 2, you see why. "But Jesus on his part did not entrust himself to them, because he knew all people (πάντας) and needed no one to bear witness about man (ἀνθρώπου), for he himself knew what was in man (ἀνθρώπῳ)" (ESV). There is a play on words being made on ἄνθρωπος, and Nicodemus is one of these "men" introduced in chapter 2.

3:2   What do you see in verse 2?

οὗτος ἦλθεν πρὸς αὐτὸν νυκτὸς καὶ εἶπεν αὐτῷ· ῥαββί, οἴδαμεν ὅτι ἀπὸ θεοῦ ἐλήλυθας διδάσκαλος· οὐδεὶς γὰρ δύναται ταῦτα τὰ σημεῖα ποιεῖν ἃ σὺ ποιεῖς, ἐὰν μὴ ᾖ ὁ θεὸς μετ᾽ αὐτοῦ.

- οὗτος is one of the demonstrative pronouns, referring back to the nearer antecedent, in other words, Nicodemus and not Jesus. Demonstratives can function adjectivally or substantivally. Which one is it here? What determines its case, number, and gender?

- ἦλθεν is an indicative verb.

- πρὸς αὐτὸν is a prepositional phrase.

- This is a strange use of the genitive, νυκτὸς. You don't know about this, so just use the translation, "by night."

- εἶπεν. This is a compound sentence, a single subject and two verbs joined with καί.

- Why is αὐτῷ dative?

- οἴδαμεν is another indicative verb.

- ὅτι introduces a dependent clause, giving the content of what Nicodemus says.

- Why is διδάσκαλος nominative? (This is tricky. It is because it is in apposition to the unexpressed subject contained in the personal ending of the verb, "you are" [lit., "you have come"]).

- The next part of the verse is introduced by the postpositive γὰρ, so how does v 2b relate to v 2a? What is the γὰρ saying?

- Why is οὐδεὶς nominative?

- Why is σημεῖα accusative? Did you remember that demonstrative pronouns are anarthrous, and therefore ταῦτα modifies σημεῖα.

- ποιεῖν is what part of speech, and how is it related to the verb?

- Did you recognize that ἃ is a relative pronoun, and therefore ἃ σὺ ποιεῖς is a relative clause and should be on its own phrasing line? But whenever you see a relative pronoun, you have to find its antecedent. In fact, what I usually do is move the relative clause further to the left (since I am often running out of room on the page) and draw a line connecting the pronoun to its antecedent. So what is the linkage between the relative pronoun and its antecedent?

  ✓ Gender and number determined by antecedent. What is its antecedent?

  ✓ Case determined by its function inside the relative clause. So if you look at the clause in isolation from the context (ἃ σὺ ποιεῖς), why is ἃ accusative?

- ἐὰν introduces another dependent clause. Where is the end of the clause? (Answer: at the end of the sentence.) By the way, ἐὰν μὴ is an idiom that means "unless."

That is a lot of detail; but as I said, I need to go slower at first and make sure you are able to move from what you have learned structurally about Greek to actually seeing the rules put into practice. So let's start phrasing.

Break it into its phrases and add in the English.

οὗτος ἦλθεν πρὸς αὐτὸν
this one came to him

νυκτὸς
by night

καὶ
and

εἶπεν αὐτῷ·
said to him

ῥαββί, οἴδαμεν
Rabbi, we know

ὅτι ἀπὸ θεοῦ ἐλήλυθας διδάσκαλος·
that from God you have come a teacher

οὐδεὶς γὰρ δύναται ταῦτα τὰ σημεῖα ποιεῖν
no one for is able these signs to do

ἃ σὺ ποιεῖς,
which you do

ἐὰν μὴ ᾖ ὁ θεὸς μετ᾽ αὐτοῦ.
unless is God with him

I am keeping the word–for–word translation in Greek word order. You actually can use English word order if it will help you.

Part of the challenge of phrasing is how to graphically represent things like two main verbs, and how to represent the Greek when English demands that you change the order of the Greek words. Here is what I would do with ellipsis (see next page).

οὗτος   ἦλθεν πρὸς αὐτὸν
this one came to him

　　νυκτὸς
　　by night

　　καὶ
　　and

　　εἶπεν αὐτῷ·
　　said to him

ῥαββί, οἴδαμεν
Rabbi, we know

　　ὅτι ἀπὸ θεοῦ ἐλήλυθας διδάσκαλος·
　　that from God you have come a teacher

　　γὰρ
　　for

οὐδεὶς ... δύναται ταῦτα τὰ σημεῖα ποιεῖν
no one is able these signs to do

　　　　ἃ σὺ ποιεῖς,
　　　　which you do

　　ἐὰν μὴ ᾖ ὁ θεὸς μετ᾽ αὐτοῦ.
　　unless is God with him

- The space after οὗτος makes it a little easier to see that ἦλθεν and εἶπεν are parallel.

- The ellipsis after οὐδεὶς means that a word has been moved, and because postpositives are so common you can see that the missing word is γὰρ.

- The ὅτι ἀπὸ θεοῦ ἐλήλυθας διδάσκαλος clause did not have to be on its own line under οἴδαμεν; it could have been on the same line: ῥαββί, οἴδαμεν.

- In this particular case, there was enough room so I left the relative clause ἃ σὺ ποιεῖς indented under its antecedent rather than moving it to the left. (Note that I indent under the Greek, even though there is an intervening English line.)

3:3　　Let's do one more verse in detail. Here is verse 3.

ἀπεκρίθη Ἰησοῦς καὶ εἶπεν αὐτῷ· ἀμὴν ἀμὴν λέγω σοι, ἐὰν μή τις γεννηθῇ ἄνωθεν, οὐ δύναται ἰδεῖν τὴν βασιλείαν τοῦ θεοῦ.

- ἀπεκρίθη is parsed as a passive, so why is its translation active?

- Interesting how Jesus turns Nicodemus's words around on him. He will do it again in v 10, but here he uses the idiom ἐὰν μή. As in v 2, here it introduces a dependent clause that will go on its own phrasing line.

- ἄνωθεν has two basic meanings, doesn't it? "Again" and "from above." What's the connection?

- The rest of the verse is pretty straightforward.

Break the verse into its phrases and phrase them. I am not going to break it down into quite as much detail as the last verse; I couldn't see any advantage in doing so.

ἀπεκρίθη Ἰησοῦς καὶ εἶπεν αὐτῷ·

ἀμὴν ἀμὴν λέγω σοι,

        ἐὰν μή τις γεννηθῇ ἄνωθεν,

    οὐ δύναται ἰδεῖν τὴν βασιλείαν τοῦ θεοῦ.

- The phrasing of an "if … then …" sentence is somewhat a matter of personal preference. The apodosis is usually the main point, so I tend to indent the protasis.

- Did you notice the Greek semicolon after αὐτῷ? In our Greek texts the editors add these before direct quotations.

- The main verb in the apodosis is δύναται, and its subject is assumed in its person ending.

- τις γεννηθῇ is the subject/verb in the protasis, referenced in the apodosis by the personal ending on δύναται.

3:4   Like the previous verse, in verse 4 you have a narrative introduction and then the actual statement.

λέγει πρὸς αὐτὸν [ὁ] Νικόδημος· πῶς δύναται ἄνθρωπος γεννηθῆναι γέρων ὤν; μὴ δύναται εἰς τὴν κοιλίαν τῆς μητρὸς αὐτοῦ δεύτερον εἰσελθεῖν καὶ γεννηθῆναι;

- You can tell from the punctuation after ὤν that this is a question. If you get confused with the grammar, turn the question into a statement. It usually helps you discover the subject, direct object, etc. "How can a man be born when he is old?" becomes, "A man can be born when he is old." This explains why ἄνθρωπος is nominative.

- What same function do γεννηθῆναι, εἰσελθεῖν, and γεννηθῆναι play in the sentence?

- γέρων ὤν is difficult. ὤν is a participle of εἰμί, and hence takes a predicate nominative (γέρων). What is a little strange is that γέρων comes before ὤν and not after. But the real question is, what function is ὤν performing?

- εἰς is a preposition, so that starts a new phrasing line.

λέγει πρὸς αὐτὸν [ὁ] Νικόδημος·
πῶς δύναται ἄνθρωπος γεννηθῆναι
                    γέρων ὤν;
μὴ δύναται
       εἰς τὴν κοιλίαν τῆς μητρὸς αὐτοῦ
       δεύτερον
    εἰσελθεῖν
   καὶ
   γεννηθῆναι;

- The three infinitives are all complementary.

- By starting the question with μή, Nicodemus is saying he expects the answer to be "No" (see 29.10).

- What does the prepositional phrase εἰς τὴν κοιλίαν τῆς μητρὸς αὐτοῦ and the adverb δεύτερον both modify?

- This is actually a good example of how Greek is willing to leave words out when they are clearly implied from the context. The second δύναται does not need a subject and so technically the subject comes from the personal ending. However, the previous ἄνθρωπος is really the subject of both verbs, δύναται and δύναται.

I have been taking up enough space going through these verses. In the remaining pages I am going to point out only the difficult Greek issues that might discourage you. But in the online class there are screen casts for each verse in which I will keep going into detail. I have also posted my phrasing for the chapter there.

3:5   The only tricky thing in verse 5 is that you have a preposition with two objects. I am not sure if you have seen that before. Did you notice the repetition of εἰς in both the compound verb εἰσελθεῖν and the following εἰς? This is considered good Greek style and is not redundant.

3:6   The key to phrasing verse 6 is to think grammatically.

- When you see ὁ followed by a verbal form, by default you should think of ὁ as making the next word (or phrase) into a noun concept. So what does τὸ γεγεννημένον mean?

- What is the subject of ἐστιν? The answer is not one individual word.

- Why is σάρξ nominative?

- Once you figure out the first half of verse 7, you will see that the second half is the same structure.

3:7   In chapter 29 you will learn that one of the ways to state a prohibition is to use μή and an aorist subjunctive verb. The only other thing in verse 7 is to know why ὑμᾶς is accusative. (Hint: it has to do with γεννηθῆναι.)

3:8   There is nothing overly difficult in verse 8, except that having οὕτως as the first word in a sentence is a little tricky.

3:9   Why do you have δύναται ταῦτα in verse 9? In chaper 28 you will learn that sometimes a verb will be singular when the subject is neuter plural. The singular verb is telling you that the speaker is thinking of the subject as a whole.

3:10   Nothing overly difficult in verse 10, but note the irony in Jesus' use of ὁ διδάσκαλος in light of Nicodemus's use of the anarthrous διδάσκαλος in verse 2. What point is Jesus making? The inclusion of the question mark is a matter of interpretation.

26.10   So that's it for Greek phrasing. In chapter 30 your will graduate to Greek Phrasing 104, and you will find that Paul's style of writing is much more compact than John's, and that Greek phrasing is that much more helpful.

Please be sure to do your homework for this chapter carefully. Greek phrasing is something that you have to do over and over and over for it to really sink in. You also really have to know the structural clues of the language, which are those items the Professor has been pointing to throughout the book.

Chapter 27

Nouns

Morphology

27.1 "Morphology" refers to how Greek actually forms a word. In our approach, you have not needed to memorize all these rules and paradigms, but in Functional Greek I thought it would be helpful to at least show you some of the patterns so you could theoretically understand what is happening. These rules and paradigms do not need to be memorized, and there is more morphological information that you can download from the online class.

27.2 A **morpheme** is the smallest amount of information in a word. For a noun, the root (e.g., λογο) and the case ending (e.g., ν) are two morphemes that together form the inflected form λόγον.

27.3 A **declension** is a basic pattern for inflecting a noun or adjective. There are three basic patterns for nouns, with many subpatterns of each. Declensions have only to do with form; they have no effect on meaning. Here are some sample paradigms of nouns.

nom sg	ὥρα	λόγος	σάρξ	ὄνομα
gen sg	ὥρας	λόγου	σαρκός	ὀνόματος
dat sg	ὥρᾳ	λόγῳ	σαρκί	ὀνόματι
acc sg	ὥραν	λόγον	σάρκα	ὄνομα
n/v pl	ὧραι	λόγοι	σάρκες	ὀνόματα
gen pl	ὡρῶν	λόγων	σαρκῶν	ὀνομάτων
dat pl	ὥραις	λόγοις	σαρξίν	ὀνόμασι(ν)
acc pl	ὥρας	λόγους	σάρκας	ὀνόματα

Four or Eight Cases

27.4 In years past there has been a debate as to whether there are four or eight cases in Greek. You may see remnants of this discussion in the commentaries so I thought I should summarize the issues.

27.5   There are four distinct forms of words in the Greek noun system, and the argument (among others) is that form should be the deciding factor: nominative, accusative, dative, and genitive.

27.6   Others have argued that there are eight distinct ideas, and form should take a back seat to meaning. In this arrangement, the genitive and ablative have the same form (e.g., θεοῦ), but the genitive is the basic idea of "of," and the basic idea of the ablative is "from." "Of God" and "from God."

Likewise, what we have been calling the dative can actually be broken down into three basic ideas: "to" (*dative*, indicating personal interest or reference/respect), "in" (*locative*), and "by" (*instrumental*).

27.7   The four case system has won the day, partially because there are many more uses of the case system than eight. Form wins over function, and I think in this case that is a good decision (pun intended).

Vocative

27.8   In the four case system, there technically is a fifth case, although it is so similar to the nominative in form (and in some ways, in function) that we still speak of the "four" cases in Greek. The vocative is the case of *direct address*. When speaking directly to a person, the word used is in the vocative (*simple address*). In the eight case system, the vocative is the eighth case.

Rev 22:20   ἔρχου κύριε Ἰησοῦ.
            come   Lord   Jesus
            Come, *Lord Jesus*!

κύριε represents one of the few forms (second declension singular) in which the vocative is distinctly different from the nominative, which would be κύριος.

27.9   ὦ may be included if there is deep emotion or emphasis (*emphatic address*).

Matt 15:28   ὁ Ἰησοῦς εἶπεν αὐτῇ, ὦ γύναι, μεγάλη σου ἡ πίστις
        Jesus   said   to her O   woman   great   your   the faith
        ESV: Then Jesus answered her, "*O woman*, great is your faith!"
        NET: Then Jesus answered her, "*Woman*, your faith is great!"

Nominative

27.10 In most instances, the nominative is used in place of the vocative (*nominative for vocative*).

> *Luke 8:54*   ἡ παῖς, ἔγειρε
> Child   arise
> NIV: My child, get up!

Accusative

27.11 It is common for Greek to drop a verb's direct object, and English translators must add them back in (since English doesn't allow this, for the most part).

> *1 Pet 1:8*   ὃν   οὐκ   ἰδόντες   ἀγαπᾶτε
> whom   not   seeing   you love
> NIV: Though you have not seen him, you love *him*.
> KJV: Whom having not seen, ye love.
>
> The implied direct object of "you love" is the "whom" in the first part of the sentence.

Translations rarely (if ever) indicate in the footnotes when they add in the direct object; it is too common of an occurrence. It often happens when there is a parallelism in the sentence, and words from the first half are assumed in the second.

> You have not seen *him*.
>
> You love *him*.

27.12 The accusative can behave as an adverb, modifying the verb (*measure, adverbial, manner*).

> *Matt 6:33*   ζητεῖτε   πρῶτον   τὴν βασιλείαν   τοῦ   θεοῦ
> seek   first   the kingdom   of   God
> Seek *first* the kingdom of God.
>
> πρῶτον is technically an adjective, but here it is functioning as an adverb.

27.13 When used with time designations, the accusative is used to indicate length of time (*accusative of time how long*). This is a subcategory of the adverbial accusative.

Mark 1:13   ἦν   ἐν τῇ ἐρήμῳ τεσσεράκοντα ἡμέρας πειραζόμενος ὑπὸ τοῦ σατανᾶ
he was in the desert   *forty*   *days*   being tempted   by   Satan
He was in the wilderness *forty days*, tempted by Satan.

Matt 20:6   τί   ὧδε   ἑστήκατε ὅλην   τὴν ἡμέραν ἀργοί;
why here   stand   *entire* *the* *day*   idle
Why are you standing here idle *all day*?

When I was learning Greek, we called this the "accusative of time how long," to keep it separate from the "dative of time when."

Dative

27.14 Some verbs take a *direct object* in the dative. If you think through the meaning of the verb, you will often see why this makes sense.

Lk 17:16   ἔπεσεν ἐπὶ πρόσωπον παρὰ τοὺς πόδας αὐτοῦ εὐχαριστῶν αὐτῷ
falling   on   face   at   feet   his   thanking   *to him*
NIV: He threw himself at Jesus' feet and thanked *him*.

You can see that εὐχαριστῶν (εὐχαριστέω) means "give thanks to," and hence is followed by the dative.

27.15 A time designation in the dative specifies when something occurs (*locative of time*).

Matt 17:23   τῇ   τρίτῃ ἡμέρᾳ ἐγερθήσεται
to the third   day   he will be raised.
NET: *On the third day* he will be raised.
NLT: *Three days later* he will be raised from the dead.

When I was learning Greek, we called this the "dative of time when" to keep it separate from the related use of the accusative.

27.16 The dative can indicate the idea of "with" (*instrumental of association*).

2 Cor 6:14   μὴ γίνεσθε   ἑτεροζυγοῦντες ἀπίστοις
Not you become   unequally yoked   *to unbelievers*
ESV: Do not be unequally yoked *with unbelievers*.

Believers are not to be yoked in association with nonbelievers.

27.17 The dative can indicate the *cause* of an action (*instrumental of cause*).

> Luke 15:17 ἐγὼ δὲ λιμῷ ὧδε ἀπόλλυμαι.
> I but *to famine* here I perish
> But I am perishing here *due to the famine.*
> ESV: I perish here *with hunger.*
> NIV: Here I am starving *to death!*

> The prodigal son was perishing, and the cause of his perishing was the famine.

27.18 The dative can indicate the manner in which something is done (*instrumental of manner*).

> John 7:26 παρρησίᾳ λαλεῖ
> in boldness he speaks
> NKJ: He speaks *boldly.*

> The manner in which he was speaking was boldness.

Genitive

27.19 Sometimes the noun in the genitive is a larger unit, while its head noun represents a smaller portion of it (*partitive*).

> Rom 11:17 τινες τῶν κλάδων
> some of the branches
> some *of the branches*

> The branches comprise the larger group, and τινες represents a part of that group.

27.20 The substantive in the genitive gives an attribute of the head noun (*attributive*). As such, it is similar to a simple adjective; however, it uses a substantive to in effect modify another substantive, and it is more emphatic in its force than an adjective. This is a common contruction and is sometimes called a *Hebraic genitive* as it reflects a Hebraic way of thinking. "Body of sin" becomes "sinful body."

> Rom 6:6 καταργηθῇ τὸ σῶμα τῆς ἁμαρτίας
> abolished the body of sin
> ESV: the body *of sin* might be brought to nothing
> NIV: the body *ruled by sin* might be done away with

Some of these constructions can be tricky, since the translator must make up his or her mind whether to use the "of" construction or to translate as an attributive. English does not have the same ambiguity as the Greek genitive in this case.

1 Tim 1:11 κατὰ   τὸ εὐαγγέλιον   τῆς δόξης   τοῦ   μακαρίου   θεοῦ
according to   the gospel   *of the glory*   of the   blessed   God

ESV: in accordance with the gospel *of the glory* of the blessed God
NASB: according to the *glorious* gospel of the blessed God
NRSV: that conforms to the *glorious* gospel of the blessed God

Is Paul saying that the gospel is glorious, or that the gospel is about the glory of God? The first printings of the ESV read, "in accordance with the glorious gospel of the blessed God."

27.21 After comparative adjectives (πολύς, ἰσχυρός, etc.) you will often find a word in the genitive (*comparison*).

Matt 6:25 οὐχὶ   ἡ ψυχὴ   πλεῖόν   ἐστιν   τῆς τροφῆς
not   life   more than   is   *food*

Is not life worth more than *food*?

27.22 The genitive can describe the content of the head term (*content*).

Col 2:3 πάντες   οἱ θησαυροὶ   τῆς σοφίας   καὶ   γνώσεως
all   the treasures   *of wisdom*   and   *of knowledge*

All the treasures of *wisdom* and *knowledge*

The treasures are comprised of wisdom and knowledge; they are the content of the treasures.

27.23 The word in the genitive can indicate something that is separate from the head noun. It will often use the helping word "from" (*separation*).[4]

Eph 2:12 ἀπηλλοτριωμένοι   τῆς πολιτείας   τοῦ Ἰσραὴλ
being alienated   *of the commonwealth*   of the Israel

ESV: alienated *from the commonwealth* of Israel

---

[4] This use of the genitive is not common, but this is an example of the ablative "case," and so I wanted to point it out to you. In the Eph 2:12 illustration, note the use of ἀπό in forming the compound verb ἀπηλλοτριωμένοι, which helps to introduce the genitive case.

27.24 The genitive can describe the kind of time, or the time within which, the head noun takes place (*time*).

John 3:2   οὗτος ἦλθεν πρὸς αὐτὸν νυκτός.
          he   came   to   him   of night
          He came to him at night.

> Nicodemus came to Jesus as one who comes in the night, either because Pharisees studied at night or else Nicodemus did not want to be seen with Jesus (hence, secretly).

Luke 18:12   νηστεύω δὶς τοῦ σαββάτου
           I fast   twice   week
           I fast twice a week.

> The Pharisee fasts two times within the week.

27.25 Some verbs take a *direct object* in the genitive. If you think through the meaning of the verb, you will often see why this makes sense.

1 Tim 3:1   Εἴ τις ἐπισκοπῆς ὀρέγεται, καλοῦ ἔργου ἐπιθυμεῖ.
           if   anyone   office of overseer   aspires   good   work   he desires
           If anyone aspires to the office of overseer, he desires *a good thing*.
           NLT: If someone aspires to be an elder, he desires *an honorable position*.

> You can see that ἐπιθυμεῖ (ἐπιθυμέω) means "to be desirous of," and hence is followed by the genitive.

27.26 The next three categories are extremely important. They occur with a head noun that expresses a verbal idea (i.e., the root of the noun can also occur as a verb). These three categories often present the translator with significantly different interpretations.

27.27 Sometimes the word in the genitive functions as if it were the subject of the verbal idea implicit in the head noun (*subjective*). In other words, if you can turn the head noun into a verb, the word in the genitive would become its subject. You can use the helping word "produced" to help identify this usage. The ambiguous "the love of Christ" becomes "The love produced by Christ," which means Christ's love for us.

Rom 8:35   τίς ἡμᾶς χωρίσει ἀπὸ τῆς ἀγάπης τοῦ Χριστοῦ;
           who   us   will separate   from   the love   of Christ
           NIV: Who shall separate us from the love *of Christ*?
           NLT: Can anything ever separate us from *Christ's* love?

27.28 The word in the genitive can function as the direct object of the verbal idea implicit in the head noun (*objective*). This is the opposite of the subjective genitive. You can use the key word "receives." "The blasphemy received by the Spirit," which would mean our blasphemy of the Spirit.

> *Matt 12:31*   ἡ   τοῦ πνεύματος   βλασφημία   οὐκ   ἀφεθήσεται
> The   *of the Spirit*   blasphemy   not   will be forgiven
>
> The blasphemy *of the Spirit* will not be forgiven.
> NIV: Blasphemy *against the Spirit* will not be forgiven.

27.29 Sometimes it appears that the word in the genitive is a combination of both the objective and subjective genitive (*plenary*).

> *2 Cor 5:14*   ἡ ἀγάπη   τοῦ Χριστοῦ   συνέχει   ἡμᾶς
> the love   *of Christ*   constrains   us
>
> NASB: The love *of Christ* controls us (i.e., both my love for Christ and his love for me).
> NIV: For *Christ's* love compels us.
> NLT: Whatever we do, it is because *Christ's* love controls us.
>
> The NIV and NLT view τοῦ Χριστοῦ as a subjective genitive.

27.30 A *Genitive Absolute* is a construction using a noun and a participle, both in the genitive. I will discuss this in chapter 29 on participles.

Partially Inflected and Uninflected

27.31 Some words inflect in some cases but not in others. For example, the four cases of Ἰησοῦς are Ἰησοῦς, Ἰησοῦ, Ἰησοῦ, Ἰησοῦν. The genitive and dative are identical.

27.32 Other words never inflect, such as many personal names and words borrowed from other languages. For example, Ἀβραάμ ("Abraham") will always be Ἀβραάμ regardless of its function in the sentence.

27.33 Even though the form does not change, the computers will parse these with the relevant case. Ἰησοῦ will be parsed as either a genitive or a dative.

Chapter 28

Verbs (Indicative)

Morphology

28.1   Although our approach does not require you to be able to identify the parts of the Greek verb, it can be helpful to understand the concepts.

28.2   The **stem** of a verb is the part of the verb that carries its basic meaning. The form λύο-μεν means "we destroy." The stem is *λυ (I put an asterisk in front of a stem). While it is possible for the stem of a verb to undergo some changes, most of the changes are to the beginning and the ending of the verb.

28.3   Greek often adds a **connecting vowel** between the stem of a verb and its personal ending. This is to aid in pronunciation. For example, λέγετε means "You say." The stem is *λεγ, the connecting vowel is the second ε, and τε is the second person plural personal ending.

28.4   In order to mark a verb as indicating a past event, an **augment** is added to the beginning of the word. If the word begins with a consonant, the augment is an ε, such as in λέγω → ἔλεγεν, "I lose → I was loosing."

28.5   Some tenses use a **tense formative** like a σ or a κ that is placed between the word's stem and the connecting vowel/personal ending. ἀγαπάω (I love) → ἀγαπήσω (I will love) → ἠγάπησα (I loved) → ἠγάπηκα (I have loved).

28.6   Some of the more common verbs use totally different stems to form their different tense forms. ἔρχομαι (I go) → ἐλεύσομαι (I will go) → ἦλθον (I went) → ἐλήλυθα (I have gone). The software will parse these confusing forms properly, but you may notice they are significantly different.

28.7   There are many examples of verbal paradigms available for download from the online class. Here is the present active indicative.

1 sg	λύω	I loose
2 sg	λύεις	You loose
3 sg	λύει	He/she/it looses
1 pl	λύομεν	We loose
2 pl	λύετε	You loose
3 pl	λύουσι(ν)	They loose

Present

28.8 The present tense can refer to a future event, and the fact that it is present tense emphasizes the immediacy or certainty of the event (*futuristic*).

> *Rom 6:9* Χριστὸς ἐγερθεὶς   ἐκ   νεκρῶν οὐκέτι ἀποθνῄσκει
> Christ   having been raised from dead   never   *dies*
> NASB: Christ, having been raised from the dead, *is* never *to die* again.
> NRSV: We know that Christ, being raised from the dead, *will* never *die* again.
>
> Paul is convinced that Christ will never die, not now and not in the future.

> *Matt 26:45* ἤγγικεν ἡ ὥρα καὶ ὁ υἱὸς τοῦ ἀνθρώπου παραδίδοται
> has come the hour and the son of man   *is betrayed*
> HCSB: The time is near. The Son of Man *is being betrayed* into the hands of sinners.
> NRSV: The hour is at hand, and the Son of Man *is betrayed*.
>
> Judas was on his way, and so technically the betrayal is still in the future when Jesus says this, but the betrayal is certain.

Future

28.9 The future can state that a generic event will occur. It does not say that a particular occurrence is in mind, but that such events do occur (*gnomic*).

> *Matt 4:4* οὐκ ἐπ᾽ ἄρτῳ μόνῳ ζήσεται ὁ ἄνθρωπος
> not on bread alone *will live* man
> NASB: Man *shall* not *live* on bread alone.
> NRSV: One *does* not *live* by bread alone.
>
> Jesus is not thinking of one particular meal, but of how life should be.

Imperfect

28.10 The imperfect can describe what a person wishes to do (*voluntative*), tries to do (*conative*), or almost does (*tendential*). Often it is difficult to tell the difference between these three, and, as always, context is the guide.

> *Rom 9:3*   ηὐχόμην   γὰρ   ἀνάθεμα   εἶναι   αὐτὸς   ἐγώ
> *I was wishing*   for   curse   to be   myself   I
> NASB: For *I could wish* that I myself were accursed.
> NLT: *I would be willing* to be forever cursed.

> *Gal 1:13*   ἐδίωκον   τὴν ἐκκλησίαν   τοῦ θεοῦ   καὶ   ἐπόρθουν   αὐτήν
> *I was persecuting*   the church   of God   and   *I was destroying*   it
> NASB: I *used to persecute* the church of God … and *tried to destroy* it.
> ESV: I *persecuted* the church of God … and *tried to destroy* it.
> NET: I *was persecuting* the church of God … and *trying to destroy* it.

> *Matt 3:14*   ὁ   δὲ   Ἰωάννης   διεκώλυεν   αὐτόν
> the   but   John   *he was preventing*   him
> NIV: But John *tried to deter* him.
> ESV: John *would have prevented* him.

Aorist

28.11 **Punctiliar.** One of the primary areas of confusion in Greek exegesis comes when people confuse the Greek aorist with the English punctiliar aspect. The English punctiliar describes an action that occurs in a single point of time. "The tidal wave *hit* the boat." However, the Greek aorist is not necessarily punctiliar. It tells you nothing about the action of the verb other than it happened.

It is interesting that Luke's version of Jesus' statement on discipleship is a little different from Mark's. He says,

> If anyone wishes to come after me, let him deny himself and *take up* his cross *daily*, and follow me. (Luke 9:23)

Luke includes the adverb "daily" to emphasize that the action of "taking up" occurs every day. Does this contradict the Markan account (Mark 8:34) that simply says, "take up"? No. Both Mark and Luke use the same undefined aspect—the aorist—when saying "take up." The verb does not specify the nature of the action; it merely says that it should occur. But Luke includes the adverb "daily" to clarify that this action is a daily action. He could have just as easily used the continuous aspect for "take up" and arrived at the same meaning.

Part of the misconception surrounding the aorist and its aspect is because it can be used to describe a punctiliar action. However, such a verb is punctiliar not because it is an aorist but because of the context and the meaning of the word. You will find this mistake in many commentaries, so be careful.

Greek Passive

28.12 Sometimes context shows that when a verb is passive, God is doing the action of the verb (*divine passive*).

Matt 5:4   μακάριοι οἱ   πενθοῦντες, ὅτι αὐτοὶ παρακληθήσονται.
           Blessed   the   mourning   for   they   *will be comforted*
           Blessed are those who mourn, for they *will be comforted*.

           Comforted by whom? God.

28.13 English style, however, prefers active verbs, and so many Greek passives are changed to actives in the standard translations.

Matt 27:63   μετὰ   τρεῖς   ἡμέρας   ἐγείρομαι.
             after   three   days   *I will be raised*
             After three days *I will be raised*.
             ESV: After three days *I will arise*.

             When it comes to the resurrection, it is unfortunate that the theologically rich passive is set aside for English style.

Neuter plural

28.14 A subject that is neuter plural can have a singular verb when the subject is being viewed as a collective whole.

2 Cor 5:17   τὰ   ἀρχαῖα   παρῆλθεν,   ἰδοὺ   γέγονεν   καινά.
             the   old   passed away   behold   has become   *new*
             NASB: *The old things* passed away; behold, *new things* have come.
             ESV: *The old* has passed away; behold, *the new* has come.

             The "old" are the "old things" (plural) that all have passed away (singular).

Chapter 29

Verbs (Nonindicative)

Prohibition

29.1   In Greek there are different ways to state a prohibition, to tell someone not to do something. One way is to use οὐ and the *future indicative*.

> *Matt 4:7*   οὐκ   ἐκπειράσεις   κύριον   τὸν θεόν   σου.
>   *not*   *put to the test*   *Lord*   *God*   *your*
> NRSV: *Do not put* the Lord your God to the test.
> ESV: *You shall not put* the Lord your God to the test.

29.2   Prohibition is also expressed with μή and the *aorist subjunctive*.

> *Matt 1:20*   μὴ   φοβηθῇς   παραλαβεῖν   Μαρίαν   τὴν γυναῖκά   σου
>   *not*   *you be afraid*   *to take*   *Mary*   *wife*   *your*
> NIV: *Do not be afraid* to take Mary home as your wife.

29.3   μή with the imperative may also forbid an action.

> *Matt 6:3*   μὴ   γνώτω   ἡ ἀριστερά σου   τί   ποιεῖ   ἡ δεξιά   σου
>   *not*   *you let*   *left*   *your*   *what*   *does*   *the right*   *your*
> ESV: *Do not let* your left hand *know* what your right hand is doing.

οὐ is used to negate the indicative, and μή in the other moods (including the infinitive and participle).

29.4   For many years it was believed that μή with a persent tense imperative was a prohibition to stop something currently in progress. μή with an aorist tense imperative was a prohibition to not even start an action. Although you will find this distinction throughout the commentaries, grammarians today are for the most part agreed that this distinction is invalid.

I comment in *BBG* (p. 317): "This has tremendously important ramifications for exegesis. For example, Paul tells Timothy to have nothing to do with silly myths, using a present imperative (παραιτοῦ; 1 Tim 4:7). If the present imperative commands cessation from an action currently under way, this means Timothy was participating in the myths. This creates a picture of Timothy that is irreconcilable with his mission at

Ephesus and what we know of him elsewhere. But if a present imperative does not carry this meaning, then Paul is stating a command regarding a "general precept" that is continuous in nature—continually stay away from the myths—and is saying nothing about Timothy's current involvement, or noninvolvement, in the Ephesian myths."[5]

Emphatic negation

29.5   If the speaker uses οὐ μή and the aorist subjunctive, the statement is exceptionally strong. Often the translator will add a word like "never" to make the prohibition more emphatic.

Matt 24:35   οἱ λόγοι   μου   οὐ   μή   παρέλθωσιν
the words   my   not   not   they will pass away
NIV: My words *will never pass away.*
NRSV: My words *will not pass away.*

"Never" is really over-translation because the construction is only an emphatic negation; it is not a statement about "forever." But English does not have a construction equal to the strength of this strong negation, so sometimes this is as close as we can get to the Greek.

29.6   Another strong way to say no is with the expression, μὴ γένοιτο.

Rom 6:15   ἁμαρτήσωμεν, ὅτι   οὐκ   ἐσμὲν   ὑπὸ   νόμον   ἀλλὰ   ὑπὸ   χάριν;   μὴ γένοιτο.
should we sin   since not   we are   under law   but   under grace   not be
ESV: Are we to sin because we are not under law but under grace? *By no means!* (also NIV)

You can watch the translations struggle with how to say "No" in the strongest possible terms.

- ■ "Absolutely not!" (HCSB, NET)

- ■ "May it never be!" (NASB)

- ■ "God forbid" (KJV)

- ■ "Of course not!" (NLT)

- ■ "Out of the question!" (NJB)

---

[5]   If someone wants the technical discussion, they can read it in *Verbal Aspect in New Testament Greek* by Buist Fanning (Oxford, pp. 325-88).

Questions

29.7 We have seen above that the subjunctive can be used in a prohibition and the emphatic negation. Here is another use. When a person asks a question and expects the audience to think about the answer, the verb in the question is put in the subjunctive (*deliberative*).

> *Matt 6:31* τί   φάγωμεν; ἤ· τί   πίωμεν; ἤ· τί   περιβαλώμεθα;
> what *we eat*   or what *we drink*   or what *we wear*
> "What *should we eat*?" or "What *should we drink*?" or "What *should we wear*?"
> ESV: "What *shall we eat*?" or "What *shall we drink*?" or "What *shall we wear*?"

29.8 Greek can ask a question and give no indication of the expected response.

> *Matt 2:2* ποῦ ἐστιν ὁ τεχθεὶς   βασιλεὺς τῶν Ἰουδαίων;
> where is   the one born   King   of the Jews
> Where is the one born King of the Jews?

29.9 Greek can ask a question such that the expected answer is, "Yes." They do this by introducing the question with οὐ (or the strengthened form οὐχί).

> *Matt 6:25* οὐχὶ ἡ ψυχὴ πλεῖόν   ἐστιν τῆς τροφῆς
> not   life   more than   is   food
> Life is more than food, *isn't it*?

29.10 Greek can also ask a question such that the expected answer is, "No." They do this by introducing the question with μή.

> *1 Cor 12:30* μὴ πάντες χαρίσματα ἔχουσιν ἰαμάτων;
> not   all   gifts   they have   of healing
> *Not* all have the gifts of healing, *do they*?

Optative

29.11 There is another mood called the optative. If the subjunctive describes an action one step removed from reality (uncertain but possible), the optative describes an action two steps removed. It is sometimes called the mood of "wish."

29.12 Since the days of Classical Greek, the optative has been falling out of use. There are only 68 uses of the optative in the New Testament, and 15 are the expression μὴ γένοιτο (see above), "may it not be," sometimes translated idiomatically as, "God forbid." Beware of any preacher or teacher placing too much weight on the optative; its nuanced meaning is often difficult to pin down.

Imperative

29.13 There are three ways to state a command. The *future indicative.*

1 Pet 1:16	ἅγιοι	ἔσεσθε,	ὅτι	ἐγὼ	ἅγιός
	holy	*you will be*	because	I	holy

NRSV: *You shall be* holy, for I am holy.
NIV: *Be* holy, because I am holy.

29.14 The *present imperative* commands an ongoing action.

Matt 3:2	μετανοεῖτε·	ἤγγικεν	γὰρ	ἡ βασιλεία	τῶν οὐρανῶν.
	repent	has come near	for	the kingdom	of heaven

Repent, for the kingdom of heaven is at hand.

29.15 The *aorist imperative* commands an undefined action.

Acts 2:38	μετανοήσατε,	καὶ βαπτισθήτω	ἕκαστος	ὑμῶν	ἐπὶ	τῷ	ὀνόματι	Ἰησοῦ
	repent	and *be baptized*	each	of you	in	the	name	of Jesus

Repent and *be baptized*, each of you, in the name of Jesus.

29.16 Sometimes the indicative and imperative are identical in form in the second person plural. In John 14:1 Jesus says,

John 14:1	πιστεύετε	εἰς	τὸν θεὸν	καὶ	εἰς	ἐμὲ	πιστεύετε.
	you believe	in	God	and	in	me	you believe

NRSV: *Believe* in God; believe also in me.
NIV: *You believe* in God; believe also in me.

πιστεύετε can be either indicative or imperative. The translator will have made a decision, but you can see how difficult this passage is to exegete, especially when you add in that the indicative is used for statements and questions ("Do you believe in God?").

Other examples are 1 Cor 12:31 and 14:1, but these are most likely imperatives. This does not happen frequently; it was just fun to point it out.

Infinitive

29.17 The infinitive is always indeclinable. When it is preceded by the article, it is neuter singular and is declined according to the function of the infinitive. For example, if the infinitive is the subject, the article will be in the nominative case.

> *2 Cor 9:1*   περισσόν μοί ἐστιν τὸ γράφειν ὑμῖν.
>   superfulous   to me   is   *to write*   to you
>   *To write* to you is unnecessary for me.
>   NIV: There is no need for me *to write* to you.

29.18 **Articular infinitive and preposition**. When the infinitive is preceded by a preposition and the article, there are specific rules of translation. This is the most difficult use of the infinitive and the most idiomatic. Any attempt to translate word for word must be abandoned because we have no construction like it in English. The translator sees what the phrase means in Greek and then says the same thing in English.

Below I have listed the preposition and have italicized the word in the translation that translates the preposition. All of the pronouns below that act as the subject of the infinitive are accusative. Remember: the infinitive uses an accusative word as if it were the subject (although the word in the accusative is optional).

μετά indicating a*ntecedent time* (i.e., the infinitive happened *before* the main verb)

> <u>μετὰ τὸ βλέψαι τὸν Ἰησοῦν</u> τοὺς ἁμαρτωλούς, ἔκλαυσεν.
>
> *After Jesus saw* the sinners, he wept.

ἐν indicating *contemporaneous time*

> ὁ κύριος κρινεῖ ἡμᾶς <u>ἐν τῷ ἔρχεσθαι αὐτὸν</u> πάλιν.
>
> The Lord will judge us *when he comes* again.

πρό indicating *prior time* (i.e., the infinitive happened *after* the main verb)

> ὁ Ἰησοῦς ἠγάπησεν ἡμᾶς <u>πρὸ τοῦ γνῶναι ἡμᾶς</u> αὐτόν.
>
> Jesus loved us *before we knew* him.

διά indicating *reason* or *cause*

> ὁ Ἰησοῦς χαρήσεται <u>διὰ τὸ βλέπειν αὐτὸν</u> ὅτι ἀγαπῶμεν αὐτόν.
>
> Jesus will rejoice *because he sees* that we love him.

εἰς indicating *purpose*

> καθίζω ἐν τῷ ναῷ <u>εἰς τὸ ἀκούειν με</u> τὸν λόγον τοῦ θεοῦ.
>
> I sit in the temple *in order that I might hear* the word of God.

πρός indicating *purpose*

> κηρύσσομεν τὸν εὐαγγέλιον <u>πρὸς τὸ βλέψαι ὑμᾶς</u> τὴν ἀλήθειαν.
>
> We proclaim the gospel *so that you may see* the truth.

29.19 There are multiple ways to express purpose using the infinitive.

■ The simple infinitive

Matt 5:17 Μὴ νομίσητε ὅτι ἦλθον καταλῦσαι τὸν νόμον ἢ   τοὺς προφήτας
not   think   that I came   *to abolish*   the law   or   the prophets

Do not think that I have come *to abolish* the Law or the Prophets.

The purpose of Jesus' coming was not to abolish the Hebrew Scriptures.

■ The articular infinitive with the article in the genitive case (τοῦ).

Acts 3:2 ἐτίθουν   καθ᾽ ἡμέραν πρὸς τὴν θύραν τοῦ ἱεροῦ ... τοῦ αἰτεῖν ἐλεημοσύνην
he was placed every   day   at   the door   of the temple ... *to ask for*   alms

NRSV: People would lay him daily at the gate of the temple ... *so that he could ask* for alms.

The lame man was placed by the gate for the purpose of asking for alms.

■ εἰς τό and the infinitive

Matt 20:19 παραδώσουσιν αὐτὸν   τοῖς ἔθνεσιν εἰς   τὸ   ἐμπαῖξαι καὶ μαστιγῶσαι
hand over   him   to the Gentiles *into* *the* *mocked*   and *flogged*

NRSV: They will hand him over to the Gentiles *to be mocked* and *flogged*.

Jesus was handed over for the purpose of being mocked and flogged.

■ πρὸς τό and the infinitive

Matt 5:28 ὁ βλέπων   γυναῖκα πρὸς τὸ   ἐπιθυμῆσαι αὐτὴν ἤδη   ἐμοίχευσεν
the one looking at woman   *to*   *the* *lust*   her   already committed adultery

ESV: Everyone who looks at a woman *with lustful intent* has already committed adultery with her.

It is looking with intent that constitutes sin.

29.20 An infinitive can stand in apposition to a substantive (*appositional*). The infinitive usually gives a specific example of the broader category expressed by the head noun.

James 1:27 θρησκεία … αὕτη ἐστίν, ἐπισκέπτεσθαι ὀρφανοὺς καὶ χήρας
religion …   this   is   *to visit*   orphans   and   widows

This is pure and undefiled religion, *to visit* orphans and widows.

True religion shows itself in many ways. One way is to visit those rejected by society.

29.21 A similar use of the infinitive is the *epexegetical.* Instead of defining the head noun (appositional), the epexegetical infinitive "clarifies, explains, or qualifies a noun or adjective" (*BNTS*, 263). The epexegetical infinitive cannot stand on its own as a substitute for the head noun; the appositional can.

1 Cor 7:39 ἐλευθέρα ἐστὶν ᾧ   θέλει   γαμηθῆναι, μόνον ἐν κυρίῳ.
free   she is   to whom   she wishes   *to marry*   only   in   Lord

NIV: She is free *to marry* anyone she wishes, but he must belong to the Lord.

She is free in respect to marriage.

Adverbial Participle

29.22 When I talk about an adjectival and an adverbial participle, I am talking only about meaning. The form of the participle is identical in both cases; ἀκούσας could be either adjectival or adverbial.

However, *the adverbial participle is always anarthrous; the adjectival is usually articular.*

Matt 2:3 ἀκούσας δὲ ὁ βασιλεὺς Ἡρῴδης ἐταράχθη
hearing   but   king   Herod   was troubled

But *when* King Herod *heard* this, he was troubled.

ἀκούσας is not immediately preceded by ὁ.

Matt 2:7 Ἡρῴδης … ἠκρίβωσεν παρ᾽ αὐτῶν τὸν χρόνον τοῦ φαινομένου ἀστέρος
Herod   learned   from   them   the time   *of the appearing*   of the star

Herod learned from them the time *of the appearing* of the star.
ESV: Herod summoned the wise men secretly and ascertained from them *what time* the star *had appeared.*

φαινομένου is preceded by the article (τοῦ) and hence is articular and therefore adjectival.

29.23 The adverbial participle can indicate the purpose of the finite verb (*purpose, telic*). These are often translated as infinitives.

> *Matt 27:49* εἰ   ἔρχεται Ἠλίας   σώσων   αὐτόν
> if   he comes Elijah   *saving* him
> NIV: Let's see if Elijah comes *to save* him.
> NLT: Let's see whether Elijah *will* come and *save* him.
>
> They waited for the purpose of seeing if Elijah would come.

29.24 The adverbial participle can indicate the result of the finite verb (*result*). This is close to the participle of purpose; the difference is whether the force of the particple is on the intention or the result.

> *Eph 2:15* τοὺς δύο   κτίσῃ ἐν αὐτῷ εἰς ἕνα καινὸν ἄνθρωπον ποιῶν εἰρήνην
> the two   he create in him   into one new   man   *making* peace
> NIV: His purpose was to create in himself one new humanity out of the two, *thus making* peace.
>
> Peace was the result of creating the one new man.

29.25 It is common to have an indicative verb indicating some type of speech, accompanied by a participle with the same basic meaning (*redundant*). This participle is often not translated.

> *Matt 11:25* ἀποκριθεὶς ὁ Ἰησοῦς εἶπεν·   ἐξομολογοῦμαί σοι πάτερ
> *answering* Jesus   said   I praise   you father
> Jesus, *answering*, said, "I praise you Father."
> ESV: Jesus declared, "I thank you, Father."
>
> "Answering" and "said" denote the same action, and hence ἀποκριθεὶς is considered redundant (to the English ear). The KJV, however, usually translates both.

29.26 An adverbial participle can describe an action that is coordinate with the regular verb (*attendant circumstances*). In most cases, the participle is translated as a regular verb and the conjunction "and" is inserted.[6]

> *Mark 1:18* εὐθὺς   ἀφέντες τὰ δίκτυα ἠκολούθησαν αὐτῷ.
> immediately *leaving* the nets they followed   him
> NASB. Immediately they *left* their nets and followed Him.
>
> ἀφέντες is a participle, and ἠκολούθησαν is the main verb.

---

[6] Wallace goes into some detail on this construction (*BNTS*, 279-80). The participle is usually aorist, usually precedes the main verb, and is found in narrative literature. The main verb is usually aorist and an indicative or imperative.

Mark 10:23 Καὶ περιβλεψάμενος ὁ Ἰησοῦς λέγει τοῖς μαθηταῖς αὐτοῦ
and *looking around* Jesus *says* to the disciples his
ESV: And Jesus *looked around* and said to his disciples

περιβλεψάμενος is a participle, and λέγει is the main verb.

This may create a problem for exegesis, because you can't distinguish between the main verb—which is normally indicative and normally contains the main thought—and the dependent participle, which normally contains a modifying thought.

29.27 When Greek sentences get too long for English translations, it is often easiest to treat a long participial phrase as an independent sentence. Ephesians 1:3-14 is one such sentence. V. 5 begins with a participial phrase, and many translations start a new English sentence by turning the participle into a finite verb, supply a subject, and hence turn a participial phrase into an independent sentence. The NET adds, "He did this," and the NRSV adds "He."

Eph 1:5 προορίσας ἡμᾶς εἰς υἱοθεσίαν διὰ Ἰησοῦ Χριστοῦ
predestining us to adoption through Jesus Christ
KJV: *Having predestinated* us unto the adoption of children by Jesus Christ to himself.
NET: *He did this by predestining* us to adoption as his sons through Jesus Christ.
NRSV: *He destined* us for adoption as his children through Jesus Christ.

This is not necessarily bad translation practice. After all, the point of translation is to make something understandable. However, because it blurs the grammatical distinction between independent and dependent constructions, and because the author's main thought tends to be in the independent clauses, this practice can make exegesis more difficult when based on the English text.

29.28 The opposite can also happen; an independent clause can be translated as dependent.

Rom 4:19 μὴ ἀσθενήσας τῇ πίστει κατενόησεν τὸ ἑαυτοῦ σῶμα
not *weakening* in faith *he considered* the his own body
NRSV: He did not *weaken* in faith when he *considered* his own body

"Did not weaken" is a participle in a subordinate clause. "When he considered" is the main verb in Greek, but in the NRSV it is a temporal subordinate clause. Paul's point is how Abraham looked at his aging body ("considered"), and adds that in doing so he "did not weaken" in his faith, a fact obscured by the NRSV. The NIV does a better job in this regard.

Without weakening in his faith, he *faced the fact* that his body was as good as dead—since he was about a hundred years old.

Another good example is the "Great Commission" (Matt 28:19-20). The NIV reads,

> Therefore *go* and *make disciples* of all nations, *baptizing* them in the name of the Father and of the Son and of the Holy Spirit, and *teaching* them to obey everything I have commanded you.

What is the main point? It appears that the apostles are told to do two things: "Go!" and "Make disciples!" However, if you look at the Greek, you will find that there is only one imperative: "Make disciples!" "Go" is a participle, like "baptizing" and "teaching." Jesus is telling his disciples (and us): "Therefore, as you go, make disciples by baptizing and by teaching." Wherever you are, wherever you go (whether, I would add, you are in full-time ministry as a missionary or as a stay-at-home Christian), you are to make disciples.[7]

29.29 Periphrastic. One of the basic differences we have seen between English and Greek is that the different Greek tenses do not use helping verbs. English uses "will" to make a verb future and "be" to make it passive. Greek just uses different tense formatives, etc.

There is one construction, however, when Greek uses εἰμί and a participle together to state a single idea, and this is called a **periphrastic construction**. Originally a periphrastic construction emphasized the continuous force of the participle (which is why the aorist participle never occurs in this construction). However, by the time of Koine Greek, this emphasis is often lost. In fact, Koine Greek normally uses a periphrastic construction for the third person plural, perfect middle/passive.

Matt 7:29	ἦν	γὰρ	διδάσκων	αὐτοὺς	ὡς	ἐξουσίαν	ἔχων
	he was	*for*	*teaching*	*them*	*as*	*authority*	*having*

For *he was teaching* them as one who had authority.

Eph 2:8	Τῇ	γὰρ	χάριτί	ἐστε	σεσῳσμένοι	διὰ	πίστεως
	by	*for*	*grace*	*you are*	*having been saved*	*through*	*faith*

For by grace *you have been saved* through faith.

---

7 It is not quite this simple. The participle does pick up some of the imperatival force of the imperative. But the basic point I am making is valid.

29.30 Here are all the different forms a periphrastic construction can take. The form of εἰμί and the participle can be separated by several words.

periphrastic tense	construction		
Present	present of εἰμί	+	present participle
Imperfect	imperfect of εἰμί	+	present participle
Future	future of εἰμί	+	present participle
Perfect	present of εἰμί	+	perfect participle
Pluperfect	imperfect of εἰμί	+	perfect participle
Future perfect	future of εἰμί	+	perfect participle

29.31 A **genitive absolute** is a noun or pronoun and a participle in the genitive that are not grammatically connected to the rest of the sentence. In other words, there will be no word in the remaining part of the sentence that the noun, pronoun, or participle modifies.

These are common constructions especially in narrative passages. They usually occur at the beginning of the sentence and are usually temporal. Translation is often idiomatic.

Mark 14:43   αὐτοῦ λαλοῦντος παραγίνεται Ἰούδας
             he   *speaking*   *comes*   *Judas*
             NASB: While He was still speaking, Judas … came up.
             NIV: Just as he was speaking, Judas … appeared.

John 5:13   ὁ Ἰησοῦς ἐξένευσεν ὄχλου ὄντος ἐν τῷ τόπῳ
             Jesus   *departed*   *crowd*   *being*   *in*   *the*   *place*
             NASB: Jesus had slipped away *while there was a crowd* in that place.
             ESV: Jesus had withdrawn, *as there was a crowd* in the place.
             NET: Jesus had slipped out *since there was a crowd* in that place.
             NRSV: Jesus had disappeared *in the crowd* that was there.

Notice how the genitive αὐτοῦ ("he") in the first example functions as the "subject" of the participle, even though technically a participle cannot have a subject. The genitive absolute is often used when the noun or pronoun doing the action of the participle is different from the subject of the sentence.

Chapter 30

Phrasing 104

In Phrasing 103 we learned Greek phrasing. In Phrasing 104 you are going to graduate to the Greek phrasing of Ephesians 1, and learn about semantic tags. This is the last chapter on phrasing; and as before, the homework is incredibly important.

30.1   Phrasing Ephesians 1 is going to be a little harder than John 3, but you will see even more reasons why this is a discipline you need to practice for the rest of your life.

As always, there are many screen casts at the online class where I go into each verse in more detail. In this text, I will cover the basics and those elements of the text that may be too difficult or unknown to you.

30.2   The final step I am going to add to phrasing is the use of semantic tags. These tags will help you be specific in seeing how the phrases are actually related to each other. For example, "Christ Jesus came into the world in order to save sinners" (1 Tim 1:15). "Christ Jesus came" is the main clause, "into the world" tells us *location*, and "in order to save sinners" tells us what? It tells us the *purpose* of Jesus' coming.

Assertion	Χριστὸς Ἰησοῦς ἦλθεν Christ Jesus came	
Place		εἰς τὸν κόσμον into the world
Purpose		ἁμαρτωλοὺς σῶσαι sinners to save

30.3 Here is another example that is less obvious. Paul writes to the Romans, in 12:3-5,

> ³For by the grace given to me I say to everyone among you not to think of himself more highly than he ought to think, but to think with sober judgment, each according to the measure of faith that God has assigned. ⁴ *For* as in one body we have many members, and the members do not all have the same function, ⁵ so we, though many, are one body in Christ, and individually members one of another. (ESV)

What is the relationship between v 3 and vv 4-5? Some translations don't start v 4 with the word "for," but the ESV has correctly translated the initial γάρ. "For" tells you that vv 4-5 are not a new topic but are giving you the *reason* for v 3. We should not be prideful *because,* despite the diversity of gifts in the church, we are one body in Christ and members one of another.

So, in phrasing we would add the semantic tags *reason* to the left of v 4.

By the way, remember that one of our goals in this text is for you to be able to read good commentaries. Specifying the precise relationship between ideas is at the heart of an exegetical commentary.

30.4 Ephesians 1:3–14. Start by preparing the Greek text as I discussed in Phrasing 103, and set up your interlinear.

1:3 Εὐλογητὸς ὁ θεὸς καὶ πατὴρ τοῦ κυρίου ἡμῶν Ἰησοῦ Χριστοῦ, ὁ εὐλογήσας ἡμᾶς ἐν πάσῃ εὐλογίᾳ πνευματικῇ ἐν τοῖς ἐπουρανίοις ἐν Χριστῷ,

1:4 καθὼς ἐξελέξατο ἡμᾶς ἐν αὐτῷ πρὸ καταβολῆς κόσμου εἶναι ἡμᾶς ἁγίους καὶ ἀμώμους κατενώπιον αὐτοῦ ἐν ἀγάπῃ,

1:5 προορίσας ἡμᾶς εἰς υἱοθεσίαν διὰ Ἰησοῦ Χριστοῦ εἰς αὐτόν, κατὰ τὴν εὐδοκίαν τοῦ θελήματος αὐτοῦ,

1:6 εἰς ἔπαινον δόξης τῆς χάριτος αὐτοῦ ἧς ἐχαρίτωσεν ἡμᾶς ἐν τῷ ἠγαπημένῳ.

1:7 Ἐν ᾧ ἔχομεν τὴν ἀπολύτρωσιν διὰ τοῦ αἵματος αὐτοῦ, τὴν ἄφεσιν τῶν παραπτωμάτων, κατὰ τὸ πλοῦτος τῆς χάριτος αὐτοῦ

1:8 ἧς ἐπερίσσευσεν εἰς ἡμᾶς, ἐν πάσῃ σοφίᾳ καὶ φρονήσει,

1:9 γνωρίσας ἡμῖν τὸ μυστήριον τοῦ θελήματος αὐτοῦ, κατὰ τὴν εὐδοκίαν αὐτοῦ ἣν προέθετο ἐν αὐτῷ

1:10 εἰς οἰκονομίαν τοῦ πληρώματος τῶν καιρῶν, ἀνακεφαλαιώσασθαι τὰ πάντα ἐν τῷ Χριστῷ, τὰ ἐπὶ τοῖς οὐρανοῖς καὶ τὰ ἐπὶ τῆς γῆς ἐν αὐτῷ.

1:11 Ἐν ᾧ καὶ ἐκληρώθημεν προορισθέντες κατὰ πρόθεσιν τοῦ τὰ πάντα ἐνεργοῦντος κατὰ τὴν βουλὴν τοῦ θελήματος αὐτοῦ

1:12 εἰς τὸ εἶναι ἡμᾶς εἰς ἔπαινον δόξης αὐτοῦ τοὺς προηλπικότας ἐν τῷ Χριστῷ.

1:13 Ἐν ᾧ καὶ ὑμεῖς ἀκούσαντες τὸν λόγον τῆς ἀληθείας, τὸ εὐαγγέλιον τῆς σωτηρίας ὑμῶν, ἐν ᾧ καὶ πιστεύσαντες ἐσφραγίσθητε τῷ πνεύματι τῆς ἐπαγγελίας τῷ ἁγίῳ,

1:14 ὅ ἐστιν ἀρραβὼν τῆς κληρονομίας ἡμῶν, εἰς ἀπολύτρωσιν τῆς περιποιήσεως, εἰς ἔπαινον τῆς δόξης αὐτοῦ.

30.5   As you scan the Greek text you can see several editorial clues.

- The editors start new sentences at vv 7, 11, and 13. Vv 3–14 actually form one long sentence, but these are natural breaks.

- You may also notice that Paul likes prepositions.

Set up your interlinears and work through verse by verse.

When we are done, I am going to encourage you to look at Clint Arnold's commentary on the passage and compare your work. If you have any questions you can't answer, be sure to save them and read what Arnold says when done. Thanks to Zondervan for allowing you to download this part of his commentary at the online class.

1:3   In verse 3, Paul starts by stating his blessing and summarizes why God is worthy of praise.

- You arrive at the first punctuation and what is missing? A verb, so you will need to decide where to insert some form of "to be."

- Are θεός and πατήρ one or two different persons? Unless your doctrine of the Trinity is really messed up, they are the same, so how is καί functioning?

- What is the grammatical relationship between Ἰησοῦ and κυρίου? Or asked another way, why is Ἰησοῦ genitive?

- ὁ εὐλογήσας. The longer I teach this class, the more important the following is: when you see ὁ followed by a verbal form of any kind (but especially the participle), it often signals to you that the article is making the verbal form function in some attributive/substantival way. Why is εὐλογήσας nominative singular masculine?

- εὐλογία and πνευματικῇ are both anarthrous, so how do you determine their relationship to each other?

1:4   As you work through the macro structure of the passage, you will see that verse 4 contains a main verb to which other verbal forms are connected. What is it?

- καθώς is a difficult word to define in this context. It normally introduces a comparison, "just as." You have to go down to BDAG's third definition before you find something that fits the context: "since."

- What kind of infinitive is εἶναι? (When I say "kind," I mean you should look on the laminated sheet for the answer.) There are several of these throughout this passage.

- The most difficult exegetical decision to make in v 4 is whether ἐν ἀγάπῃ goes with v 4 or v 5. What do you think?

1:5   Regardless of what some translations do, verse 5 is still in the same sentence.

- προορίσας is an anarthrous participle, so what determines its case, number, and gender?

- Four prepositional phrases! Even for Paul that is a bit extreme, but it makes phrasing fun.

1:6   The main challenge in verse 6 is the string of genitives.

- There are two possible interpretations of δόξης. What would be the difference if it were an attributive genitive or an objective genitive?

- ἧς gives us a good opportunity to review our understanding of relative pronouns. The prepositional phrase is ἧς ἐχαρίτωσεν ἡμᾶς ἐν τῷ ἠγαπημένῳ. What determines the number and gender of a relative pronoun? Antecedent. Be sure to draw a line from ἧς to its antecedent. But what determines its case? Its function inside the relative clause. But this is where it gets tricky. Inside the clause it is functioning as part of a double accusative; just replace ἧς with its antecedent and you will see this. But in that case ἧς should be accusative, but it is genitive. Why? This is an example of "attraction" (25.13). Its case has been attracted to the case of its antecedent χάριτος (genitive) as if ἧς were an adjective.

- Did you see that τῷ ἠγαπημένῳ is an articular participle? What is the article doing?

1:7   As in v 5, translations often start a new sentence at verse 7, turning ἔχομεν into the main verb of the sentence even though in Greek it is inside a dependent relative clause.

- Why is ἄφεσιν accusative? What "kind" of accusative is it?

1:8   Verse 8 is pretty straightforward.

- What is the antecedent of ἧς, and how do you explain its case?

- As in v 5, do you think the final prepositional phrase, ἐν πάσῃ σοφίᾳ καὶ φρονήσει, goes with v 8 or v 9?

- I don't know if this is the first time you have seen this construction, but did you notice that the preposition ἐν has two objects, σοφίᾳ and φρονήσει?

1:9 Don't forget to rejoice in the meaning of verse 9 and following. God's motivation for what he is doing is his εὐδοκίαν. Arnold writes, "Long ago, John Eadie noted that the term 'defines His will as being something more than a mere decree resting on sovereignty.' God took great delight in thinking of his future people and being kindly disposed toward them" (83).

- γνωρίσας is another anarthrous participle, and hence probably adverbial. Remember, all adverbial participles must be anarthrous; most adjectival participles are articular (holding out the possibility of an anarthrous adjectival participle). But seeing as γνωρίσας is the first word in the verse, it would be strange indeed if it were not adverbial.

- How nice to have a relative pronoun, ἥν, that forms its case "correctly."

1:10 There are two prepositional phrases in verse 10, each introduced by τὰ. What is τὰ doing?

1:11 τοῦ τὰ πάντα ἐνεργοῦντος in verse 11 is difficult, unless you figure out why πάντα is accusative. Any thoughts? It is the direct object of ἐνεργοῦντος; what is strange is its placement between τοῦ and ἐνεργοῦντος. Once you see this, however, you can see that the article is making the participle substantival: "the one who works all things."

1:12 There are a couple challenges in verse 12.

- εἰς τὸ εἶναι ἡμᾶς is a specific grammatical construction. Do you remember it? It is the preposition + articular infinitive, in which case a word in the accusative (ἡμᾶς) is functioning as the subject of the infinitive (29.19).

- There is also an unusual use of εἰς (the second occurrence). It means something close to "for."

- Explain the case of προηλπικότας and its relationship to τούς.

1:13 Building off the mention of Χριστῷ, signaled by the repeated phrase ἐν ᾧ (which repeats the first ἐν ᾧ), Paul now turns his full attention to Jesus in verse 13.

- The key here is to find the main verb and its subject. After that, clearly define each of the phrases and tie them to the word they modify.

- Why is εὐαγγέλιον accusative? Unless you know this, you wouldn't know how to phrase the verse.

- Hint: whereas ἀκούσαντες has a direct object, πιστεύσαντες does not. Both are anarthrous adverbial participles.

- τῷ πνεύματι τῆς ἐπαγγελίας τῷ ἁγίῳ could also have been written τῷ πνεύματι τῷ ἁγίῳ τῆς ἐπαγγελίας. Perhaps that will help.

1:14 Verse 14 is our last verse. As in v 13, Paul uses a relative pronoun to switch attention from Jesus to the Holy Spirit.

- The first use of εἰς is a tad peculiar; Arnold will talk about it.

30.6 There you have it, Eph 1:3–14. Please remember what I said at the beginning. It is your practice, practice, practice, that will make all the difference in whether you really learn Greek well enough to use it. This is why there are so many screen cast videos at the website. When I teach people this material, we spend a significant amount of time going over verse after verse after verse. Without this practice, all the theoretical information you have learned will dissipate into nothingness in the recesses of your mind. You need to practice.

30.7 There is one more step you should do. Zondervan graciously has allowed me to post a pdf of Clint Arnold's commentary on Ephesians 1:3-14. It is from the *Zondervan Exegetical Commentary* series, which is based around phrasing. The series is designed for people who have had two years of Greek, and it should be a tremendous encouragement for you. If you had tried to read this commentary before working through *Greek for the Rest of Us,* it is doubtful you could have understood much of it. But now you should be able to understand almost everything Arnold says. So download it from the online class, read it, check your phrasing, and rejoice in your newly earned ability to read better commentaries. Good job!

Diagramming tools in software

30.8 There are some helpful tools in the software, and no doubt the software companies will continue to improve these. As is true of all tools, be sure not to let them ruin your fun; don't let them do your work of phrasing. But they are helpful as cross-references, or if you just don't have enough time to get ready for Sunday's sermon.

30.9 Accordance has a tool called the GNT Syntax module (page 243). It is a work in progress; currently they have Matthew through Acts. You should read the instructions carefully in order to understand the diagramming, but this is pretty cool.

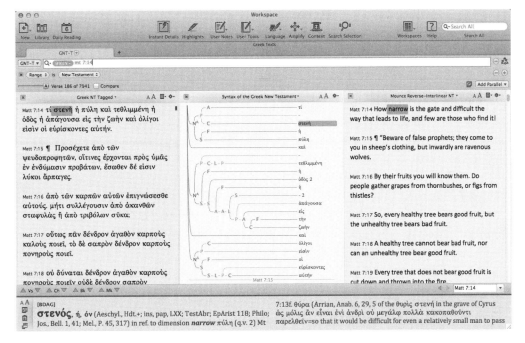

Accordance: GNT Syntax

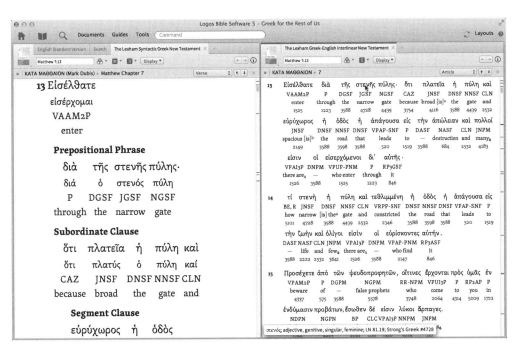

Logos: Lexham Syntactic Greek New Testament

30.10 Logos also has a nice tool called the Lexham Syntactic Greek New Testament, which lays the phrases out and includes grammatical labels (page 243).

30.11 Recognize that these tools, and others like them, are helpful, but they represent exegetical decisions by the editors. Their editors are highly qualified scholars, but they still represent opinion; they are not infallible. So use them as you would any other tool, respecting the scholarship but making your own decisions.

Semantic tags

30.12 The following is only for students who want to go even further into phrasing. Much of the discussion in commentaries is concerned with the precise nature of the relationships between phrases, and the writer will use a label to describe the relationship such as "manner" or "temporal." These terms overlap some with the terms you have seen in parentheses and italics throughout Functional Greek.

30.13 If you come up with your own labels for the connections between the major phrases, you will be doing well. But sometimes it is difficult to come up with the right terminology, so here are some suggestions. They have been taken (with permission) from a textbook written by some good friends of mine, George Guthrie and Scott Duvall. If you want to know more, see their book *Biblical Greek Exegesis* (Zondervan, 1998). The terminology is also being employed in the *Zondervan Exegetical Commentary on the New Testament* series. (Check out the download file on Ephesians 1:3-14 for a sample of their phrasing: bit.ly/16Jg7CH.) I also included these terms on the laminated sheet for this textbook. Many of these terms listed below are the technical terms used in the better commentaries

Foundational Expressions

Many of the main phrases you come across can be categorized in one of these "foundational" categories.

1. **Assertion**. Making a statement.

   I am the true vine *(John 15:1)*.

2. **Event/Action**. Something that happened.

   The life was made manifest *(1 John 1:2)*.

3. **Rhetorical question**. A question used to make a declaration.

For to which of the angels did God ever say,"You are my Son?" *(Heb 1:5)*.

4. **Desire** (wish/hope). Expression of a wish or hope.

   I hope to see you soon *(3 John 1:14)*.

5. **Exclamation**.

   I am a miserable man *(Rom 7:24)*.

6. **Exhortation** (command/encouragement).

   "Get behind me, Satan!" *(Mark 8:33)*

7. **Warning**.

> For if we go on sinning deliberately after receiving the knowledge of the truth, there no longer remains a sacrifice for sins (Heb 10:26).

8. **Promise**.

> I will never leave you nor forsake you (Heb 13:5).

9. **Problem/Resolution**. The stating of a problem followed by its resolution.

> And you were dead in your trespasses and sins.… But God … made us alive together with Christ (Eph 2:1-5).

10. **Entreaty**. A polite request made to a superior.

> Give us this day our daily bread (Matt 6:11).

11. **Prayer** (Col 1:9-10). See p. 249

Modifications

These are different ways to modify the main assertion.

Temporal

1. **Time**. A simple statement of the time an event, action, or state occurred. It answers the question, "When did this occur?"

> Then *after fasting and praying* they laid their hands on them and sent them off (Acts 13:3).

2. **Simultaneous**. Two or more events or states expressed as happening at the same time.

> Then, when they had *fasted and prayed* and laid hands on them, they sent them off (Acts 13:3).

3. **Sequence**. Two or more events expressed as happening one after the other.

> He appeared to Cephas, *then* to the twelve (1 Cor 15:5).

4. **Progression**. Same as "sequence," but the emphasis is placed on the developmental nature of the actions.

> I planted, Apollos watered (1 Cor 3:6a).

Location

5. **Place**. Where the event, action, or state occurred. Answers the question, "Where?"

> They came *to Thessalonica* (Acts 17:1).

6. **Sphere**. The domain or realm of existence.

> But you are not in the flesh, you are *in the Spirit* (Rom 8:9a).

7. **Source**. The point of origin. Answers the question, "From where?"

> But we have this treasure in earthen vessels, to show that the transcendent power *belongs to God* and not to us (2 Cor 4:7).

8. **Separation**. Creating distance between two parties.

> And lead us not into temptation, but deliver us *from evil* (Matt 6:13).

9. **Posture**. A frame of mind, an attitude, or an approach toward something or someone.

> Unlike so many, we do not peddle the word of God for profit (2 Cor 2:17).

Adverbial

10. Measure. Answers the question, "How long?" "How many?" or, "How far?"

> Why do you stand here idle *all day*? *(Matt 20:6).*

11. Circumstance. Situations surrounding events or actions.

> … *leaving all* they followed him *(Luke 5:11).*

12. Object

> … whom God presented as a propitiation through faith in his blood for a demonstration *of his righteousness (Rom 3:25).*

13. Cause. An event or state that produces some result. Answers the question, "What brought this about?"

> Therefore, *having been justified by faith,* we have peace with God through our Lord Jesus Christ *(Rom 5:1a).*

14. Result. An outcome of some action or attitude.

> Having shut your door, pray to your Father who is in secret, and *your Father who sees in secret will repay you (Matt 6:6).*

15. Purpose. An outcome that one intends to take place. Answers the question, "What did he wish to occur?"

> For God so loved the world, that he gave his only Son, *that whoever believes in him should not perish but have eternal life (John 3:16).*

16. Means. The tool or instrument used in carrying out an action. Answers the question, "How did he do that?"

But *by the grace of God* I am what I am *(1 Cor. 15:10a).*

17. Manner. How the instrument is used. Answers the question, "In what way did he do this?"

> Only that *in every way,* whether *in pretense* or *in truth,* Christ is proclaimed *(Phil 1:18).*

18. Agency. The personal agent who performs the action. Answers the question, "By whom?" or, "Through whom?"

> We have peace with God *through our Lord Jesus Christ (Rom 5:1).*

19. Substance. The material or reality of which something is made.

> Asking that you may be filled with the knowledge *of his will* (Col 1:9). ("His will" makes up the "knowledge.")

20. Reference. An expression of relation. Answers the question, "With reference to whom or what?"

> You were taught, *with regard to your former way of life,* to put off your old self *(Eph 4:22).*

21. Advantage or Disadvantage. For whom or against whom an action takes place.

> For one will scarcely die *for a righteous person (Rom 5:7).*

> Thus you witness *against yourselves* that you are sons of those who murdered the prophets *(Matt 23:31).*

22. Association. Expresses the idea of accompaniment.

> And if anyone forces you to go one mile, go *with him* two miles *(Matt 5:41).*

23. **Relationship**. Expresses some form of personal relationship.

> We always thank God, the Father *of our Lord* Jesus Christ (*Col 1:3*).

24. **Possession**. Expresses ownership.

> And if anyone would sue you and take *your* tunic, let him have *your* cloak as well (*Matt 5:40*).

Logic

25. **Basis**. The grounds upon which a statement or command is made.

> *For the one who enters God's rest has also rested from his works, as God did from his.* Let us, therefore, make every effort to enter that rest (*Heb 4:10-11*).

26. **Inference**. The logical conclusion drawn from an idea.

> If anyone does not stumble in what he says, *he is a perfect man* (*Jam 3:2*).

27. **Condition**. A requirement that must be fulfilled.

> *If anyone does not stumble in what he says,* he is a perfect man (*Jam 3:2*).

28. **Concession/Contra-expectation**. A reservation or qualification.

> *Although he was a son,* he learned obedience through what he suffered (*Heb 5:8*).

29. **Contrast/Comparison**. Two conditions, ideas, or actions put together in order to point out differences.

> Therefore *do not be foolish, but understand* what the will of the Lord is (*Eph 5:17*).

30. **General/Specific**. When a general and a specific statement are put side-by-side to show the relationship between a broader and a particular concept, truth, or action.

> *No one takes this honor for himself,* but only when called by God, just as Aaron was. So also *Christ did not exalt himself to be made a high priest,* but was appointed (*Heb 5:4-5*).

Clarification

31. **Restatement**. The same idea is expressed in a different way.

> For I will be merciful toward their iniquities, and *I will remember their sins no more* (*Heb 8:12*).

32. **Description**. Functions to provide vivid detail of a person, event, state, or object.

> A *great red dragon,* with *seven heads and ten horns,* and on his heads *seven diadems* (*Rev 12:3*).

33. **Identification**. Information used to specify a person or thing. Answers the question, "Which one?"

> Now there was a man of the Pharisees *named Nicodemus,* a ruler of the Jews (*John 3:1*).

34. **Illustration/Example**. To elucidate by use of examples.

> God, having promised to Abraham … swore by himself … And so having waited pateintly [Abraham] obtained the promise (*Heb 6:13-15*). The whole of vv 13–15 function as the illustration.

35. **Apposition**. A noun or participle that follows immediately another noun or participle

with which it shares a common referent.

> For this reason I, Paul, *a prisoner* for Christ Jesus *(Eph 3:1)*.

36. **Explanation**. The addition of clarifying statements to a main proposition.

> And when you pray, do not heap up empty phrases as the Gentiles do, *for they think that they will be heard for their many words (Matt 6:7)*.

37. **Expansion**. Adding to a previous statement.

> Therefore, it is necessary for an overseer to be above reproach: *a man of one woman, clear-minded, self-controlled (1 Tim 3:2)*.

38. **Alternative** (either . . . or). When one condition, action, or place is expressed as a possible substitute for another.

> Either he will hate the one and love the other, *or he will be devoted to the one and despise the other (Matt 6:24)*.

39. **Question/Answer**. I'll let you figure this one out.

> And he asked them, *"But who do you say that I am?"* Peter answered him, *"You are the Christ" (Mark 8:29)*.

40. **Content**. The material or reality that something contains.

> Therefore let us leave standing the elementary teaching about Christ and let us move on to maturity, not laying again a foundation of *repentance from dead works*

and of faith in God, instruction about cleansing rites and laying on of hands (Heb 6:1-2).

41. **Verification**. Something by which a truth is established.

> For David did not ascend into the heavens, but he himself says, *"The Lord said to my Lord, Sit at my right hand, until I make your enemies a footstool for your feet."* (Acts 2:34-35).

Form

38. **Introduction**. A passage that presents the opening of a discussion or narrative, such as Hebrews 1:1-4 or Mark 1:1.

38. **Conclusion/Summary**. To bring to an end by way of summary or final decisive statement, such as Mark 7:28–29.

39. **List**. A number of things, normally of the same kind, mentioned one after the other.

> To God's elect, strangers in the world, scattered throughout *Pontus, Galatia, Cappadocia, Asia and Bithynia* (1 Pet 1:1).

40. **Series**. The joining of equally prominent assertions or commands in a loose association.

> *Rejoice always, pray without ceasing, give thanks in all circumstances (1 Thess 5:16-18)*.

41. **Parallel**. Two or more elements correspond verbally or conceptually.

> You are the salt of the earth.... *You are the light of the world (Matt 5:13-14)*.

On the next page is a sample of how you can use these tags to define the relationships between phrases. It is Col 1:9–14 (ESV).

9a		And so,
b	duration	from the day we heard,
c	**assertion**	**we have not ceased to pray for you,**
d	content	asking that you may be filled
e	content	with the knowledge of his will
f	manner	in all spiritual wisdom and understanding,
10a	purpose	so as to walk
b	manner	in a manner worthy of the Lord,
c	manner	fully pleasing to him,
d	result	bearing fruit in every good work and
e	result	increasing in the knowledge of God.
11a	result	May you be strengthened
b	instrument	with all power,
c	accordance	according to his glorious might,
d	purpose	for all endurance and patience with joy,
12a	result	giving thanks to the Father,
b	description	who has qualified you to share in the inheritance of the saints in light.
13a	description	He has delivered us from the domain of darkness and
b		transferred us to the kingdom of his beloved Son,
14	description	in whom we have redemption, the forgiveness of sins.

Chapter 31

The History of the Bible and Textual Criticism

In my opening discussion, "What Would It Look Like If You Knew a Little Greek?" (pp. xi–xvii), I give two examples of different translations. The first was what the angels said to the shepherds, and I pointed out how these two are substantially different.

> Glory to God in the highest, and on earth *peace, good will toward men.* (KJV)

> Glory to God in the highest, and on earth *peace among men with whom he is pleased.* (RSV)

I also talked about how some translations stop at Mark 16:8 while others go on to verse 20, including v 18, which talks about Christians handling snakes and drinking poison.

These differences are not due to different translations of the same Greek words. The differences are due to the fact that there are variations among the many Greek manuscripts we have of the New Testament; some translations follow certain selected manuscripts and other translations follow others. If you are going to know why translations are different, you need to have some awareness of this issue.

To put it another way, along the bottom of many Bibles you will see the constant mention of what "other manuscripts" say. These footnotes are talking about the differences that exist among the different Greek manuscripts. The easiest way to explain these dif-

ferences is to walk through church history and see how the Bible has come down to us through the centuries. All Bible citations below are from the ESV unless otherwise stated.

Writing of the New Testament

The New Testament authors wrote for many different reasons. The gospels were written to slightly different audiences, and while they had the same basic message, they also had their own themes the authors wanted to stress. Matthew appears to have been written more for a Jewish audience as is seen, among other things, by his frequent assertion that a certain act fulfilled prophecy. Matthew wanted his audience to understand that Jesus was the Messiah. It is generally believed that Mark was written for a Roman audience and, among other things, wanted to show that Jesus was the Son of God. Luke, we believe, was written more for Gentiles; many of the passages that occur only in Luke address this specific audience. He also tells us that he wanted people (specifically Theophilus) to understand the "certainty" of the gospel story (Luke 1:4). John was written so that his audience "may believe that Jesus is the Christ, the Son of God, and that by believing you may have life in his name" (20:31). When these gospels were first writ-

There are several books I will be citing. Each is worth reading if you want more information.

Paul Wegner, *The Journey from Texts to Translations* (Baker, 1999). A college-length textbook with many pictures and original citations. An excellent reference book as well as an enjoyable book just to read.

Philip Comfort, *Essential Guide to Bible Versions* (Tyndale, 2000). A lay-level discussion of the history of the Bible and its translations, written by the chair of the New Testament Committee for the New Living Bible.

Bruce Metzger, *The Bible in Translation* (Baker, 2001). An authoritative discussion by one of the preeminent translators and textual critics of our day, who was part of the translation team of the RSV and convener of the New Testament division for the NRSV. Prof. Metzger was a scholar and a gentleman.

Bruce Metzger, *The Text of the New Testament: Its Transmission, Corruption, and Restoration* (Oxford, 1992, third, enlarged edition). This is the best discussion of the history of the Greek text.

ten, they were probably sent to the author's specific audience.

The letters (or epistles) are another matter. Most of Paul's letters were written to a church. They were written to answer specific questions (e.g., 1 Corinthians, 1 and 2 Thessalonians), deal with specific problems (e.g., Galatians), thank the church (Philippians), or to prepare the way for future ministry (Romans). He also wrote letters to an old friend (Philemon) and two of his associates (1 and 2 Timothy, Titus). Some of the letters don't tell us much about to whom they were written (e.g., Hebrews, James, 1 and 2 Peter, 1 John). The short letters of 2 and 3 John were written to a specific church and to a friend, Gaius. Even more so than the Gospels, these letters would have been sent to a specific audience.

These original writings, or what we call the "autographs," would have been written on papyrus (2 John 12) or possibly parchment (2 Timothy 4:13). They were then delivered to the churches/people to whom they were written, perhaps by friends traveling to the area or by people specifically sent (e.g., Eph 6:21-22; Col 4:7-9). When the New Testament was written, there were no printing presses, no photocopy machines, no Internet. They were not broadcast to the widest possible audience. They were written to specific audiences, and it was to each audience that the writing was first sent.

Spread of the Writings

So how were the writings spread? Obviously, when Paul's letter to a church arrived, it was read to everyone in that church (e.g., 1 Thess 5:27). We can assume that different individuals wanted copies of the letters, either for their own reading or to share with other people in the city. It is also safe to assume that as people traveled, they wanted to take copies of these writings to people and churches in other cities, as well as obtain copies of the gospels/letters that perhaps had been written to the other churches. In fact, Paul tells the Colossians to share their letter with the church at Laodicea, and to be sure to read the one he wrote the Laodiceans (Col 4:16). This type of sharing occurred throughout the ancient world.

So how were the copies made? It does not appear that the early church used professional scribes to make the copies, and the church was growing quickly and the word needed to get out. People either sat down and copied the letter/gospel, or sometimes, perhaps rarely, a person would read it aloud and a small group would write what they heard. As you might imagine, this is where a problem arose. If you were to sit down and copy the letter of Romans, or if you were to read it and have others write what they heard, you can imagine how many and what types of errors would creep into the copies. The fact of the matter is that no two manuscripts of the Greek New Testament are identical. There are differences among all of them.

This is not a made-up problem. This is not some problem created by a "liberal bias" against Scripture. These "mistakes," these differences among the copies of the New Testament writings, are real. You can look at them and see the differences.

It was merely a matter of time before the autographs, written as they were on biodegradable materials, would deteriorate, become unusable, and be discarded. All that the church had, then, were manuscript copies, with all their differences.

The Types of Differences Among the Manuscripts

If you sit down and look at the differences among the Greek manuscripts of the New Testament, they fall into one of two categories, unintentional and intentional. Many of the mistakes are **unintentional**, such as misspellings and transposition of words.

- The name John can be spelled Ἰωάνης or Ἰωάννης. While the shift from a double to a single ν is a difference, it is not that significant especially in terms of meaning. There are, likewise, multiple spellings of

---

Autograph. The original document written by the biblical author. **Manuscript**. Copies made of the autograph or other manuscripts. **Papyrus**. A writing material made of strips from papyrus reeds that were laid vertically, and another layer laid horizontally, and then pressed together. **Parchment** and **Vellum**. Writing materials made from animal hides, parchment from sheep and goats, and vellum from younger calves and kids. **Reading**. The word(s) used by a specific manuscript in a specific location. For example, I can talk about the reading "peace, good will toward men" and the reading "peace among men with whom he is pleased." **Textual Criticism**. The science of studying the differences among the manuscripts and deciding which reading is most likely to be original. **Translation**. Moving what was written from one language to another. Also called versions. The obvious bears repeating: no translation is inspired; all translations are interpretive. **Lectionary**. Biblical texts prepared for church reading in the liturgy. **Codex**. As opposed to a single piece of writing material or a scroll, the codex is like our modern books. Individual leaves were folded and then sewed together.

the names "Gerasenes" (Mark 5:1), "Bethesda" (John 5:2), and others.

Mistakes include the omission of a word, transposing letters, or even transposing words.

- In several places we are not sure whether the author wrote "Jesus Christ" or "Christ Jesus" (e.g., 1 Tim 1:16).

- In some places we are not sure whether the author included the definite article or not (e.g., "the resurrection" in 2 Tim 2:18).

Some of these differences can be traced to similar sounding letters.

- Romans 5:1 says either "we have peace" (ἔχομεν) or "let us have peace" (ἔχωμεν); the difference in pronunciation between o and ω was slight to negligible.

- Does John write "And we are writing these things so that our (ἡμῶν) joy may be complete" or "so that your (ὑμῶν) joy may be complete" (1 John 1:4)? Again, the difference in sound between η and υ is so slight, especially in medieval manuscripts, that they could easily be mistaken.

These types of differences constitute the bulk of the differences among manuscripts. Rarely do they affect the theological meaning of the verse; the last two examples constitute two of the more significant differences. For an excellent chart of these types of mistakes, see Wegner, *Journey*.

Intentional changes can be more difficult to detect, and just because a change appears to be intentional does not mean that the change was necessarily ill-intentioned. Sometimes we see a scribe changing what evidently he thought was an error. Either he was right, or in changing the text he introduced an error. Sometimes we see scribes trying to improve grammar, using a fancier word to dress-up the verse, or using a simpler word to make the verse more understandable. Sometimes words are added to help explain the text. (These additions may originally have been written in the margins and in later centuries moved into the text itself.) When the same account appears in more than one gospel, we can see the scribes trying to make sure the gospels do not contradict each other (i.e., "harmonization"). They do the same with harmonizing Old Testament citations in the New Testament with the Old Testament itself, as well as harmonizing similar statements in different New Testament passages. Scribes tended to add to the name of Jesus (e.g., changing "Jesus" to "Jesus Christ the Lord") out of reverence.

- Matt 9:17 reads, "But new wine is put into fresh wineskins, and so both are preserved." The parallel in Luke 5:38 reads, "But new wine must be put into fresh wineskins." Some Lukan manuscripts add, "and so both are preserved" to harmonize the saying.

- The manuscripts of Matthew 16:20 read "the Christ," "Jesus Christ," or "Christ Jesus" (cf. Gal 6:17).

- Matthew 15:8 reads,

"This people honors me with their lips,
    but their heart is far from me."
It is a citation of Isaiah 29:13, which reads,

"Because this people draw near with their mouth
    and honor me with their lips,
    while their hearts are far from me."

Some manuscripts of Matthew 15:8 begin, "This people draws near to me with their mouth," to make the citations closer.

- Matthew 9:13 reads, "Go and learn what this means, 'I desire mercy, and not sacrifice.' For I came not to call the righteous, but sinners." Some manuscripts add "to repentance" after "sinners" for clarity's sake or to harmonize with Luke 5:32.

- John 5 contains the account of Jesus healing the paralytic in the pool of Bethesda. Vv 3, 5 read, "³In these lay a multitude of invalids—blind, lame, and paralyzed. ⁵One man was there who had been an invalid for thirty-eight years." Where did v 4 go, which talks about the angel stirring the water? It doesn't exist in the oldest and best manuscripts; and in about twenty manuscripts that include v 4, the scribes indicated that the words are an addition to the original text. It is easy to imagine a scribe reading v 3 and v 5, knowing that readers will wonder why the paralytic was lying there for so long, and perhaps at first adding a comment in the margin, and then eventually the marginal note being added to the text. Vv 3b- 4 read, "waiting for the moving of the water, ⁴for an angel of the Lord went down at certain seasons into the pool, and stirred the water: whoever stepped in first after the stirring of the water was healed of whatever disease he had."

Why didn't God superintend the process? Why didn't God's providence control the copying process so that mistakes didn't creep into the copies? This is an interesting question, especially for those who hold to a high view of Scripture. There are several answers.

1. Regardless of one's theological position on Scripture, it is in fact remarkable how well the copies of the New Testament made it through the centuries. As we will see below, we have over 5,600 Greek manuscripts of the New Testament (most of them only partial), which is significantly more than any other writing from antiquity. It is because we have so many manuscripts that it is possible to look at all of them and come to a relatively comfortable conclusion as to what was originally written.

2. The vast majority of the differences are inconsequential (misspellings, a word left out), and no cardinal doctrine is brought into question by any viable variant.

3. From this I would conclude that God did superintend the process of copying the gospels/letters of the New Testament. For whatever reason he chose to allow mistakes to creep in, he evidently did make sure that the basic message of the New Testament was never corrupted.

All of these scribal tendencies are natural and not necessarily the result of a desire to pervert Scriptures. Granted, there was some of this. The heretic Marcion tried to remove all the Jewishness from Jesus and the New Testament. But usually the changes appear to be well-intentioned.

Do scribes always add to Scripture? Couldn't they also drop out? It certainly is a possibility, but it appears that they rarely did; when they did omit, it was almost always due to accidental oversight. It is sometimes said today that the scribes tended to omit words and verses because of their heretical belief, but that is an unsubstantiated claim.

If nothing else, this should help you understand many of the footnotes in your Bible. When the translators are not sure of the original reading, they will sometimes list the other reading(s) in the footnotes. Jude 5 reads, "Now I want to remind you, although you once fully knew it, that Jesus, who saved a people out of the land of Egypt," an amazing statement missed in some manuscripts, because it means the God of the Exodus was Jesus. The footnote on "Jesus" in the ESV reads, "Some manuscripts *although you fully knew it, that the Lord who once saved*." Footnotes are sometimes included when the translators are confident of the correct Greek reading, but out of deference to the KJV and the familiarity of the verse they list an alternate reading. For example, most modern translations recognize that the Lord's Prayer ends, "but deliver us from evil" (Matthew 6:13). But they add the footnote, "some manuscripts add *For yours is the kingdom and the power and the glory forever. Amen.*" While this ending of the prayer is well known, beloved by most, and without it the prayer "feels" incomplete, there is little question that it was added centuries after Matthew wrote down Christ's prayer.

Historical Events

There are several major events in the early history of the church that had a significant impact on the spread of the Greek manuscripts. The first is persecution. Christians have been persecuted from the earliest days, and their writings were often destroyed. During the persecution by the Roman emperors, many Christians were martyred and their sacred writings destroyed. In 303 Diocletian ordered the destruction of all Christian Scriptures. Fortunately, a few years later the emperor Constantine guaranteed the safety of religion, specifically Christianity, throughout the Roman empire, and the mass destruction of the Bible ceased.

The church grew publicly, and the need for Bibles increased greatly. The copying of manuscripts continued, more now by monks. Not only did they copy the text but they embellished it cosmetically with color and fancy edging. The fracture between the Eastern and the Western Church was also becoming significant. The Eastern Church was based in Constantinople and used Greek. The Western Church was centered in Rome, and Latin was becoming its official language.

The other major event had to do with a man named Lucian of Antioch. Before the Diocletian persecution, Lucian produced an edited version of the Greek New Testament (Jerome, *Patrologia Latina* 29, column 527). This means that he looked at different Greek manuscripts, and instead of

---

Uncials are a form of capital letters used in the 2nd through the 9th century. The script was written with more curves than the previous form of the alphabet, curves that make it easier to write. **Cursive** script was used from the 9th through the 16th century. It is like our handwriting where the letters are connected. **Lectionaries** are biblical texts prepared for church reading in the liturgy. **Papyri** refers to the type of writing material. (All extant Greek New Testament papyri use uncial script.)

---

simply copying one, he merged all the manuscripts into one. In the process he smoothed over difficult readings, modified grammar, harmonized passages, and the like. When the Diocletian persecution began, many of the Bibles were destroyed, both some of Lucian's and the manuscripts he used. When Constantine reversed the policy and actually asked Eusebius to have fifty copies of the Bible made for the church at Constantinople, it was the remaining copies of Lucian's work that evidently were copied. (See Metzger, *Text*, for more details; this account is simplified.) Because the Eastern Church used Greek, it became the primary source of Greek manuscripts, and many copies were made. Despite their number, they were an altered text, significantly different from the citations of the New Testament that we read in the early Greek Church Fathers.

Latin Translations

In the Western Church, the Bible was translated into Latin. As early as 160 Tertullian evidently used a Latin Bible. By the end of the fourth century, there were so many versions of the Bible in Latin that Pope Damasus I (366-384) commissioned Jerome (c. 345-420) to standardize the Latin Bible. He began his work in Rome and finished many years later in Bethlehem. The New Testament was a revision of the older Latin versions as Jerome compared them to the Greek. The Gospels were published in 383. However, he translated the Old Testament afresh into Latin from the Hebrew (390-405). He was severely criticized for doing so because, in the eyes of many, the Septuagint was the "inspired translation" and therefore of abiding authority. It appears that many people of all times have struggled with a

new translation of the Bible, preferring the more familiar. Jerome called his opponents "two-legged asses" (F. F. Bruce, *The Books and the Parchments*, p. 205).

Jerome expressed his concern to Damasus about the nature of translating in the preface to his work:

> You urge me to revise the old Latin version, and, as it were, to sit in judgment on the copies of the Scriptures which are now scattered throughout the whole world; and, inasmuch as they differ from one another, you would have me decide which of them agree with the Greek original. The labour is one of love, but at the same time both perilous and presumptuous; for in judging others I must be content to be judged by all; and how can I dare to change the language of the world in its hoary old age, and carry it back to the early days of its infancy? Is there a man, learned or unlearned, who will not, when he takes the volume into his hands, and perceives that what he reads does not suit his settled tastes, break out immediately into violent language, and call me a forger and a profane person for having the audacity to add anything to the ancient books, or to make any changes or corrections therein? (in Wegner, *Journey*, p. 255)

Eventually Jerome's translation became the dominant translation in the West for 1,000 years. It is called the Latin Vulgate, "Vulgate" meaning "common" or "plain," the standard Bible of the church. It was a revised edition of Jerome's Vulgate that Wycliffe translated into English (see below). When Gutenberg (c. 1398-1468) adapted the Chinese invention of printing with moveable type to the much simpler Latin alphabet, the face of publication—both quantity and quality—was changed forever. Gutenberg's first printed book was a two-volume Vulgate. It was not until the Council of Trent (1546-1563) that the Catholic Church officially made it their authorized Bible and pronounced an anathema on anyone using any other translation.

Greek Texts

There were many forces at work in the world that had an effect on the Bible. The Eastern and Western Church continued to divide. With the downfall of the Byzantine Empire and the conquering of Constantinople (1453), the Greek scholars fled with their ancient manuscripts to the West. The Renaissance (14th - 16th centuries) and Reformation fostered a new interest in the Greek and Hebrew texts lying beneath the Latin.

The Complutensian Polyglot Bible was begun in 1502, with four columns of Hebrew, Aramaic, Greek, and Latin. The Greek manuscripts upon which it was based were evidently quite good (and a little different from Erasmus' text), and the project had significant funding. The New Testament was finished in 1514 and the Old Testament in 1517, but it was not published until 1522.

However, in 1515 a Swiss printer named Froben wanted to get a Greek Bible to market before the Complutensian Polyglot. He contacted the Dutch scholar Desiderius Erasmus (1469-1536), who then came to Basel, Switzerland, in July to begin his work. Metzger describes Erasmus' work as follows.

> For most of the text he relied on two rather inferior manuscripts from a monastic library at Basle, one of the Gospels … and one of the Acts and Epistles, both dating from about the twelfth century. Erasmus compared them with two or three others of the same books and entered occasional corrections for the printer in the margins or between the lines of the Greek script. For the Book of Revelation he had but one manuscript, dating from the twelfth century, which he had borrowed from

his friend Reuchlin. Unfortunately, this manuscript lacked the final leaf, which had contained the last six verses of the book. For these verses, as well as a few other passages throughout the book where the Greek text of the Apocalypse and the adjoining Greek commentary with which the manuscript was supplied are so mixed up as to be almost indistinguishable, Erasmus depended upon the Latin Vulgate, translating this text into Greek. (*Text*, 99-100)

The three manuscripts are Codex 1, 2, and 2814 (earlier named 1ʳ).

Erasmus' work was hurried and poor in many cases. Not only were there hundreds of typographical errors, but he added words that could not be found in any current Greek manuscripts. The most famous was his inclusion of Paul's question, "What shall I do, Lord?" in Acts 9:6, copied from the parallel account in Acts 22:10. His translation from Latin to Greek in Revelation includes words that do not exist in the Greek language (see Metzger, *Text*, p. 100n1). But Erasmus finished his work in ten months and beat the Complutensian Polyglot to market on March 1, 1516.

It was published as a diglot, with a parallel translation in Latin that Erasmus had been working on for several years. At first it was not well received. Because his Latin translation was different from the more familiar Vulgate, he was viewed with suspicion, and the typographical errors brought him ridicule from many quarters. The Greek was also suspect because Latin had been the language of the Western Church for a thousand years, and many could not believe that the Greek texts were more reliable than the Latin translations. Strange but true (although the Greek texts Jerome used were evidently superior to those Erasmus used, and consequently his overall resultant translation was better, too). But the fact that it was published first, combined with the fact that it was smaller and cheaper than the Complutensian Polyglot, were major forces in its eventual acceptance and dominance in the market.

Erasmus' text went through five editions. The second (1519) was used by Luther as the basis for his German translation in 1522. The third edition (1522) was used by Tyndale. The fourth edition (1527) became the standard, an edition corrected by comparisons with the now-published and superior Complutensian Polyglot (about 90 changes in Revelation alone). Future editions by Stephanus and Beza were based on this fourth edition. The King James translators (1611) used Beza's editions of 1588-1589 and 1598. In 1633 two relatives, Bonaventure and Abraham Elzevir, printed a copy of Beza's 1565 edition with the following advertisement: "[The reader has] the text which is now received by all, in which we give nothing changed or corrupted" (Metzger, *Text*, 106). The Latin behind "text … received" is "textum … receptum," from which the phrase "Textus Receptus," or the "Received Text," came. This became the dominant Greek text for the next two and a half centuries. Even so, variants began to be noted. The TR was used, after a while, out of attrition. Variants to it were listed in footnotes.

Metzger concludes, "So superstitious has been the reverence accorded the Textus Receptus that in some cases attempts to criticize or emend it have been regarded as akin to sacrilege. Yet its textual basis is essentially a handful of late and haphazardly collected

As of today, there are 5,824 Greek New Testament manuscripts: 128 papyri; 322 majuscules; 2,914 minuscules; 2,460 lectionaries. However, a few of these are actually parts of the same document. But taking these into consideration, there are more than 5,600 manuscripts. The most recent numbers can be found at the website for Institut für neutestamentliche Textforschung, at:

http://intf.uni-muenster.de/vmr/NTVMR/

Be sure to check out the work at The Center for the Study of New Testament Manuscripts, at:

http://csntm.com

minuscule manuscripts, and in a dozen passages its reading is supported by no known Greek witness" (*Text*, 106).

English Translations

Over the centuries most people did not know how to read Latin or Greek, and it unfortunately became the teaching of the church that only the clergy were able to read and interpret the Bible. John Wycliffe (c. 1329-1384) was a pastor and a scholar who was highly critical of the current church, opposing its corruption and much of its teaching. As such Wycliffe has earned the title "Morning Star of the Reformation." Wycliffe believed that the Bible, not the Pope, had the right to determine biblical doctrine, and therefore he translated the Vulgate into English, along with the help of his students. Then his students and other people, nicknamed the Lollards, carried his translation and teaching throughout England. For his efforts Wycliffe was branded a heretic, anyone caught reading his translation was excommunicated, and some of his students were burned at the stake. Wegner (p. 282) writes,

> Archbishop Arundel denounces Wycliffe in a letter to Pope John XXIII in 1411: "This pestilent and wretched John Wyclif, of cursed memory, that son of the old serpent ... endeavored by every means to attack the very faith and sacred doctrine of the Holy Church, devising—to fill up the measure of his malice—the expedient of a new translation of the Scriptures into the mother tongue."

Even after Wycliffe's death, his work was continued by his followers. John Purvey produced a second edition (1388), which became the main English Bible until the time of Tyndale. In 1428 Pope Martin V had Wycliffe's body exhumed, burned, and the ashes thrown into the local river. Metzger poetically concludes, "But just as his ashes were carried by that river to multiple points, so his message went far and wide during the following centuries" (*Translation,* 57).

William Tyndale (c. 1494-1536) produced the first English translation from the Greek and Hebrew. One of the more famous quotations comes from his debate with a cleric.

> Not long after, Tindall happened to be in the company of a certain divine, recounted for a learned man, and in disputing with him drave him to that issue, that the great doctor burst out into these blasphemous words: "We are better to be without God's law than the Pope's." Master Tindall, replied, "I defy the Pope and all his laws," and added that if God spared him life, ere many years he would cause a boy that driveth the plough to know more of the Scripture than he did. (from *Foxe's Book of Martyrs,* in Wegner, pp. 285-86)

Tyndale was required to obtain ecclesiastical permission to write a new translation.

Unable to do so, he went to London and for six months, supported by a wealthy cloth merchant, started his translation. Eventually he fled to Europe to finish. He translated the New Testament from the Textus Receptus and published it in 1526, with a second edition in 1534. In 1536 he was kidnapped, tried, killed by strangulation, and burned at the stake. His final words were, "Lord, open the King of England's eyes."

All this happened while King Henry VIII was married and without a male heir. The King eventually broke with the Roman Catholic Church, divorced his wife to marry Anne Boleyn, and within one year of Tyndale's death allowed the printing of an English Bible based largely on Tyndale's work. In fact, the long line of English translations that followed (Coverdale, Great Bible, Bishops' Bible) were all heavily indebted to Tyndale's work. It is estimated that over 80 percent of the English Bible, from the King James Version through the Revised Version (1881), was the work of Tyndale. It is fascinating to read about the opposition mounted toward these translations, how they were condemned as perversions written by "damnable" men who sought to destroy the faith. History is a record of entrenched thought preferring the comfortable to anything new, regardless of the quality of the new.

When Catholic persecution under Queen Mary I made Bible translation nearly impossible in England, many Protestant scholars fled to Geneva, Switzerland, for safety. The Geneva Bible was due primarily to the work of William Whittingham, brother-in-law to John Calvin. (The New Testament was published in 1557, the Old Testament in 1560.) Its margins were covered in notes, some doctrinal (Calvinist obviously), others political (e.g., the pope was identified with "the angel of the bottomless pit" [Rev 9:11]). It was the first

English Bible with numbered verses, and continued the practice of italicizing English words not in the Greek. Its smaller size and cheaper price aided its popularity, dominating the market from 1560 through 1666. This was the Bible of Shakespeare, John Bunyan, the Puritan pilgrims, and the young King James.

In 1604 King James I held a conference at Hampton Court in an attempt to reconcile religious differences between the Church of England and the Puritans. It was there that the suggestion came for a revision of the Bishops' Bible. The revision was to stay as close to the Bishops' Bible as the Greek and Hebrew would allow, and the translators were to pay special attention to previous translations (except the Geneva Bible), ecclesiastical terminology was to be kept, and no notes critical of the church were to be included. The translation team was comprised of most of the best scholars of the day, and their work became the most dominating force in the history of English literature. The original title page reads,

> The Holy Bible, Conteyning the Old Testament, and the New: Newly Translated out of the Originall tongues: & with the former Translations diligently compared and revised, by his Maiesties speciall Commandment. Appointed to be read in Churches. Anno Dom. 1611. (in Metzger, *Translation*, 75)

The Greek, of course, was basically that of Beza (Erasmus; Textus Receptus), and the translation became known in America as the King James Version, in England as the Authorized Version.

Textual Criticism

So why is the King James Version of the Bible (and its most recent American revision,

the New King James Bible) different in so many places from all other modern translations? I have been working slowly through history (actually, it was a sprint) so you can understand the issues in the following discussion.

Erasmus had very few Greek manuscripts from which to work, and they were late. Regardless of how many Greek manuscripts might have been available in 1611—and the number is considerably less than we now possess—the King James translators slavishly followed just Beza's edition. However, since that time thousands of additional Greek New Testament manuscripts (most containing only part of the New Testament) have been found in libraries and monasteries, and by archaeologists.

There are more than 5,600 Greek manuscripts of the New Testament. Most of them are parts of the New Testament; only about 50 are of the entire New Testament, only one of those being an uncial (Sinaiticus). Along with these manuscripts we also have about 10,000 manuscripts of the Bible in different languages (such as Coptic, Syriac, Armenian, Georgian, and Latin) as well over one million citations in the Church Fathers in Latin alone.

When we consider these manuscripts, especially the uncials and papyri, which were written centuries before the minuscules used by Erasmus, the question then becomes which of the readings are most likely to be original. The science of textual criticism was born in order to answer this question.

Basic to the science is the concept of "text-types." As the manuscripts were studied, it was found that they fall into four basic groupings. Manuscripts that showed the same types of changes, corrections, readings, and physical location were said to belong to a text-type. Four text-types are hypothesized: Alexandrian, Caesarean, Western, and Byzantine. The basic conclusion of textual criticism is that the manuscripts that belong to the Alexandrian text-type are most likely to consistently contain the original wording. They show less willingness on the scribes' part to change, add to, harmonize, or otherwise alter the text. They are also some of the oldest manuscripts, having been written as far back as the second century. Two of the more famous Alexandrian manuscripts are Sinaiticus, written about 350-375, and Vaticanus, also fourth century. On the other hand, textual critics are nearly unanimous that the Byzantine text-type is the least reliable, showing the greatest willingness on the part of the scribes to amend the text. These manuscripts stem, it is hypothesized, from the creative work of Lucian that I discussed above.

So convincing is the work of textual critics that all modern translations give significantly greater weight to the readings of the Alexandrian manuscripts. Erasmus, on the other hand, and therefore the King James translators had access only to a few manuscripts that stem from the Byzantine text-type. Because the Alexandrian and the Byzantine manuscripts are so different in places, because the King James Version is based on Byzantine manuscripts, and because all translations in the last century are based primarily on the Alexandrian manuscripts, you can see why recent translations are often different from the KJV.

Now here is the interesting point. There is little debate among scholars, whether they are on the evangelical or liberal side of the theological spectrum, as to the superiority of the Alexandrian text-type and the overall findings of textual criticism. However, in certain circles, what is called the "King James Debate" rages on, and the debate can often

turn ugly. It is not my purpose here to defend my position. I primarily wanted to show you why there are manuscript differences and how those differences are reflected in the KJV and other translations. I would simply refer you to D. A. Carson, *The King James Version Debate* (Baker, 1979), for further reading. The basic contention of the minority view is that the Byzantine text-type is the best witness.

I will make one point, however. The science of textual criticism is unbelievably difficult. Very few world-class textual critics do anything but text criticism, and it is a lifelong endeavor. Their knowledge of Greek and the biblical texts is staggering. Many people who can read Greek with proficiency will quickly admit that they are not competent to enter into detailed debate on the topic. Of course, that doesn't always stop a person who lacks proficiency from jumping in. My encouragement is, if you find yourself embroiled in this debate, unless you have committed your life to Greek and have earned a proficiency in the field, defer to the experts and walk away.

Principles of Textual Criticism

1. Manuscripts are not to be counted but weighed. In other words, a simple counting of how many manuscripts support one reading as opposed to another does not arrive at the original. Let's say that two copies were made of an autograph. Scribe "A" was concerned to be as faithful as possible. Scribe "B," while perhaps well intentioned, wanted to make his copy more readable, more understandable, and more consistent (in his mind) with other books of the New Testament, and so he altered the text at will. What if manuscript "A" was never recopied, but manuscript "B" was taken to a large city where Greek was still spoken and 100 copies were made? You now have 102 manuscripts, assuming the autograph has been lost. Are the 100 copies necessarily more reliable than the single manuscript A? Of course not. You can't simply count manuscripts.

Part of this "weighing" process looks at what text-type the manuscript is from. The reading of an Alexandrian manuscript is more likely to be original than a Byzantine, since the manuscript as a whole shows more restraint at changing the biblical text. A related principle is that the older the manuscript, the closer it is to the time of the original, and the less time has passed for errors to creep in.

But let's throw a monkey wrench into the mix. What if you have an eleventh-century minuscule that is an excellent copy of a third-century uncial, and you have another minuscule that was compiled in the ninth century. Which is to be preferred? The eleventh-century will be viewed as superior to the ninth-century one, even though it was written two centuries later. Textual criticism is a complicated field that lies in the realm of the specialist.

2. The shorter reading is preferred. In general, it is easier to believe that the scribe would add to the text rather than drop out parts. (The defenders of the Byzantine text argue that the scribal tendency was to omit words.) An example is the final part of the Lord's Prayer as found in the KJV. "For thine is the kingdom and the power and the glory forever. Amen." The oldest manuscripts do not have the phrase, and it seems more likely that the words were added rather than subtracted from the text.

3. What reading best explains the other readings? When a textual critic compares two readings, he or she will ask which reading most likely gave rise to the other. For example, if you have the same story in Matthew and Luke, and in one manuscript the accounts are identical and in the other manuscript they are slightly different, which is to be preferred? The general assumption is that the manuscript that has slightly different accounts is original, since it is more believable that a scribe changed them to agree ("harmonization").

If you want to see textual criticism at work, you can read Bruce Metzger's *A Textual Commentary on the Greek New Testament* (second edition, 1994, American Bible Society). In it Metzger walks you through how the committee preparing the United Bible Societies' *Greek New Testament* made its decisions.

There are two editions of the Greek New Testament used as the basis of most modern translations. The text is identical in both, although their discussion of the various readings are different and complementary: *Novum Testamentum Graece,* 27th edition revised, German Bible Society; *Greek New Testament,* 4th edition revised, American Bible Society. (GBS just released version 28, and the fifth ABS edition is to be released soon.)

Zane Hodges and Arthur Farstad have done an excellent job collating the Byzantine manuscripts in *The Greek New Testament According to the Majority Text* (Thomas Nelson, 1985, 2nd edition, revised), so it is easy to see where the Byzantine text-type differs.

Conclusion

Thankfully, as I said earlier, no cardinal doctrine is brought into question by any viable variant. Despite claims to the contrary, the Alexandrian text has not dropped words because of the scribes' heretical beliefs.

The KJV is a beautiful translation written by the best scholars of their day, scholars who also had a command of the English language that has not since been paralleled. But the English language has changed substantially, superior Greek manuscripts have been found, and the purpose of translation is to convey the beautiful message of God's salvation in terms that the untrained person can understand. After all, the New Testament is written in "Koine" Greek—not the fancy Greek of previous centuries, but the language most familiar to Jesus, Paul, and their contemporaries. So should our translations be understandable.

Thank you

I have spent quite a bit of time walking you through the history of the Bible. It was partly so you could see why the KJV is different from more recent translations. But it was also to give you one final encouragement as we complete our study of Greek. The Bible is a precious book. Learned men and women have given their lives so we can read and understand it, in Greek, Hebrew, English, and many other languages. It is a message of truth and freedom, often opposed by the religious hierarchy currently in power. Throughout history people have been told that they are not able to read and understand the Bible, both in Catholicism as well as, ironically, in Protestantism. But when the Bible is made available in a form that we can study and from which we can learn, people can and do understand its basic message. I trust that after six weeks of study you now have the tools to better understand both your English and Greek Bibles.

Chapter 32

Translations

Communication isn't as easy as we might think. When was the last time you used plain English words and your friend looked at you with with a deadpan face and said, "What did you say?" You think, "I was crystal clear. Why can't you understand me?" But that's just the nature of communication. Even in speaking the same language in the same culture to someone you know, words don't always convey the meaning you intend them to.

Let me give you some examples. Getting used to the road signs when we first moved to New England was a treat and a half. I still remember going up Monument Street and seeing the sign, "Thickly Settled," and I thought, "What does that mean?" I stopped the car and turned to Robin (my wife) and said, "This must be where the really stupid people live because they're thick in the head." (I knew that wasn't what the sign meant, but I really had no idea what it did mean.) It turns out that "thickly settled" is a legal designation based on how closely the homes are built, and areas that are "thickly settled" have specific speed limits.

When we drove around Wenham Lake for the first time, we saw the sign "Lightly Salted." We had never seen a sign like that before and really had no idea what it meant until about the fourth time we saw the same sign elsewhere and realized the signs were all located next to lakes, which we later learned are used for reservoirs. They don't salt the roads in winter there so the salt doesn't run off and contaminate the drinking water. Now someone who is from New England might say that I am thick in the head for not understanding what the sign so "obviously" meant. No, not really. For someone who's not from New England, and it's during the summer, and who's never seen a sign like that, its meaning isn't immediately obvious.

What about communicating in the same language but in different countries? I will never forget the time when I first went to Aberdeen in Scotland and was on Princess Street. I was asking for directions to a store and a lady said, "It's at the top of the street." I wanted to say, "Ma'am, the street is level. What do you mean, 'top?'" I knew she didn't mean "on top of the pavement," but how can you have a "top" on a flat street? She was communicating with me, but I didn't have the foggiest idea what she meant.

What if you speak a different language but live in the same century? When I was learning German, I went to school in Germany for a few months. I learned that "Ich" means "I," "bin" means "am," and "kalt" means "cold." So one day I said to my friends, "Ich bin kalt," and they literally rolled on the ground laughing hysterically. When they finally regained some composure, they informed me that I had said, "I am sexually frigid." If I wanted to say, "I am cold," I had to say, "Es ist zu mir kalt," "It is to me cold."

What happens when you get all the way down this progression and you have different languages from different countries separated by the centuries, which is the position we are in with the Bible? Acts 20:37 says, if you translate word for word, "They fell on his neck." What does that mean? It means they were hugging and kissing him, in our terminology. They were falling on his neck and embracing him. How did you get that from "fall on the neck"? I think of my young son, hiding around the corner, and when I'm not looking he falls on my neck and any other part of my body that he can hit. (He's in a hitting stage.)

What is the point? The point is that communication is not simple. If there is miscommunication between two people speaking the same language, living in the same culture, looking directly at each other and being able to see body language and all the other clues we use in communication, then how much more difficult it is to understand communication coming from two thousand years ago, through a different language, stemming from a different culture.

Why am I talking about this? It is because one of the first steps toward learning to study your Bible is to understand the nature of language. It is the *meaning* conveyed by the words of Scripture that is so important to us, but to get to that meaning we have to go through *words* and *grammar*. And you probably still must rely on the translators' understanding of the words and grammar as they attempt to convey the passage's meaning. But why are the translations so different if they are working with the same words and the same grammar? All the translators I know are good people and highly qualified in their field; but each translation team is working with its own philosophy, and that is what makes all the difference. Each transla-

tion has its own answers to a set of questions. (I need to tell you up front that I was the chair of the New Testament committee for the ESV, and am currently serving on the CBT [Committee for Bible Translation] for the NIV.)

1. Words or Meaning

The most basic question is, "Am I going to translate *words* or *meaning*?

As a caveat I need to say something about the word "literal," because it is a poor word. It appears to mean one thing, but it means something else. If you ask most evangelical Christians, "What kind of Bible do you want?" they will say, "I want a literal translation." But for some people "literal" means "word for word." If the Greek has eight words, then the English should have eight words. If the first word is a participle in Greek, then the first word should be a participle in English. If the Greek doesn't have a word, then we're not going to add one unless we absolutely have to and then we will italicize it. (So we have the italics in the NASB and the KJV.) The implication is that there's minimal interpretation in this type of translation process.

However, if you look up the word "literal" in Webster's dictionary, its first meaning has to do with *meaning*, not *form*. "Literal" means, "in accordance with, involving or being the primary or strict meaning of the word or words, not figurative or metaphorical."

In other words, technically, if you say, "I want a literal translation," what you're saying is that you want a translation that *means* the same as what the author meant. We call this "authorial intent," reproducing the intention of the author. I want to hear what was meant for me to hear, not what the translator may want me to hear. When I am reading Matthew, I want to hear Matthew. And yet many people think of "literal" in terms of *form*, of a word-for-word equivalence.

What I would like to do is simply not use the word "literal" because people use it in a way that begs the question. The real question is how do I translate meaning from Greek into English so that to an English American reader, in my case, it means the same as what Matthew wrote to his original audience.

Back to the second question of translating words or meaning. There are two ways to translate. You can either translate words, or you can translate meaning. The NASB is an example of translating words, or what is technically called "formal equivalence." The "formal" means that there is grammatical formal equivalence: if the Greek has a participle, the English has a participle; if the Greek has a conjunction, the English has a conjunction; and if the Greek has ten words, the English tries to have ten words. Again the assumption is that there's minimal interpretation in this method of translation. There also is often the desire to use the same English word for the same Greek word, no matter where the Greek occurs. This is called "concordance."

The other way to translate is to translate meaning. The technical term for this is "dynamic equivalence," or what is now called "functional equivalence." The dynamism has to do with the grammatical forms. In a dynamic translation you don't care whether the Greek uses a participle or not. You don't care whether the Greek uses ten or twenty words. That's not the point. Dynamic translation chooses whatever

words the English requires in order to convey the *same meaning*. This is where the NIV fits. We often use the word "paraphrase" for this type of translation because instead of going word for word, it goes thought for thought. The problem is that the term "paraphrase" has been identified with being overly interpretive, and if you call something a paraphrase, you generally are not complementing it.

So you can translate words or meaning. There are advantages and difficulties with both of these approaches, but if you want to understand why Bibles are different, there are differences with which you must wrestle.

Problems with Formal Equivalence

Let me give you two problems of the "word-for-word" approach. The first is that it's interpretive. The very reason that people want a word-for-word translation is that they believe there's not going to be any interpretation, and that's simply not true. *All translation involves interpretation.* It is impossible to translate without being interpretive. Anyone who disagrees with this statement simply does not know Greek, Hebrew, or probably any other language well.

For example, in John 2:4 the Greek, word for word, reads, "Jesus says to her, 'What to me and to you?'" Almost no one is going to go word for word on this one, so they say,

> What do I have to do with you? (NASB)
>
> What does that have to do with us? (NASB 95)
>
> What have you to do with me? (RSV)
>
> What concern is that to you and to me? (NRSV)
>
> Why do you involve me? (NIV)
>
> How does that concern you and me? (NLT)

What does your concern have to do with Me? (NKJV)

What have I to do with thee? (KJV)

You must not tell me what to do. (TEV)

What do you want from me? (NJB)

Even the NASB will not go word for word because it means nothing at all.

In John 10:24 the RSV reads,

So the Jews gathered round him and said to him, "How long will you keep us in suspense? If you are the Christ, tell us plainly."

That sounds pretty straight forward, until you look at each word. Here is a word-for-word translation from the Greek of the phrase, "How long will you keep us in suspense":

Until when the soul of us will you lift up?

That's what the words say in the Greek. You have to be interpretive. What does it mean to "lift up the soul"? Even the NASB must be interpretive.

The NIV translates Romans 16:1,

I commend to you our sister Phoebe, a *servant* of the church in Cenchrea.

The RSV translates,

I commend to you our sister Phoebe, a *deaconess* of the church at Cenchreae.

That's an important difference. Was Phoebe part of the official structure of the church, a deaconess? Was there an official structure of the church? Was there, in the official structure of the church, a place for a woman? How are you going to translate διάκονον? "Servant," "deacon," or "deaconess"? The interesting thing here is that the noun is masculine, but you can still legitimately translate it "deaconess." The translator must make an interpretive decision.

John 5:6 is about the paralytic at the pool of Bethesda. The RSV translates,

When Jesus saw him and knew that he'd been lying there for a long time he said to him, "Do you want to be healed?"

One of the more interesting questions in all of Scripture, it seems to me. "No, I've been lying here for thirty-eight years because I like the view! Yes, I want to be healed!" But as we know, Jesus often calls for a public commitment before he heals. The important part for our discussion is that Jesus "knew," which is one of the legitimate translations of the Greek word. But the NIV reads,

When Jesus saw him lying there and learned that he had been in this condition....

What just happened? We moved from superhuman knowledge (RSV) to Jesus asking for information (NIV). Both are legitimate translations of the same word, but the translator must make a choice. He or she has to make an exegetical decision as to whether Jesus knew that this man had been lying there for a long time, or whether he had asked somebody about him. All translation is interpretive.

First Corinthians 6:9-10 is another good example. How do you translate μαλακός? If you look up the word in a dictionary, it refers to the passive member in a homosexual relationship. So the RSV says,

Do you not know that the unrighteous will not inherit the kingdom of God. Do not be deceived neither the immoral nor the idolators nor the adulterers nor *sexual perverts* nor thieves, nor the greedy, nor drunkards, nor revilers, nor robbers will inherit the kingdom of God.

Their translation of μαλακός is *sexual perverts,* which is quite general. The phrase "sexual perverts" can refer to a lot of things. But the NIV translates it as "male prostitutes" and the NASB uses the word "effeminate." "Effeminate" has a lot of meanings other than "homosexual." A person can be effeminate and not be a homosexual. How are you going to translate the word? Is it a general word for sexual perversion? Is it a specific word for male prostitutes, or does it refer to effeminate people? It's an issue of interpretation. All translation is interpretive.

So one of the problems of going word for word is that it's interpretive, the very thing that it tries not to be. A second problem of going word for word is that, frankly, word-for-word translations can lose or distort meaning. For example, the NASB usually translates πόλις as "city," both Nazareth (Matt 2:23) and Jerusalem (Matt 4:5). But what does the word "city" mean to you? It is a rather large place, isn't it? And while Jerusalem was a large city, Nazareth was a wide spot in the road, perhaps a "village" or a "hamlet." While there are advantages at times to using the same English word for the same Greek or Hebrew word, at times it distorts the meaning of the original word.

The KJV translates Romans 12:16 as, "Mind not high things," which sounds as if we are not to think about important or significant issues. While this may be more word for word, it obscures the fact that Paul is telling the Roman church to not be proud, as most modern translations agree.

Problems with Dynamic Equivalence

There are also significant problems with the dynamic equivalent approach to translation. The first relates to the translators' view of grammatical structure. Because they generally do not view the structure of the language as having much connection with meaning, they often exercise considerable freedom in translating. I certainly agree that many times there is no real significance in structure. What Greek says best with a prepositional phrase may be best said in English with a relative clause.

However, there is one distinction that I think is critical; and because dynamic translations often ignore this distinction, I cannot recommend dynamic translations for serious Bible study. (There, I showed my hand.) The distinction between a dependent and independent clause is critical in exegesis. A dependent clause is one that cannot stand on its own; it is not a complete sentence. An independent clause can stand alone; it contains a subject and finite verb. Usually, we put our main thought in the independent clause and secondary thoughts in dependent clauses. As we saw, finding the main point is the key to Bible study.

For example, if I said, "I want to learn Greek and to study my Bible," what is the main point I am making? Is there a main point? You may infer from your own sense of worth that I want to learn Greek *in order to* study my Bible, but you really can't tell; and when it comes to interpreting Scripture, we shouldn't be guessing if possible. But if I said, "After learning Greek, I can study my Bible better," then you can clearly see my priorities.

What if I said, "Go, make disciples." What is the main point? I have heard sermons on the "Great Commission" that placed almost all the weight on the "Go." But "Go" is a dependent construction (a participle), and the only independent verbal form in the verse is "make disciples." The Great Commission is not to go; it is to make disciples.

This can also be reversed. Sometimes an independent clause will be made dependent. Ephesians 4:26 in the NIV reads, "In your anger do not sin." The problem is that Ephesians 4:26 has two separate commands: "be angry; do not sin." While it is a controversial verse, the NIV has removed one of the two possible meanings. Formal equivalent theory tends to respect this distinction between dependent and independent constructions, and hence (in my opinion) formal equivalent translations are better for serious, in-depth Bible study.

A second problem with dynamic equivalence is that it is often overly interpretive. While it is certainly true that all translation involves interpretation, sometimes I think some translators give up and feel free to be as interpretive as they want. I personally don't feel the need to make something clearer in English than it is in the Greek.

This willingness to be overly (in my opinion) interpretive comes up with gender language. I will discuss gender language in detail below, but a few examples will suffice here. Some translators have concluded that words like "brother," "man," and "he" for the most part no longer function as generic terms referring to both men and women (NIV, NLT, NRSV). Fair enough, but how do you make this decision? The TNIV translates James 3:1 as "Not many of you should presume to be teachers, my brothers and sisters," interpreting ἀδελφός as "brothers and sisters." Therefore, they have removed from debate whether the early church had women teachers. (My opinion or yours on this issue is not the point. The point is that the TNIV removed the discussion entirely when they translated the one word ἀδελφός not as "brothers" but as the multiple "brothers and sisters," suggesting that James is addressing women and men teachers.) This was changed in the NIV 2011; "Not many of you should become teachers, my fellow believers."

The TNIV also translates John 19:12 as, "Pilate tried to set Jesus free, but the *Jewish leaders* kept shouting, 'If you let this man go, you are no friend of Caesar,'" despite the fact that the Greek just says "Jews." The translators' motives are not necessarily bad; they want to keep people from misunderstanding the Bible (see point 6 below). However, because of their willingness to be quite free in translating, they have laid the crucifixion at the feet of the Jewish leaders. Only the Jewish leaders called for Jesus' crucifixion. The point here is not whether they are right or not. The point is that dynamic equivalence lends itself to a type of translation that can be much more interpretive than formal equivalence.

Third, dynamic equivalence allows English style more sway than does formal equivalence. For example, Greek style does not mind repeating the same word over and over again in the same context; English avoids this, using synonyms if possible. But then in translation you lose the fact that the same word is used throughout a passage and in fact could be the theme that ties the paragraph together.

For example, here is 1 Timothy 2:1-6 in the NLT. The Greek words in parentheses are all forms of the same Greek word. When you see this repeated word, you can understand the flow of Paul's thought.

¹ I urge you, first of all, to pray for all people (ἀνθρώπων). As you make your requests, plead for God's mercy upon them, and give thanks. ² Pray this way for kings and all others who are in authority, so that we can live in peace and quietness, in godliness and dignity. ³ This is good and pleases God our

Savior, ⁴ for he wants everyone (πάντας ἀνθρώπους) to be saved and to understand the truth. ⁵ For there is only one God and one Mediator who can reconcile God and people (ἀνθρώπων). He is the man (ἄνθρωπος) Christ Jesus.

Timothy is to pray for all "people" because God wants all "people" to be saved through the one mediator between God and "people," the "human being" Christ Jesus. The NIV more clearly connects the four Greek words.

> ¹ I urge, then, first of all, that requests, prayers, intercession and thanksgiving be made for everyone—² for kings and all those in authority, that we may live peaceful and quiet lives in all godliness and holiness. ³ This is good, and pleases God our Savior, ⁴ who wants all men to be saved and to come to a knowledge of the truth. ⁵ For there is one God and one mediator between God and men, the man Christ Jesus.

Conclusion

Both formal and dynamic equivalent methods of translation suffer from the same problems because of the nature of language and communication; they both are interpretive. The translator's beliefs and knowledge, or lack of knowledge, all come into play in the translation process. In a dynamic equivalent translation the possibility for (mis)interpretation is greater. As you try to write more smoothly and with better English, the only way to do so is to become more and more interpretive. So the NLT is more interpretive than the NIV, and the NIV is more interpretive than the RSV, and the RSV is more interpretive than the ESV, and the ESV is more interpretive than the NASB, but they're all interpretive, every last one of them.

There is an Italian proverb that says, "Translators are traitors" (*Traddutore, traditore*; "Translators, traitors"), and it's true. All translation loses meaning. All translators are traitors to the actual meaning. There is no such thing as a noninterpretive translation. Anyone who says otherwise probably has a limited exposure to translation theory, and it may not be worth discussing the point with them.

That was the first and the biggest of the issues as to how we go about translating. Are you going to translate words and be interpretive, or are you going to translate meaning and be more interpretive?

2. Audience

Translators need to ask, "To whom am I writing? Who is my audience?"

There are different ways to look at this question. The first is in terms of age. Am I writing for adults or children? This will affect a lot of things, such as word choice. In the RSV, 1 John 2:2 says, "God presented Christ as a sacrifice of atonement." What's "sacrifice of atonement"? (The Greek word is ἱλασμός.) The ESV uses the word "propitiation." The NRSV uses the word "expiation." Maybe if you are an adult, you could figure out what these terms mean. The NLT simplifies it even further and says Jesus is a "sacrifice for sin." What should the translator do with ἱλασμός? If you're translating for adults, you can say, "I'm going to use the word 'propitiation' and they'll look it up if they want to know what it means; adults can see the difference between 'expiation' and 'propitiation.'" If you're translating for children, they generally can't.

Another issue when it comes to the reader's age is the complexity of the sentence structure. Greek can write long sentences, like German. A good example is Ephesians 1:3-14. It's one sentence in Greek, so what will you do? The answer largely depends on your audience. If you are translating for children, you're going to divide it into about ten smaller sentences. If you are writing to adults, you will turn it into less. The NIrV (New International Reader's Verion) uses 36 sentences and 7 paragraphs; the NIV uses eight sentences and two paragraphs; the ESV has five sentences and two paragraphs; the KJV I have uses three sentences.

The KJV is written at about a twelfth-grade level. The NIV is written at about the ninth-grade level. The NIrV is written firmly at the third-grade level. So, for example, the word "fort" is considered a fourth-grade word and the translators couldn't use it. They could use the word "stronghold," probably because you can look at its two parts and figure out what it means. They couldn't use the word "manure" but could use the word "poop." (There is stuff about poop in the Bible and you have to have a word for it.)

Another issue about the translator's audience is whether they are Christian or non-Christian. Vocabulary can be broken down into two parts, active and passive. Your active vocabulary is words that you use; passive vocabulary is words that you don't use but can understand. Someone who became a Christian at a young age and was raised in a church has a much larger passive Christian vocabulary (what we call, "translationese") than someone who is a recent Christian or not a Christian at all. That's going to affect how you translate. For example, in Romans 11:16, Paul discusses how Jews and Gentiles relate to each other in the church. The RSV translates,

> If the dough offered as first fruits is holy, so is the whole lump; and if the root is holy, so are the branches.

If you were raised in a church and understand the Old Testament background of Abraham and the patriarchs, you could figure it out. The NLT says,

> And since Abraham and the other patriarchs were holy, their children will also be holy. For if the roots of the tree are holy, the branches will be, too.

In other words the NLT interprets the metaphor for you. You might think, "Isn't that being pretty free with their translation?" In one sense, perhaps it is too much. Under inspiration Paul decided to use a metaphor. But on the other hand, the NLT does not assume that its readership is Christian and they're translating with that in mind. I don't think you can fault them for their intent, but it does illustrate why translations can be radically different.

Another example is Luke 2:7. The RSV translates,

> And she gave birth to her first-born son and wrapped him in swaddling cloths, and laid him in a manger, because there was no place for them in the inn.

What are "swaddling cloths"? Whatever it means, I am used to the expression, and when I read other translations of this passage that don't use "swaddling cloths," it feels as if they left something out. The NIV reads, "she wrapped him in cloths." The NLT has a good translation, "She wrapped him snugly in strips of cloth." In other words, the translators are trying to help you understand what swaddling cloths are. Actually I've been wrong on this my whole life. I thought swaddling cloths were diapers, but they're not. When my three children were born, they were cleaned up and wrapped tightly in a blanket. It's like the baby is back in the womb. That's what swaddling cloths are, and that's why the NLT says, "she wrapped him snugly." The translators are trying to help you understand not only the words but what the words mean.

Other issues in terms of audience are whether you want to write a translation that can be used for public readings, perhaps liturgical readings, and whether you want people to be able to memorize it easily. This controls word choice, how many words you use, whether alliteration is helpful, and so on. These and other issues related to audience have a significant impact on how the translator works, and hence one reason why translations are different.

3. Ambiguity

Translators have to ask themselves, "What am I going to do with ambiguity?" If the Greek or Hebrew isn't clear, when it can mean several different things, what am I going to do? The KJV, NASB, NRSV, and ESV generally answer that question, "Leave it alone. If the original is ambiguous, we will leave the ambiguity; and if we can reproduce in English the same ambiguity that is present in the Greek, then we will do so. We will not make up the reader's mind." But the NIV will remove some of the ambiguity, and the NLT goes to even greater lengths than the NIV.

Second Corinthians 5:14 in the RSV reads,

For the love of Christ controls us.

What does "love of Christ" mean? The same ambiguity in the Greek is present in the English, and there are two possible mean-

ings. It is Christ's love for me that controls, or it is my love for Christ that controls. The RSV says, "I'll keep it 'the love of Christ.' You figure it out for yourself." But the NIV wants to make it clear what they think it means: "For Christ's love compels us." In other words, it's Christ's love for me. The NLT says, "Whatever we do it is because Christ's love controls us." See what they're doing? They are saying that because of their audience, because of their translation philosophy, they want to tell you what they think this ambiguous construction means.

When I started writing this book, I thought I would find many places where the translations differed sharply from each other. To my surprise and delight, that proved not to be the case. Rather, what I found was that some translations leave a verse ambiguous, and others take a more interpretive stance and remove the ambiguity; but the majority of the time the latter group of translations take the same interpretive stance. The NIV and NLT are remarkably similar in what they understand Scripture to mean.

4. Move Implicit to Explicit

Some translations feel the need to fill out the story. In other words, there will be things that are perhaps *implicit* in the Greek and they'll make it *explicit* in English.

Sometimes this is just necessary. For example, Greek does not always require a direct object; English does (usually for transitive verbs), and so the translators must add one in, as in 1 Peter 1:8.

Though you have not seen him, you love *him.*

Other times, in order to avoid misunderstanding, the translator supplies the antecedent for the pronoun. Romans 6:10 in the NIV reads,

> The *death* he died, he died to sin once for all; but the *life* he lives, he lives to God.

"Death" and "life" in Greek are both the relative pronoun, whose antecedent is clear from the context.

Other times the translator will add words to help clarify meaning. For example, Philippians 1:7 says,

> It is right for me to feel thus about you because I hold you in my heart, for you are all partakers with me of grace.

The NIV says, "All of you share in *God's grace.*" The NLT writes, "We have shared together the *blessings of God.*" The word "God" is not in the Greek, but the translators felt that the verse was not fully understandable without identifying the source of the grace, and so they included it.

Matthew 10:29 in the RSV reads,

> Are not two sparrows sold for a penny?

The NLT has, "Not even a sparrow, worth only half a penny." They were trying to say it's even less than a penny. In the KJV, it is a "farthing."

5. Fill Out the Story

If you take this a step further, some translations will add to the story. They will add things that are not even implied, and this is where eyebrows should start to be raised, in my opinion. At some point you have to say this is God's Word, and this is how the Holy Spirit inspired the author to say it. If you want to know what it means, study, but don't change the biblical text.

A good example is 1 Peter 1:7b. The RSV writes,

> your faith, more precious than gold which though perishable is tested by fire, may redound to praise and glory and honor at the revelation of Jesus Christ.

It is not clear about whose "glory" Peter is speaking. The NLT makes the decision for the reader.

> So if your faith remains strong after being tried by fiery trials, it will bring you much praise and glory and honor on the day when Jesus Christ is revealed to the whole world.

"It will bring *you*," they write, so it is our glory.

In Acts 28:11. Paul is leaving Malta and the RSV says,

> After three months we set sail in a ship which had wintered in the island, a ship of Alexandria, with the Twin Brothers as figurehead.

However, the NIV adds to the end of the verse, "Castor and Pollux," identifying the twin brothers. (The ESV lists their names in a footnote.) The Greek word is Διόσκουροι, which is a transliteration of the Latin *Dioscuri.* The Dioscuri were the twin sons of Zeus (Δίος κοῦροι), Castor and Pollux. You can see why the translators added the names, but should they?

6. Possible Misunderstanding

Translators will look at the possibility of misunderstanding. I don't know how many times in the ESV meetings we would come up with a good translation, but then somebody would notice that the original was clear but our translation was open to misunderstanding.

For example, the RSV translates Matthew 5:28,

> But I say to you that every one who looks at a woman lustfully has already committed adultery with her in his heart.

The problem with this translation is that it can give the impression that if a man has a passing lustful thought, that he has sinned. Is temptation to sin actually sin? However, the Greek explicitly says that if a man looks at a woman *for the purpose of* lusting, he has committed adultery. I don't believe that a temptation that shoots through your mind constitutes sin; it is the intention, the dwelling on it, that is a sin. So when you read the RSV translation, you don't understand that the Greek is clearly saying, "looks for the purpose of lusting." But if you read some of the other translations, you can see that they're struggling with this specific issue. The NASB says "but I say to you, that everyone who looks on a woman *to lust for her* has committed adultery with her already in his heart." They're trying to make you see that there's intent involved. This is why the ESV reads, "I say to you that everyone who looks at a woman *with lustful intent.*" We wanted to be as clear as the Greek is and not open up the text to misunderstanding.

7. Sensitivity and Euphemisms

There are passages in Scripture where the Greek is painfully explicit, but because of our culture we cannot say it. Translators, out of deference perhaps to the fact that children will be listening, thus turn it into a euphemism.

On the ESV translation committee we called this the "giggle factor." One of the people on the oversight committee was a pastor; we'd come up with a translation that perhaps was more sexually explicit than we were comfortable with and we'd ask him, "Can you preach this?" Often he shook his head and said, "I will not be able to get control of my high school students for at least ten minutes if we put that into the translation."

For example, in Genesis 31:10, the story of Jacob's dream about Laban and the spotted goats, the RSV says,

> In the mating season of the flock I lifted up my eyes, and saw in a dream that the he-goats which leaped upon the flock were striped, spotted, and mottled.

The pastor said, "I can't read that. As soon as my high-school students realize the animals are mating, the euphemism of 'leaping' is so evocative that I will lose their attention." So we came up with "the goats that mated with the flock." We said what was happening.

What do you do with sexually explicit language such as in the Song of Songs? The Jews knew what they were doing when they prohibited Jewish boys who were under the age of 30 from reading it because the language, the anatomical language, is unbelievably specific.

What about what I call "potty language"? In the New Testament the most famous passage is Philippians 3:8,

> Indeed I count everything as loss because of the surpassing worth of knowing Christ Jesus my Lord. For his sake I have suffered the loss of all things, and count them as *refuse.* (RSV)

The NIV says "rubbish." The NLT says, "garbage." The problem is that the word usually refers to human or animal excrement.

In 1 Kings 18:27, the RSV says,

And at noon Elijah mocked them, saying, "Cry aloud, for he is a god; either he is musing, or he has *gone aside.*"

The NLT says, "Perhaps he is deep in thought, or he is *relieving* himself." The Hebrew is a sarcastic, rather crude statement, suggesting that Baal has gone to the bathroom and wasn't paying any attention. Everyone I know agrees that you can't translate that literally. Several translations use the metaphor of being asleep and the need to be awakened. The translator is massaging Scripture because of what is socially unacceptable, and all translations do it.

8. Theological Biases

Another thing that affects translation are theological biases, and it doesn't matter whether you are liberal or conservative. Your theological assumptions will affect your translation. When the RSV came out, it created a tremendous uproar in evangelical circles; the National Council of Churches (who owned the RSV) was branded the anti-Christ, because if you go to some of the key theological passages, the translators significantly changed the KJV. In the prophecy in Isaiah 7:14, which Matthew applies to Mary and Jesus, they translate, "For behold a *young woman* shall conceive and bear a child," instead of a "virgin."

In Romans 9:5, depending upon how you punctuate it, Jesus is or is not called "God."

to them belong the patriarchs, and of their race, according to the flesh, is the Christ. God who is over all be blessed for ever. Amen. (RSV)

Theirs are the patriarchs, and from them is

traced the human ancestry of Christ, who is God over all, forever praised! Amen. (NIV)

The same kind of thing happens in the evangelical church. At Acts 13:48, the RSV says,

And when the Gentiles heard this, they were glad and glorified the word of God; and as many as were *ordained* to eternal life believed.

In the original Living Bible, not the New Living Translation, this is how Kenneth Taylor translates it:

When the Gentiles heard this they were very glad and rejoiced in Paul's message and as many as *wanted* eternal life believed.

It is impossible to get the word "wanted" out of the Greek. This is an issue of theological disposition. Theological biases are everywhere.

9. Inclusive Language

What is a translator to do with inclusive language? Can "he" mean "he" and "she?" Can the English words "man" and "brother" be used generically of men and women or not?

The ESV committee spent a tremendous amount of its translation time dealing with this issue. The use of "man," and the use of the third person singular "he," are so pervasive throughout the biblical text that if you cannot use "man" and "he," you must significantly alter much of the biblical text, as has been done by the NRSV. They do this by changing third person "he" to second person "you," changing singular "he" to plural "they," or changing active verbs to passive.

The story I like to tell is of my nine-year-old daughter Kiersten. One day I walked into her bedroom and noticed she had xeroxed a verse from the Bible, cut it out, crossed out the "him" and written "her" over it, and stuck it on her bulletin board. I called Robin and said, "Do you know about this?" She said, "I've never seen this before in my life." We called Kiersten in and asked her, "Why did you do this?" She said, "Because I wanted to." "Do you feel, Kiersten, that by saying 'him' it doesn't include you?" "Oh, yes!" Kiersten replied. Kiersten was not responding to external feminist pressure; she felt "he" meant "male" and no one else.

So what are we going to do with passages such as, "Blessed are the peacemakers, for they shall be called sons of God" (Matt 5:9). Now I personally believe there are times because of Old Testament backgrounds that you want to keep the word "sons," "sons of Israel," "sons of God," etc. But this particular verse is not one of them. I thought this should have been translated, "children of God." (I lost the vote.)

Kiersten has provided an interesting learning situation for me as she constantly makes me reassess the words I use. I'm trying to change my vocabulary, not because of feminism but because I don't want to offend my daughter, and I don't want to unnecessarily offend any of you. But when it comes to the Bible, it's really hard to remove its patriarchal character, and it is a legitimate question as to whether we should. In fact, the only way to get rid of its patriarchal character is to so radically retranslate it that we are becoming so interpretive that the translation, in my mind, is of limited value. In my opinion, this is the problem with the NRSV. The Bible is an ancient, patriarchal book, and if we turn it into a modern inclusive book to get rid of every "he" used in a generic sense, we significantly change what it says.

Perhaps the best illustration is Matthew 18:15. The RSV translates it,

> If your *brother* sins against you, go and tell him his fault, between you and him alone. If he listens to you, you have gained your brother.

The NRSV will not use the word "brother" here so it says,

> If another *member of the church* sins against you, go and point out the fault when the two of you are alone. If the member listens to you, you have regained that one.

First of all, there is no "church," not in the sense that we think of it today, at this stage of Jesus' ministry. Second, it leads to misunderstanding. Does this mean that I have to deal with people who go to the same church (building) that I do, but if the person goes to "that other church" down the road, then Jesus' instructions are not applicable? I am sure some may say this is a silly argument and that obviously it is not true, but I guarantee you that people today are making just that mistake.

The NLT is inclusive, and I think they have done a better job. It reads,

> If another believer sins against you, go privately and point out the fault. If the other person listens and confesses it, you have won that person back.

That's about as good as you can do on that verse if you want to get rid of the "brother."

Another example is Philippians 4:21. Paul says,

> The *brethren* who are with me greet you. (RSV)

In other words, the people who accompanied Paul, who were a part of his inner circle, were sending their greetings to the Philippian church. The TNIV says, "The brothers and sisters who are with me send greetings." They have forced the interpretation. Just about everywhere else the NRSV translates ἀδελφοί as "brothers and sisters," but here they write, "The *friends* who are with me greet you." Even the NRSV isn't willing to say that women were *necessarily* part of Paul's inner traveling circle. They properly left the interpretive issue open for the reader.

Hebrews 2:17 in the RSV reads,

Therefore he had to be made like his brethren in every respect, so that he might become a merciful and faithful high priest in the service of God, to make expiation for the sins of the people.

But the TNIV writes,

For this reason he had to be made like his brothers and sisters in every way.

Jesus had to be made like his "sisters" *in every way*? I think the NLT does a better job on this verse:

Therefore, it was necessary for Jesus to be in every respect like us, his brothers and sisters, so that he could be our merciful and faithful High Priest before God. He then could offer a sacrifice that would take away the sins of the people.

The NIV 2011 has fixed this passage.

For this reason he had to be made like them, fully human in every way, in order that he might become a merciful and faithful high priest in service to God, and that he might make atonement for the sins of the people.

Another problem is what to do with the phrase "son of man?" This is Jesus' main term for himself, and it is deeply Christological, drawing its terminology and theology from Ezekiel and Daniel. The NRSV uses the phrase "son of man" in the New Testament. However, in Ezekiel they translate the phrase, "O mortal," thus losing the possibility of readers seeing the link. Their desire for inclusive translation makes it impossible for the reader of their translation to see the connection. (They kept "a son of man" in Daniel 7:13.)

Fortunately, all these translations I have been discussing have continued to call God "Father" and have not made him our "mother" or "parent."

What Bible Should I Use?

Given these considerations, what Bible would I recommend? Here are my suggestions. (1) Adopt one as your main Bible. For study purposes, I believe formal is better than dynamic. (2) When you are studying a passage, always check at least one other translation. If your main Bible is dynamic, check with a formal translation, and vice versa. (3) I enjoy checking a passage in several dynamic translations, telling myself that I am reading the translators' opinions of what the text means.

Conclusion

There are other issues I could go into detail on, but these are the main issues in my experience that illustrate why translations are different. Translations are different because translators have different translation philosophies. And that's not necessarily bad, but it does make it even more important for you to learn a little Greek, so you can know why they are different.

While it perhaps does not need to be stated, I want to stress that ultimately we do not know why the translators chose the specific wording they did unless you can ask one of them. We are only guessing.

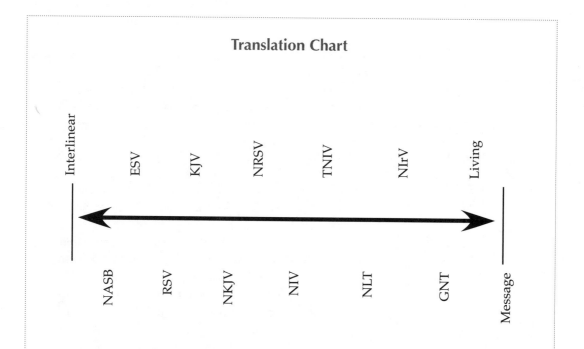

The TNIV and NRSV are difficult to place. If you remove the issue of gender translation, both are a little closer toward the formal equivalent side than the NIV and RSV, but where gender is concerned they move decidedly toward to functional equivalent side.

Please note that there is no midpoint. I do not want to suggest that there is a translation that is necessarily right and all others err to one side or the other. Each is positioned relative to the other translations.

Chapter 33

How to Read a Commentary

Congratulations. You have learned all the Greek grammar you need to know in order to accomplish our goals. However, one of our goals is to be able to read good commentaries. We have seen many of the bits and pieces necessary to do this, and it is time to pull them together.

What We Have Learned So Far

In many of the previous chapters, we have studied the same issues that a good commentary will discuss, and in so doing you have been learning how to read commentaries. We learned how words are ambiguous and open to different interpretations, how words have a range of meaning, and how it is the role of context to specify which specific meaning was intended in a particular context. We were learning to identify the main point(s) of the passage, how that point was modified, and how to discover the author's flow of thought. We saw the flexibility and ambiguity of grammar in the cases, tenses, and moods. We have looked at some of the tools that will help us to interpret the Bible more accurately—translations, concordances, word studies, software. When looking at translation theory, we were learning about the nature of language and communication and about the necessity of interpretation. Now it is time to pull together what we have learned so that we can learn to use our final tool—commentaries. I want to do this

by walking you through the basic process of what is called exegesis, a technical word for biblical interpretation, which is the primary task of a commentary.

But first I want to stress the proper role of a commentary. The best exegesis is begun with you and your Bible. I cannot emphasize this enough. Read the passage over and over. Do your phrasing. Pray that the Holy Spirit show you things you normally would miss. This is the best kind of Bible study, and certainly the most rewarding. I don't know how many times I have been struggling with a passage for a sermon or a lecture, and I am not sure what phrase modifies what, or even what the main point is; and I read and reread the passage, move things around in my phrasing, and then, eventually, the light dawns and I see what the author is saying. This is the joy of independent exegesis.

However, you must not stop here. What if you are wrong? What if your interpretation sounds great to you but is really out-to-lunch? This is where commentaries come in. If you cannot find a major commentary to agree with your position, especially if they don't list it even as a possibility, then humility requires that you accept the error of your position and change your interpretation. It is a dangerous thing to say that you understand the passage correctly and all the people who have studied the passage for years totally missed its meaning. I guess it is possible you are right and everybody else is wrong, but it is highly unlikely. Even Luther had historical precedent for what he taught, even though he stood against the teaching of the current church.

I know there is a strong anti-intellectual bias out there. I have heard pastors tell their congregation not even to look at commentaries. Certainly there are commentaries from which I want to protect my friends. And certainly there are commentaries that major in the minutia and trivia and will bore a layperson into a coma (as well as a few seminary students). But don't think of a commentary as a book. Think of it as a chance to listen to a person who probably has substantially more formal training and experience than you have, a person who possibly has spent most of his or her life thinking about this one area. I spent fourteen years working on my commentary on the Pastoral Epistles. I know of people who have spent almost their entire careers working on just one biblical book or one area of theology. To have someone say that the fruit of a person's life's work should not even be read is—well, it is just wrong.

When you read a commentary, it will provide checks and balances against your possible mistakes. If you read more than one commentary, they provide checks and balances against each other as well. I am not saying that the commentary is automatically right. I have read many interpretations in commentaries that I believe to be wrong. But as I study the text for myself and then check myself with at least two commentaries, and especially when I find myself agreeing with the commentaries, then when I stand to preach before my church, I can preach with the full conviction of "thus saith the Lord."

But commentaries do more than provide checks and balances. They can answer questions that a reading of the text can never provide or ask questions that you may never

think of asking. They can give a depth to your study beyond phrasing as they fill in the holes, so to speak. So how do you read commentaries?

Hermeneutics

Hermeneutics has been defined as the science and art of biblical interpretation. Hermeneutics helps us understand the Bible. It is a science because there are specific rules the interpreter must follow. It is an art because it takes years of practice to develop the ability to employ those rules properly. There is a difference between a novice and a seasoned interpreter. Just look at how much better you handle Scripture now than you did when you were young in Christ. I could go to an art class and learn about colors, but if you put a paintbrush in my hand, I will only be able to produce the dabbling of a child. Hermeneutics is an art that takes years to develop.

Hermeneutics has two basic steps, finding what the text meant to its original audience, and then seeing how it applies to our current situation. As wise people who not only want to hear the words of the Lord but also put them into practice (Matt 7:24-27), we must be concerned with traveling the entire hermeneutical circle, of knowing what the text *meant* to its original audience and what it *means* to me today.

Step 1: Meant

The first step in hermeneutics is to learn what the author meant to convey to his original audience. This is the role of exegesis. The word "exegesis" was formed with the Greek preposition ἐκ, which means "out of" (which of course you know); exegesis is drawing the meaning out of the text, of learning what the author wanted to say. Exegesis is often contrasted with "eisegesis"; the Greek preposition εἰς means "into," and hence eisegesis means reading your own meaning into the text. Bible study is not reading your personal theology into some biblical passage. Bible study is letting the text talk to us; we are the listeners, not the talkers.

The commentary writer will therefore try to discover the meaning intended by the author. This is called "authorial intent." In a few places the author may have intended multiple meanings, as with a pun, or God may have intended a deeper meaning, such as a prophecy. But the vast majority of the time the author meant something, one thing, and the goal is to find that one meaning.

Hard work

This can be hard work for both you and the commentary writer. It is easy to skim over a passage and then share with your Bible study group what the passage "means to me." But the cover on my Bible does not say "Bill's Holy Word." It says "God's Holy Word." If I have integrity, then I want to know what the biblical author meant, and through him what God meant. And this takes time and often hard work. The question you have to answer for yourself is, with your own view of Scripture, does it deserve the hard work? If you don't believe the Bible is God's Word, then perhaps all you think it deserves is a quick skim. But if Scripture did come from the very mouth of God (2 Tim 3:16), then I suspect it deserves more than a skim.

The Bible is not a novel. It is not a made-up story designed primarily to entertain, and hence it is not an easy read. While I enjoy

reading the Bible, it was designed primarily to be life-changing, and this takes study. That is why we call it "Bible Study," not "Bible Skim."

Don't Skip This Step

Some people attending the proverbial Bible study want to skip this first step of exegesis. They want to know what the Bible "means to me." If you stop to think about it, this is impossible. We must do the hard work of learning the author's original meaning first, and without that we can't ever know "what it means to me." Fee and Stuart say, "A text cannot mean what it never meant."[8] A biblical passage can never carry a meaning for you that was not intended by the author (except perhaps prophecy)—if we have integrity in our interpretation. So one of the safeguards against reading our own ideas into the Bible, or against misunderstanding the Bible, is always to learn what it meant, and only after this to see what it means to me, today.

We do this automatically with every other kind of literature. If you read a Victorian novel, it is so full of English history and culture that you automatically understand what it is saying in its historical context, and only afterwards do you reapply its message in our own culture. Would anyone reading *Pride and Prejudice* think that Jane Austin is speaking directly to me, in 2013, in Washougal, Washington? The same is true of reading the Bible.

So the central goal of a good exegetical commentary is to learn the biblical author's intention, and only after that is done do we move into learning what it means for me

---

8   *How to Read the Bible for All Its Worth*, Zondervan, 26.

today. How does the writer go about accomplishing this task?

Different Elements of Exegesis

Words, phrases, sentences, and paragraphs. People communicate with words, bound together into phrases, joined into sentences, that flow into paragraphs. The commentator's job is to look at each one of these components in order to learn the author's intent. In a sense, it is like the commentator is trying to restate what the author said in such as way that if the author were present, he would say, "Yes, that's what I meant."

Commentary writers will identify the main theme(s) in a passage and discuss the relationships among the phrases. They will discuss at least the major words, especially the theologically significant words. When you are done reading a good commentary, you should leave with a sense that you have spent time with the Biblical author and understand better the message he was trying to convey.

We sometimes talk about the "Grammatical-Historical Method" (spelled variously). This means that we use grammar and an understanding of the book's historical setting as the primary tool of exegesis. This method is sometimes set against the allegorical method of interpretation, which could make the Bible say almost anything the interpreter wanted it to say. One of the more famous examples is a typical allegorical interpretation of the parable of the Good Samaritan. Instead of being Jesus' answer to the question, "Who is my neighbor," it becomes an allegory of human creation (the man going down from Jerusalem to Jericho is Adam), the inability of the Law and Prophets to solve the human dilemma of sin (the priest and the Levite), and eventually of Jesus' coming (the "Good Samaritan") to care for sin, taking the robbery victim (you and me) to the Inn (the church) and paying the two denarii (baptism and the Lord's Supper). Let's not do this. Let's look at the words, phrases, sentences, and paragraphs and seek to learn what the biblical author meant.

Genres. A genre is a type of literature, like narrative, epistle, parable, prophecy, poetry, apocalyptic, and so on. Each of these genres has its own specific rules of interpretation. For example, when the author of the Song of Songs says of his beloved, "your eyes are doves" (1:15), we don't imagine some grotesque science fiction type of genetically engineered monstrosity. We understand it as poetry, and that his beloved's eyes are *like* doves in their beauty. A commentary writer will take a passage's genre into consideration and apply the rules of interpretation appropriate for that genre. Any book on hermeneutics will discuss genre, but one of the best is *How to Read the Bible for All its Worth* by Gordon Fee and Douglas Stuart (Zondervan). Others are *A Basic Guide to Interpreting the Bible; Playing by the Rules* by Robert Stein (Baker), and *Grasping God's Word; A Hands-On Approach to Reading, Interpreting, and Applying the Bible* by J. Scott Duvall and J. Daniel Hays (Zondervan), the latter being a college textbook.

Setting. A good commentary will discuss the historical, cultural, geographic, and possibly theological setting of the passage. The point is to give the reader enough background information so as to understand the text. The biblical words do not exist in a vacuum. They were written to people who were as much a part of their world as you are a part of your world, and their meaning can only be understood when we read it within their ancient context.

Introduction. Almost every commentary has an introduction. Here the author is giving you the background necessary to understand the biblical book as a whole. He or she will discuss who the biblical author is, when he wrote, where he was in his life when he wrote, the occasion that prompted the writing, and his purposes in writing. The commentary writer will give an outline of the book and will summarize its basic themes, especially the theological themes. Trying to understand a biblical book without knowing something of these issues is like trying to understand a newspaper article written on September 12, 2001, without knowing what happened on September 11 in New York City. Without the background, much of the commentary (and biblical book) become nothing but disconnected pieces of information.

It is also in the introduction that the author may present arguments more geared for scholars than for most people. For example, in my commentary on the Pastorals I spend pages arguing that Paul wrote the Pastorals (1 and 2 Timothy, Titus) and more pages defending my understanding of the nature of the problems Paul is addressing and the basics of Paul's theological refutation of those problems. Much of what I wrote is of little consequence to a nonscholar who believes Paul wrote the Pastorals. But this is part of choosing the correct commentary for your needs; you have to match your needs with the commentary's purpose.

Analogy of Faith

One of the hermeneutical principles that came out of the Reformation is the "analogy of faith." It basically means that the biblical authors do not contradict themselves. In practice, this means that if you are having

trouble interpreting one passage of Scripture, and the same biblical author writes on the same topic elsewhere, you can use the second passage to help interpret the first.

Of course, if the commentator does not agree with this Reformation (and biblical) doctrine, then he or she will be free to claim that a biblical author contradicts himself. But as a general rule, most commentaries will compare the passage you are studying with other biblical discussions of the same topic.

Textual Issues

Some commentaries will talk about the differences that exist among the different Greek manuscripts of the Bible. For example, many Greek manuscripts of Ephesians lack the words "in Ephesus" in 1:1. It is important in the exegesis of Ephesians to know if Paul is writing to the church at Ephesus, or (if the words are not original) writing to the area of Asia Minor in general, of which Ephesus is a major city. Most commentaries do not go into detail on this issue; it is complicated and very much the realm of the specialist.

Between the Lines

In the advanced commentaries there will often be discussion about details that, for lack of a better expression, are between the lines. For example, commentaries on the Synoptic Gospels (Matthew, Mark, and Luke) will often compare the wording of one account with the wording of the same account in another gospel, and then ask why they are different. Commentaries on Paul's letters will often talk about the source of some of his statements; the assumption is that Paul borrowed bits and pieces, especially hymns and creeds, from other sources. Some commentaries on John will talk about the "community" that supposedly exerted pressure on the gospel and to some degree affected how it was written. These types of discussions often punctuate, and in some cases permeate, a commentary. For you, I recommend that if the commentary writer is preoccupied with these types of issues rather than the meaning of the biblical text, don't use the commentary.

Step 2: Means

The second step of hermeneutics is to take what the passage meant and to see what it means today. Sometimes the word "hermeneutics" is used exclusively of this step. The idea is to bring the passage through the centuries, from the biblical culture to our culture, and to understand its meaning and application in our lives.

Few commentaries deal with this step. Most are content to work in the original context, and some writers even consider it wrong to try and apply the biblical message to today. The NIV Application Commentary series provides a welcomed relief to this practice. The volumes are written by true scholars and move through the issue of cultural context into the passages' contemporary significance. Individual volumes sometimes move in this direction as well; Gordon Fee's commentary on 1 Corinthians, in an excellent but scholarly series, concludes each section with a discussion helping the reader move beyond meant into means. If you struggle with the issue of application, see *Applying the Bible*, a short book by Jack Kuhatschek (Zondervan).

How to Choose a Commentary

1. The best thing you can do is read several commentaries on a biblical passage. There is

nothing like getting your "feet wet" to decide whether or not a commentary will be useful. Of course, in this day and age, many Christian bookstores are more concerned with inspirational writings and "Jesus Junk" (as one bookstore owner described it to me) than with books dealing with study and content, so you may not be able to check out different commentaries. Maybe there is a Christian school nearby or the library of a trained pastor, or Google books (www.bit.ly/12LbVCr).

2. You want to find a commentary whose philosophy matches your needs. Do you want to read the author's interaction with Greek and Hebrew? Do you want to walk through the author's reasoning process, or just hear her or his conclusions? Do you want to know about every word, or just the flow of thought and discussion of the difficult passages?

3. When you are done reading a passage in the commentary, do you know more about the biblical text or just things about it? This is a crucial distinction. Some commentaries appear to be written more for other commentary writers and scholars than for you. Many of the books lining my shelves have little to offer the pastor or Bible study leader who wants help preparing for the next week. Many of the discussions are technical and geared for scholarship. My suggestion for you is to avoid commentaries that enter into scholarly debate and concentrate on those that help you understand the text.

4. Does the author understand hermeneutics? Some commentaries, traditionally those considered more "devotional," spend little time with the meaning of the text and move quickly into application. But how do you know if the application is based on truth? Be careful of these.

5. Does the author argue fairly? Some authors are committed to presenting all interpretive decisions so fairly that even those with whom they disagree would appreciate the presentation. Dispensa–tionalists used to compliment George Ladd in how fairly he presented the dispensational position, even though he argued against it.

But some writers skew the other positions, do not give all the counterarguments, basically set up a "straw man" argument, and then shoot it down with ease. Some authors like to label those who hold another position and attack them as people, not dealing with the actual interpretation and the arguments. This is grostesquely unfair and un-Christian. Some authors like to make wide-sweeping claims that go beyond the facts and give the appearance of wisdom. Beware also of someone using words like "clearly" and "obviously." If the answers to the questions raised by the text were truly "clear" and "obvious," then there wouldn't be much debate.

There is a tendency on the part of some people to think that the canons of Christian behavior—charity, fairness, kindness—have no relevance in book writing. But while it is true that commentary writing demands that you take a position and therefore disagree with another writer, it does not demand that we leave our Christian character at the door to the study and rationalize writing that can only be termed "cruel." These types of books should themselves be left at the door or simply discarded.

6. Does the author treat the biblical text with respect? It will be hard for you to tell this right away, but after a while you will probably be able to tell whether the commentary writer believes the Bible is worthy of respect. This is part of the difficulty for an evangelical in commentary writing. In a sense, you are standing over it and trying to understand it. But at the same time an evangelical will submit to its teaching. This is a difficult balance.

7. We all see the Bible through a grid, usually through a theological grid. It is impossible to write a commentary that does not reflect your theological bias, and you should know your author's grid. Where was he trained? Where does he teach? Who published the book? If it is an academic work published by Zondervan, Baker, or Crossway, you can probably trust it. (I am speaking as an evangelical—that's my grid.)

One of the harder lessons I had to learn in college was that people considerably outside the orthodox definition of Christianity write books about the Bible. I remember one book that I simply could not understand, until I realized that the author did not believe in the physical resurrection.

The commentary series by William Barclay is wildly successful, if you judge by the number sold. He writes beautifully in ways that are easy to quote. But later in his life Barclay could be seen to be wondering about the possibility of the supernatural, specifically miracles. Be careful. And when you are reading his applications, make sure they actually come from the biblical text.

Some Bibles have notes along the bottom of the page. These are normally succinct but somewhat helpful. Just be aware that the notes are not part of the Bible, and each study Bible has its own theological bias. The *NIV Study Bible* is broadly evangelical. The *Scofield Reference Bible* is dispensational. The *Geneva Study Bible* is Calvinist.

8. Some people are impressed by length of pages, weight of the book, and the number of foot-

notes. I can still remember talking to someone at church who said that I must believe this one writer because there were so many footnotes in his book. Anybody can write with footnotes. Anybody can give the appearance of scholarship by listing long bibliographies. This has no necessary connection with truth.

My Favorite New Testament Commentaries

As far as specific recommendations are concerned, I will be keeping the list at the online class current and encourage you to go there before buying, or follow the QR code below.

Vocabulary

NOUNS

ἄγγελος, -ου, ὁ, angel, messenger
ἀδελφός, -οῦ, ὁ, brother
ἀνήρ, ἀνδρός, ὁ, man, male, husband
ἄνθρωπος, -ου, ὁ, man, mankind, person, people, humankind, human being
ἀπόστολος, -ου, ὁ, apostle, envoy, messenger
γῆ, γῆς, ἡ, earth, land, region, humanity
γυνή, γυναικός, ἡ, woman, wife
ἡμέρα, -ας, ἡ, day
θεός -οῦ, ὁ, God, god
Ἰησοῦς, -οῦ, ὁ, Jesus, Joshua
κύριος -ου, ὁ, Lord, lord, master, sir
λόγος, -ου, ὁ, word, Word, statement, message
μαθητής, -οῦ, ὁ, disciple
ὄνομα, -ατος, τό, name, reputation
οὐρανός, -οῦ, ὁ, heaven, sky
πατήρ, πατρός, ὁ, father
πίστις, -εως, ἡ, faith, belief
πνεῦμα, -ατος, τό, spirit, Spirit, wind, breath, inner life
σωτήρ, -ῆρος, ὁ, savior, deliverer
υἱός, -οῦ, ὁ, son, descendant
Χριστός, -οῦ, ὁ, Christ, Messiah, Anointed One

ADJECTIVES

ἅγιος, -ία, -ιον, adjective: holy; plural noun: saints
μέγας, μεγάλη, μέγα, large, great
ὁ, ἡ, τό, the
πᾶς, πᾶσα, πᾶν, singular: each, every; plural: all
πολύς, πολλή, πολύ, singular: much; plural: many adverb: often

PRONOUNS

αὐτός, -ή, -ό, he, she, it; him/her/itself; same
ἑαυτοῦ, -ῆς, -οῦ, singular: of himself/herself/itself; plural: of themselves
ἐγώ (ἡμεῖς), I (we) (1,178)
εἷς, μία, ἕν, one
ἐκεῖνος, -η, -ο, singular: that (man/woman/thing); plural: those (men/women, things)
ὅς, ἥ, ὅ, who (whom)
οὐδείς, οὐδεμία, οὐδέν, no one, none, nothing
οὗτος, αὕτη, τοῦτο, singular: this; he, she, it; plural: these; they
σύ (ὑμεῖς), you
τίς, τί, who? what? which? why?
τις, τι, someone/thing, certain one/thing, anyone/thing

INTERJECTIONS, ADVERBS, ETC.

ἀμήν, verily, truly, amen, so let it be
μή, not, lest
οὐ (οὐκ, οὐχ), not
οὕτως, thus, so, in this manner

VERBS

ἀκούω, I hear, learn, obey, understand
ἀποκρίνομαι, I answer
γίνομαι, I become, am, exist, happen, am born, am created
γινώσκω, I know, come to know, realize, learn
δίδωμι, I give (out), entrust, give back, put
δύναμαι, I am able, am powerful
εἰμί, I am, exist, live, am present
ἐξέρχομαι, I go out
ἔρχομαι, I come, go

ἔχω I have, hold
θέλω, I will, wish, desire, enjoy
λαλέω I speak, say
λαμβάνω, I take, receive
λέγω, I say, speak
οἶδα, I know, understand
ὁράω, I see, notice, experience
πιστεύω, I believe, I have faith (in), trust
ποιέω, I do, make

CONJUNCTIONS

Coordinating

καί, and; even, also; but; namely
δέ (δ᾽), and; now, then; but
γάρ, for, then
ἀλλά (ἀλλ᾽), but, yet, except
οὖν, therefore, then, accordingly
ἤ, or, than
τε, and (so), so

Subordinating

ὅτι, that, because
ἵνα, in order that, so that, that
εἰ, if
ἐάν, if
ὅτε, when
ὡς, as, like, when, that, how, about

Correlative

μέν ... δέ, on the one hand ... but on the other
καί ... καί, both ... and
ἤ ... ἤ, either ... or
μήτε ... μήτε, neither ... nor
οὔτε ... οὔτε, neither ... not
οὐκ ... ἀλλά, (δέ), not ... but
τε ... καί, both ... and

PREPOSITIONS

ἀπό (ἀπ᾽, ἀφ᾽), gen: (away) from
διά (δι᾽), gen: through; acc: on account of
εἰς, acc: into, in, among
ἐκ, ἐξ, gen: from, out of
ἐν, dat: in, on, among
ἐπί (ἐπ᾽, ἐφ᾽), gen: on, over, when; dat: on the basis of, at; acc: on, to, against
κατά (κατ᾽, καθ᾽), gen: down from, against; acc: according to, throughout, during
μετά (μετ᾽, μεθ᾽) gen: with; acc: after
παρά, gen: from; dat: beside, in the presence of; acc: alongside of
περί, gen: concerning, about; acc: around
πρός, acc: to, toward, with
ὑπέρ, gen: in behalf of; above
ὑπό (ὑπ᾽, ὑφ᾽) gen: by; acc: under

Index

D

dative case 20, 74–77, 75
    dative of interest 75
    direct object 217
    object of preposition 75
    reference 76
    respect 76
    simple apposition 76
declension 214
definite article 182–83
demonstratives 180–81
dependent clause 92
diacriticals 184
diaeresis 184
diphthongs 8, 9, 12, 184
    improper 6
direct object 13, 14, 15, 20, 71, 72, 73, 125

E

eight cases 214–15
elision 87, 184
emphatic negation 227
enclitics 177

F

Foundational Greek viii
Functional Greek viii
future indicative 34
future tense 116, 129
    future indicative as prohibition 226
    gnomic 223
    imperatival 129
    predictive 129

G

gamma nasal 6
gender 16, 18–19, 82, 84, 85
gender language 269
genitive absolute 221
genitive case 21, 77–79, 218
    attributive 218
    comparison 78, 219
    content 219
    descriptive 21, 77, 127

    direct object 220
    genitive of apposition, epexegetical genitive 78
    Hebraic genitive 218
    objective 220
    object of preposition 78
    partitive 218
    plenary 221
    possessive 77
    separation 219
    simple apposition 78
    subjective 220
    time 220
gerund 141
GK numbers 31
Gloss 19
Greek Alphabet 4–7
Greek Language 2–3
    Classical Greek 2
    Koine 2

H

head noun 21, 77, 78, 218, 219, 220, 232
Hebrew 3
hermeneutics 280–84

I

identical adjective 180
imperative mood 27, 38, 136–37, 229
    command 38, 136
    entreaty 136
    person 38
    prohibition 137
    request 136
imperfect tense 33, 34, 40, 116, 117, 120, 123, 129–30, 130, 236
    conative 224
    customary 130
    durative 129
    ingressive 130
    iterative 130
    progressive 129
    tendential 224
    voluntative 224
indefinite relative pronoun 90
independent clause 92

Learn Biblical Greek Pack

William D. Mounce

This pack contains everything you need to learn the original language of the New Testament, whether you are already enrolled in a class or learning on your own. It includes 36 video lessons on six DVDs, the most popular introductory Greek grammar today (*Basics of Biblical Greek*), along with the corresponding workbook, audio, and other necessary tools.

First published in 1993, William Mounce's *Basics of Biblical Greek Grammar*, now in its third edition, has consistently been rated as the most helpful introduction to the field, and a collection of complementary tools provides readers with a holistic learning experience. In addition to the textbook, the pack includes:

Basics of Biblical Greek Video Lectures, featuring 36 video lessons accompanying the passages in the textbook.

Basics of Biblical Greek Workbook, with study exercises and passages for translation practice.

Basics of Biblical Greek Vocabulary Cards, including 1,000 vocabulary flashcards for studying.

Basics of Biblical Greek Vocabulary Audio, to help with correct pronunciation and ordered according to the textbook.

Biblical Greek Laminated Sheet, for a quick reference guide to common language questions.

All resources also available individually.

Curriculum, Kit: 978-0-310-51438-1

Available in stores and online!

Interlinear for the Rest of Us

The Reverse Interlinear for New Testament Word Studies

William D. Mounce

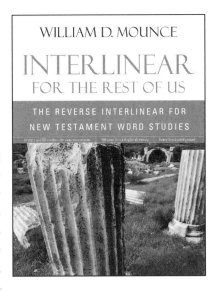

Most interlinear Bibles are superb resources for Greek students. But what about the rest of us who don't know Greek? Here is the answer. While other interlinear Bibles assume that you know Greek, *Interlinear for the Rest of Us* assumes that you don't, or that you've forgotten much of what you once knew. Designed for busy pastors, Sunday school teachers, and anyone who wants a practical tool for studying the Scriptures, this interlinear makes reading easy by flip-flopping the usual order of appearance. It uses the English text as the main text rather than the Greek, so there is absolutely no confusion about the meaning of what you're reading.

Discover the Greek words behind the English translation. Conduct your own word studies using Greek word study books—without knowing Greek. *Interlinear for the Rest of Us* offers these features: Interlinear passages appear in a "staff" with four interrelated lines. From top to bottom, the lines are: (1) English text in New International Version; (2) Corresponding Greek words; (3) Parsing information; (4) Goodrick-Kohlenberger numbers. The Greek text is given in normal Greek order at the bottom of the page. At the end of the book is Mounce's Greek-English Dictionary, keyed to both Goodrick-Kohlenberger and Strong's numbering systems.

Ideal for use with *Greek for the Rest of Us* and other Greek study tools

Softcover: 978-0-310-51394-0

Available in stores and online!

The Zondervan Greek and English Interlinear New Testament (NASB/NIV)

William D. Mounce and Robert H. Mounce, General Editors

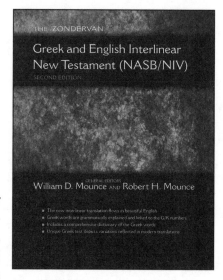

The Zondervan Greek and English Interlinear New Testament (NASB/NIV) includes an interlinear translation based on the Greek New Testament. This new, user-friendly reference tool for pastors, students, and scholars greatly enhances understanding of the Greek New Testament, as well as how to do word studies based on the G/K numbers.

Featuring the interlinear text as a third translation, this interlinear Greek and English New Testament sets the NASB side by side with the NIV. In the back is a unique Greek/English dictionary keyed to G/K numbers for easy accessibility to all users, as well as parsing and G/K numbers for each Greek word. This Zondervan interlinear Bible offers the following features:

- The new interlinear translation flows in beautiful English
- Greek words are grammatically explained and linked to the GK numbers
- Includes a comprehensive dictionary of the Greek words

Hardcover, Printed: 978-0-310-49296-2

Available in stores and online!

Mounce's Complete Expository Dictionary of Old and New Testament Words

William D. Mounce

For years, *Vine's Expository Dictionary* has been the standard word study tool for pastors and laypeople, selling millions of copies. But sixty-plus years of scholarship have shed extensive new light on the use of biblical Greek and Hebrew, creating the need for a new, more accurate, more thorough dictionary of Bible words. William Mounce, whose Greek grammar has been used by more than 150,000 college and seminary students, is the editor of this new dictionary, which will become the layperson's gold standard for biblical word studies.

Mounce's Dictionary is ideal for the reader with limited or no knowledge of Greek or Hebrew who wants greater insight into the meanings of biblical words to enhance Bible study. It is also the perfect reference for busy pastors needing to quickly get at the heart of a word's meaning without wading through more technical studies.

Hardcover, Jacketed: 978-0-310-24878-1

Available in stores and online!

New International Dictionary of New Testament Theology

Abridged Edition

Verlyn D. Verbrugge

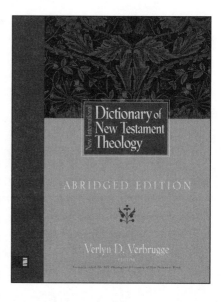

This abridgment of Colin Brown's original four-volume work is arranged with its entries in Greek alphabet order, which makes it easy to find the discussion of a particular word. All the essential information of the original work is contained in this abridgment. Greek words are transliterated into English and linked with their Goodrick/Kohlenberger numbers, which makes it ideal to use with concordances based on GK numbers. This book was formerly titled *The NIV Theological Dictionary of New Testament Words*. Now it has been reset in double columns and wider margins.

Hardcover, Printed: 978-0-310-25620-5

Available in stores and online!

Basics of Biblical Greek
Vocabulary Cards App

William D. Mounce

The cards in this vocabulary app are automatically sortable in various ways, including by *Basics of Biblical Greek* chapter, by parts of speech, alphabetically, randomly, and by frequency.

They also include two key features to greatly enhance their usability: (1) A quiz feature that can be turned on for any possible sorting of the cards, and (2) the ability to sort cards not just by the chapter order of Zondervan's language manuals, but also by chapter order of any of the most popular Greek grammars on the market. This last feature makes the cards tailor-fit to the study needs of nearly every biblical Greek student in the United States.

App: 978-0-310-49412-6

Available in the iTunes store!

We want to hear from you. Please send your comments about this
book to us in care of zreview@zondervan.com. Thank you.